Clive Finlayson

AL-ANDALUS

How nature has shaped history

Photography by the author

S

SANTANA BOOKS

al-Andalus

Published by Ediciones SANTANA, S.L.
Apartado 41
29650 Mijas-Pueblo (Málaga)
Spain

Tel: (0034) 952 48 58 38
Fax: (0034) 952 48 53 67
E-Mail: info@santanabooks.com

Copyright © 2007 Clive Finlayson

Designed by New Image Communications, S.L.

No part of this book may be reproduced or transmitted in any form or by any means without the prior written permission of the publishers.

Printed in Spain by Grafisur

ISBN: 978-84-89954-69-4

Depósito Legal: CA-805/07

To Geraldine, my source of inspiration

CONTENTS

Foreword

Preface

Chapter 1:   Dances without wolves   p12

Chapter 2:   Where the griffon still soars   p28

Chapter 3:   A May day in the Strait of Gibraltar   p48

Chapter 4:   The earliest inhabitants of al-Andalus   p62

Chapter 5:   In the Coto Doñana   p78

Chapter 6:   Africa in Europe   p96

Chapter 7:   On the road to Tarifa   p108

Chapter 8:   In the land of knights and conquistadores   p126

Chapter 9:   Janda   p144

Chapter 10:   The eagle and the fox   p166

Chapter 11:   Europe in Africa   p180

Chapter 12:   Among canes and mud   p198

Chapter 13:   Gibraltar and Cádiz   p216

Chapter 14:   Civilising al-Andalus   p226

Chapter 15:   Meltdown   p242

Chapter 16:   Refuges and refugees   p258

Chapter 17:   Eden lost   p276

Chapter 18:   Original sin   p292

Appendix 1   p313

Appendix 2   p316

Appendix 3   p321

Gorham's Cave, Gibraltar (Photo by Stewart Finlayson)

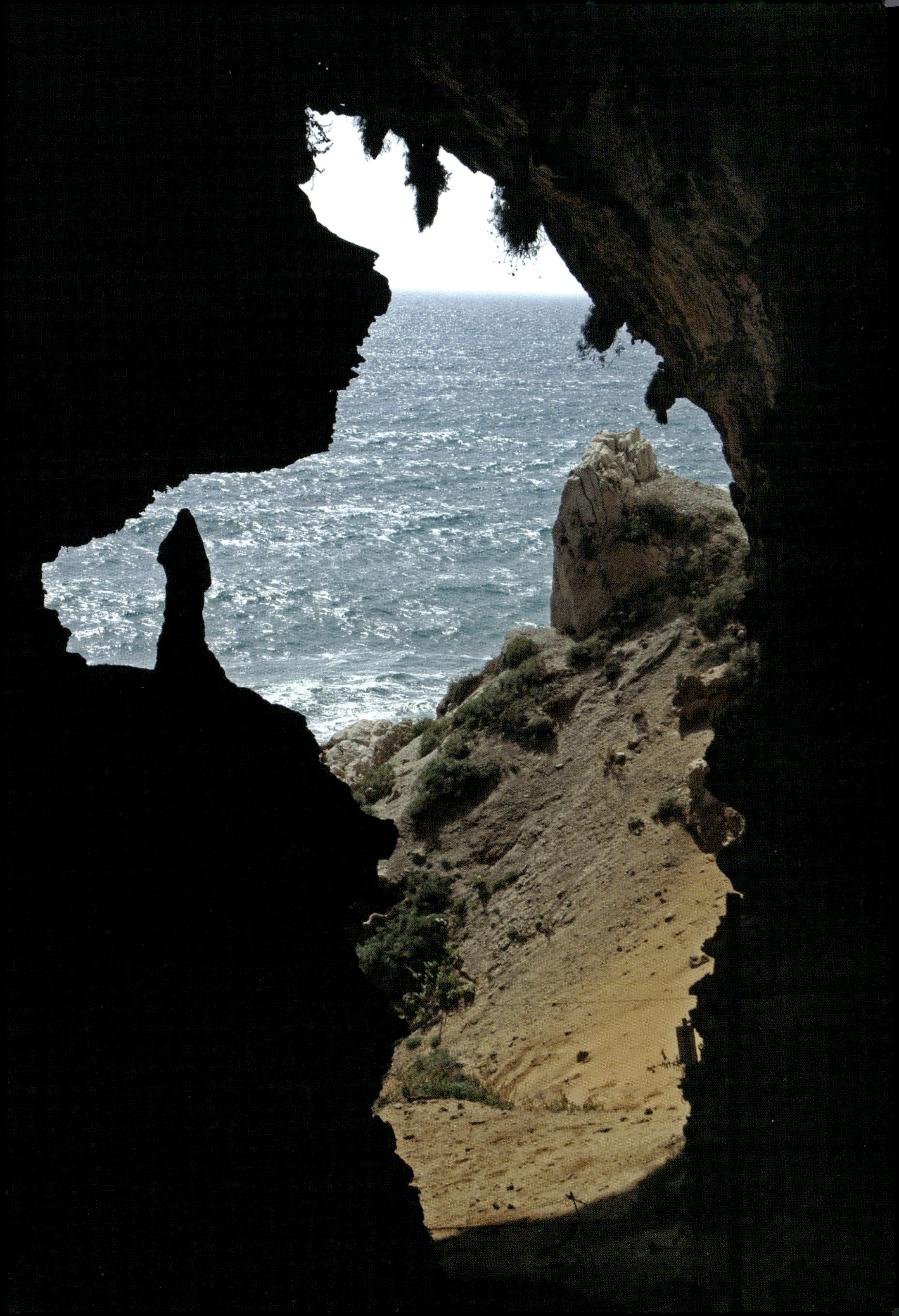

Foreword

by José S Carrión, Professor of Evolutionary Botany, University of Murcia

The natural inheritance of everyone who is capable of spiritual life is an unsubdued forest where the wolf howls and the obscene bird of night chatters
– Henry James, Sr.

Al-Andalus is a book on natural history. It is also a survey on individual wonders and collective stupidities, a novel and an account, an essay and a report, everything written with chatty style and deep knowledge of the facts. This is a masterpiece, and I feel honoured to write the foreword for this book.

I do not share the common viewpoint that we scientists must keep professional activity free from emotional input. I simply cannot believe our brain allows us to do that anyway. On the contrary, every report we write, project we start and every decision we take is coloured by our personal background. Only then are we free to think for ourselves and recount our discoveries to students and non-scientists.

It follows that these lines were unavoidably affected by the moods this book has rescued from deep inside me. Interestingly, it deals with interactions, boundaries, and jumps of scale among conceptual things that science and philosophy have traditionally considered disparate, if not opposing. I am talking especially of the artificial abyss that "academics" have created between social and natural sciences. But, like art or poetry, they all depend for progress on inspiration. And this book is the outcome of a surely long-time gestated stock of good ideas about the interplay between individual men, societies and environment.

First at all, it is pertinent to introduce the author. Finlayson´s scientific output has been prodigious. He is a confirmed evolutionary ecologist, although I have never seen him completely happy with the air of apparent inevitability of explanations based on natural selection. It is clear that both ecological and evolutionary patterns arise, in his eyes, from something more erratic, let me say more wonderful.

As a researcher, Finlayson has mounted two major campaigns. The first has been in support of the late survival of Neanderthals in the south-western extreme of Europe and about the circumstances of this unexpected permanence. He has been able to build a model of survival and extinction from a very complex set of interacting factors, a balanced scenario depicted from patterns of climatic variability, catastrophic events, genetics and ecology. The second bone of contention in Finlayson´s scientific career, has been that an ecological approach would facilitate getting out of the impasses in the debate on human origins. The solution to Finlayson has been to go decidedly for a population approach which would make many issues that remain conjectures or are unresolved accessible to research.

As a scientist, too, Clive Finlayson is one of the brightest I have ever met. He has been blessed by quick intelligence, artistic temperament, and a great ability to communicate - maybe of such success as to encourage plagiarism among reputed colleagues. I must confess to have become astonished while listening to conferences and reading papers including Finlayson´s theses without due recognition of the authorship. This is the tax of being imaginative. After all, there is also great diversity of behaviours and temperaments within the scientific community. Some make trees, others survive with detritus, and there is also space for symbiosis, parasitism and camouflage.

My main excuse for meeting Finlayson has been our joint research into the prehistoric landscapes of southern Iberia, largely under the auspices of the Gorham´s Cave excavations and related ongoing projects. From this encounter I believed that I knew him well but admittedly, after reading through this book, Prof. Finlayson has become a surprise package to me. It amazes me how a specialist can become a generalist, and then a popular writer in such a short time. I passionately conclude that if he was something else in a previous life, he might be one of those raptors that fly every year from the northern Namib to nest in southern Iberia, a long-distance migrant. For there is a serious distance between the way a limestone is formed, the collapse of Bronze Age cultures, the cave paintings of La Pileta and Ardales in Málaga, and the contrasting biographies of Willoughby Cole Verner and Pablo Larios. Thus, unexpectedly, this book includes incursions in the palaeontological arena (Neanderthals, the first Europeans), exploration, battles, trade, dynastic conflicts, the influence of fundamentalist attitude, ... all themes of paramount importance to illustrate ecological corollaries. The reader will certainly find a large number of well-selected case studies.

This is not intended to be a preface but I would like, nevertheless, to give some guide of what the reader will find in these pages if he decides to adventure within, especially because the content and format are a little unusual. I think there is a basic claim that understanding the links between people and landscape demands a millennial-scale perspective. What is emerging is that these interactions are substantially not so different in the Palaeolithic and modern times because the laws of physics continue to be the same, and the main transforming agents, humans, have kept unaltered a behaviour that eventually provokes that vulnerable ecological systems cross their thresholds of resistance and enter irreversibly into a kind of fatal uniformity. I would say that the main purpose of this book is to make an argument for a compelling association between biodiversity and human past and future. The emphasis is on making readable a modern approach to historical ecology; how to cook chance and constraint, and make the meal enjoyable. Ultimately this book is about the thin, although not straight, line that exists between the fate of humans and the fates of other living beings. The final taste is that something crucial is at stake.

Ecologists and activists of conservationism may also get in conflict. For while acknowledging the brave defence of ecosystem protection measurements, they may become crossed at reading Finlayson´s viewpoint of bull fighting and fox hunting as casual environmental preservers. And some statements may sound heretical to anyone who has been taught the usual versions of the global change paradigm. Nevertheless, be

Foreword

sure that most of the stories are firmly grounded on new data as well as on new ideas. Finlayson has taken courage. It is always difficult to buck the trend. That is true in any aspect of life and it is certainly true in science.

In connection with the former, and at the heart of this book lies a paradox. The more we learn about the relationships between physical setting, plants, animals, and humans, the more complicated it appears to be for the purposes of conservation policy. But Finlayson gives here several good examples of how beneath that complexity may lie deep simplicity. Take, for instance, the case of Griffon Vulture's recovery in the last few decades (chapter 2).

The reading of this book can be started where you like. A nice way would be taking first Chapter 16, which tells the magnificent story of José María El Tempranillo, a kind of Robin Hood of the Betic Mountains during the XIXth century. Chapter 18 (Eden Lost) is superb. It documents how, while Iberia still preserves today comparatively high levels of biodiversity, the situation was much better until the recent past.

Al-Andalus is shown by Finlayson like a contrasting land of glory and misery, of complexity, movement and flow, a land of all. Modern – politically correct – concepts of historical nationalisms get demolished in the face of history. The reader will see here how boundaries can dance and how identities may be diluted so fast.

I bet Finlayson will attain a huge level of public popularity in the near future. This piece is immensely readable. And even from the position of a specialist, I love when a colleague is able to write in a manner that make people see that science can be fun.

"Ultimately, this book is about the thin, although not straight, line that exists between the fate of humans and that of other living things. Something crucial is at stake..."

Preface

This book is the product of many years of thinking about the relationship between people and the landscape. Having started my career as an ecologist, I was always concerned about the rather constrained manner in which my discipline looked at the world. Ecology was about studying animals and plants in pristine settings, in settings where Man had not made his mark. It was also a somewhat static view that looked at the present, largely without reference to the past.

Chance has a lot to do with the content of this book, as it had to do with my own trajectory to the present. A chance meeting in 1989 with scientists interested in the Gibraltar caves drew me into the world of the past. Here in these wonderful caves I could find not only Neanderthals but the remains of the animals and plants that lived in the Mediterranean more than 100,000 years ago. I had found a window into the past, the nearest thing to time travel.

Working in the Gibraltar Museum inevitably exposed me to many latent interests that aroused my curiosity. It would have been impossible, living in a place like Gibraltar that is so steeped in history, not to have become engrossed in such disparate subjects as the evolution of fortifications, early contacts between Phoenicians and Iberian peoples, the Islamic conquest of al-Andalus and so much more. Gradually, my mind embraced these subjects and began to see the links between them. Ecology had to be understood in the wider historical context and no environment on the planet could be regarded as truly natural and untouched by the hand of Man. In any case, if Man was a natural consequence of evolution, then his hand in the landscape was, whether we liked it or not, natural. So the idea of this book was born.

Having spent much of the past 25 years exploring the old territory of al-Andalus conquered by the Muslims in the eighth century, it was logical that the setting for a book on people and nature should be that wonderful land. At one time al-Andalus stretched well beyond the limits of present-day Andalusia. It was effectively the whole of the Iberian peninsula, bar the wet and inhospitable mountains of the northwest that were inhabited since time immemorial by indomitable peoples. This book, then, is about this large territory, south of the Pyrenees, which is the Iberian peninsula.

Many books have been written about Iberia, al-Andalus and related subjects. Some are classics in their own right. When I set down this personal adventure, I could not find any book that could tell the story of al-Andalus as I had personally experienced it. History had influenced ecology, but ecology had also influenced history; there were books on history and others on ecology but I could find nothing to link the two. So I set off on the journey that led to this book.

Many chance events have affected my trajectory and consequently that of this book. The greatest and happiest one was meeting Geraldine, now my wife. She has been my life-long companion, the person with whom I have been able to share every experience in the field, the excitement of a new discovery, and the person who has always kept my feet on the ground. She is a wonderful professional and scientist and that chance encounter long ago lit up my path. I am also grateful to my son, Stewart, for his companionship in the field and for gracing this book with some of his photographs.

Many other people have influenced my thinking over the years or have shared the insights that nature so unexpectedly provides every so often. How many wonderful hours have I spent in the field with my good friend Mario Mosquera, watching migrating raptors over the Rock or wading after elusive waterbirds in Doñana? Long ago, when I wanted to study zoology in school and there was nobody who could teach it, William Guillem found the time from his busy schedule to teach me in the evenings. I shall always be grateful for that opportunity. Later, as an undergraduate, I met my mentor, the brilliant Professor Arthur Cain. Arthur had amazing vision and insight and was responsible for harnessing my youthful enthusiasm to something useful.

I have been very lucky to meet many great scientists, archaeologists and historians, many of whom have influenced my thinking. I have learned that with scientific collaboration can come friendship and genuine camaraderie, an unexpected find in an otherwise cut-throat world. Those colleagues who became friends have been the greatest source of inspiration and the most special among them are Darren Fa, Pepe Carrión, Andy Currant, Joaquín Rodríguez-Vidal, Larry Sawchuk and – greatest of greats among Iberian archaeologists – Paco Giles Pacheco. What a privilege it has been to have known and worked with them. None of this would have happened had it not been for my dear father who gave so much so that I could one day write these lines...

Finally, I am most grateful to Alan and Gertrud Roberts of Santana for placing their trust in me and in the subject of this book. I also thank David Baird and Cheryl Gatward, who have managed to tidy up and put my manuscript and photographs into a wonderful design.

I have enjoyed every second writing this book. I hope that you experience at least some of that enjoyment and that you will find a new world here, one that inspires you as much as it has inspired me.

Clive Finlayson, Gibraltar, October 8, 2007

dAnceS wit

CHAPTER ONE

Dances without wolves

AL-ANDALUS

I was driving across the maritime pine forests of the Sierra de Cazorla in southeastern Andalusia. From time to time the forest opened up to reveal a wonderful scene of mountains and deep valleys as far as the eye could see. The Guadalquivir, the great river of the Arabs, the Baetis of the Romans, is born here and it cuts deep gorges through the limestone as it makes its way north. A small flock of griffon vultures circled on a rising thermal as they started the morning search for a carcass. Cazorla provides the shelter and protection for them to nest but, as we will discover later in this book, they search far and wide beyond the sierra for their food. The road took a turn to the left and all of a sudden the landscape below me was violently different. It was no longer beautiful in its complexity but instead strangely captivating by its regularity. The view was reminiscent of a plaited hairstyle, rows of trees running parallel to each other across a slope to be met by rows running at a different angle on the next slope and so into infinity. The trees were olives and in front of me was Europe's largest monoculture of this tree. As I descended into this landscape, the temperature rose from the 28 degrees C of the forested mountain, first to 30, then 32, eventually to 38 degrees. In 20 kilometres of road, 1,000 metres of altitude and a jump from the irregularity of the forest to the extreme order of the cultivation, the temperature had risen by 10 degrees.

The road took me through endless rows of olives. The white soil, mixed with fertiliser and insecticide, dazzled as the strong sun reflected off it. There were no shrubs, no grasses, except on the narrow roadside verge. This was July in the upper Guadalquivir valley of Jaén, but as I accelerated in search of reprieve not a single insect hit my windscreen despite the heat. There were no birds either, save for a lonely turtle dove that looked lost in this desert of olives. This is what our greed and voracity can do to a land. This is what the European Community subsidises and encourages with one hand while seemingly promoting the protection of Europe's natural heritage with the other.

The wolf inhabited the Guadalquivir valley until the mid-19th century. At that time vast tracts of oak, carob and pine woodland and dehesa (a kind of savannah) covered the valley from Jaén and Córdoba in the east to its estuary in Doñana in the west. The low-lying ground in the province of Huelva, that included the great forest of Doñana, was richly wooded. This woodland continued inland into the Sierra Morena so that Doñana was not the ecological island that it is today but rather the coastal extension of a vast forest.

In the reign of King Alfonso XI (1311-50), herds of semi-wild cattle roamed freely and widely across this fallow land, providing ample food for the wolf. Red and fallow deer and wild boar, common animals throughout the Guadalquivir valley as recently as the 16th century, would also have been hunted by wolves. These carnivores moved around with impunity across this territory, to the point that an observer in the 1470s noted how two wolves had entered the city of Sevilla itself, causing panic in the population until one was eventually shot dead and the other ran off. The wolf's head, which was taken

Stone pine wood with lentisc understorey at La Algaida on the east bank of the Guadalquivir near its estuary.

to the Duke of Medina Sidonia, was considered an omen of an imminent disaster. It is hardly surprising that in those days a bounty was paid to those who managed to kill an adult wolf or destroy a litter.

In spite of the fragmentation of the once-vast woodland, leaving islands of forest surrounded by open fields, by the end of the 18th century the wolf population remained within the valley. We get an idea of their numbers from a record of 47 wolves killed just in the territory of Utrera, in the lower Guadalquivir, between January 19, 1683, and March 21, 1714. Even so, their habitat was being seriously destroyed in favour of agriculture. Some towns had by this time turned 90 per cent of their lands over to the cultivation of cereal, olive and vines, leaving little pristine woodland. The wolf would soon become a rare animal in the valley and the strongholds would be reduced to the inaccessible mountains surrounding it.

Wolves continued to roam the valley of the Guadalquivir, in much smaller numbers than previously, into the 19th century. They were still considered a nuisance close to Sevilla itself in 1838. They probably managed to survive well away from the natural forests in a similar manner to those wolves that still roam the plains of upper Castile today, in such areas as Villafáfila. These animals would have been able to survive by sheltering in olive groves and among the large wheat fields and vineyards and feeding from human waste and domestic cattle.

More and more the incursions by wolves into the valley were sporadic and from remote outposts in the Sierra Morena. The increasing transformation of the Guadalquivir valley through human activities, the absence of natural habitat, huge persecution including the use of poisons, and the intensification of agriculture, especially the massive exploitation of the olive monoculture, caused the extinction of the species in the valley during the 20th century. In the 1950s and 1960s wolves descended occasionally from nearby hills, but none were left when the century came to its end.

At the lower end of the Guadalquivir, the protection afforded to the hunting grounds of Doñana and its hinterland meant that there was still a healthy population of wolves, and bears, at the end of the 15th century. At the start of the 16th century some lands were turned to pasture for work oxen. Wolves were then a threat to the livestock in the lands of the Duke of Medina Sidonia and an active campaign against them started. It was one that would continue, with small breaks, until the middle of the 20th century. One such interruption occurred during the 17th and 18th centuries and allowed a partial recovery inside Doñana. It was caused by the increasing pressure on cattle farming on its edges that reduced the hunting intensity inside Doñana itself.

The wolf population in the rich lands of Doñana must have been huge. In 1654, the damage caused by wolves on the eastern shore of the Guadalquivir, near Sanlúcar, was considered unstoppable. The inadequacy of organised hunts in controlling such large numbers was soon recognised. Many were thought to hide in the lentisc scrub within the stone pine wood of La Algaida. The solution was the cutting down of the entire pine wood. The area was, once again, reforested in 1681 and remains part of the National Park of Doñana today. Another measure of the enormous size of the Doñana wolf population comes from the figures of animals killed inside it: 27 in 1630; 16 in 1657; 23 in 1683; 20 in 1699; 10 in 1720; 24 in 1760; and 12 in 1761.

Wolves were still plentiful in Doñana at the start of the 19th century: 30 were hunted there in 1803, two years before the Battle of Trafalgar, and 15 in 1815, the year of the Battle of Waterloo. By the end of that century they were all but gone. The Victorian naturalists Abel Chapman and Walter Buck, who probably knew Doñana as well as any contemporary, never saw a wolf there at the end of the 19th century. When King Alfonso XIII hunted there in 1924, there was no wolf among the impressive array of animals shot. A wolf was shot near Hinojos, in lands adjacent to Doñana in 1907 and another in Doñana itself in 1927. Although another one was shot north of Doñana in 1972, the last ones in Doñana itself were killed in 1951. Hunting probably finished off the last survivors, or others that strayed from nearby areas, but the real culprit was the large-scale agricultural activity of the late 19th century. It wiped out the remaining natural forest and made Doñana an ecological island, no longer connected to the forests of Sierra Morena. The wolves of the 20th century were living dead. They had nowhere to go and the gun simply accelerated the inevitable.

CHAPTER ONE *Dances without wolves*

Another carnivore, the Spanish lynx, managed to hold out and is now the subject of intense conservation. Ironically, these lynxes are trapped. On a number of occasions lynxes that have tried to disperse from the park to reach new areas have been killed, usually by traffic, when passing the fence that delimits Doñana today. There are lynxes in the Sierra Morena and in the Montes de Toledo, but those in Doñana simply cannot reach them as there is no longer any natural habitat between these areas. Doñana is their graveyard.

What of the rest of Andalusia? What happened to wolves in the mountains of the south? Sadly, the story was very similar to that of the lowlands of the Guadalquivir. Poisoning with strychnine was a major cause in the mountains. Chapman, Buck and Verner already highlighted the problem at the end of the 19th century when they warned that the laying down of poisoned food for wolves by goatherds seriously affected other animals as well as the wolves themselves. They saw the rarefaction of the bearded vulture in the mountains between Jaén and Granada, and also in Cádiz, as the result of the uncontrolled use of poison. The bearded vulture, once a common bird in the skies of all the sierras of al-Andalus, almost disappeared altogether. Poisoned baits, though illegal, are still used in parts of Andalusia.

Wolves had gone from the inland mountains of Jaén and the Córdoba sub-Betics by the beginning of the 20th century. In the southern Betic mountains, around Ronda, Grazalema and the mountains bordering the plains of Jerez, the wolf was extinct by 1925. To the east it disappeared in the 1930s from the mountains of Málaga, Antequera, Tejeda, Alhama and Almijara. They were last seen in the Sierra Nevada in 1933. To the northeast, they were practically extinct in the Sierra de Cazorla y Segura in the 1930s even though stray animals from nearby mountains were seen there up to the end of the 1970s. Eastern Andalusia suffered a similar fate. Wolves disappeared in the early 1930s from the sierras of Baza, Gor and Filabres.

Wolves once roamed across the whole of Andalusia and the vast expanses of woodland on the Sierra Morena were a major stronghold. Even though the wolf had been considered extinct from Andalusia in the 1980s, two small pockets have been rediscovered by scientists in recent years. One population survives in the eastern Sierra Morena, between the provinces of Jaén and eastern Córdoba. A second nucleus is in the central Sierra Morena in the area of Hornachuelos. They have gone from the western Sierra Morena of Huelva and Sevilla. The last ones were reported there in 1985. How much longer will the Andalusian wolves survive? With protection of their habitat in the vast and depopulated Sierra Morena they could do so, and even recover as they are doing in other parts of their natural range.

In his wonderful book on the history of the wolf in Andalusia, Victor Gutiérrez Alba says that there are two kinds of sierras: those that have wolves and those that do not. Those that still do, retain the charm and magic of their presence and they conserve a small piece of what the rural al-Andalus of our forefathers was like. In these few places,

Valley of the Guadalquivir near Carmona in Sevilla Province showing treeless landscape devoted to monocultures

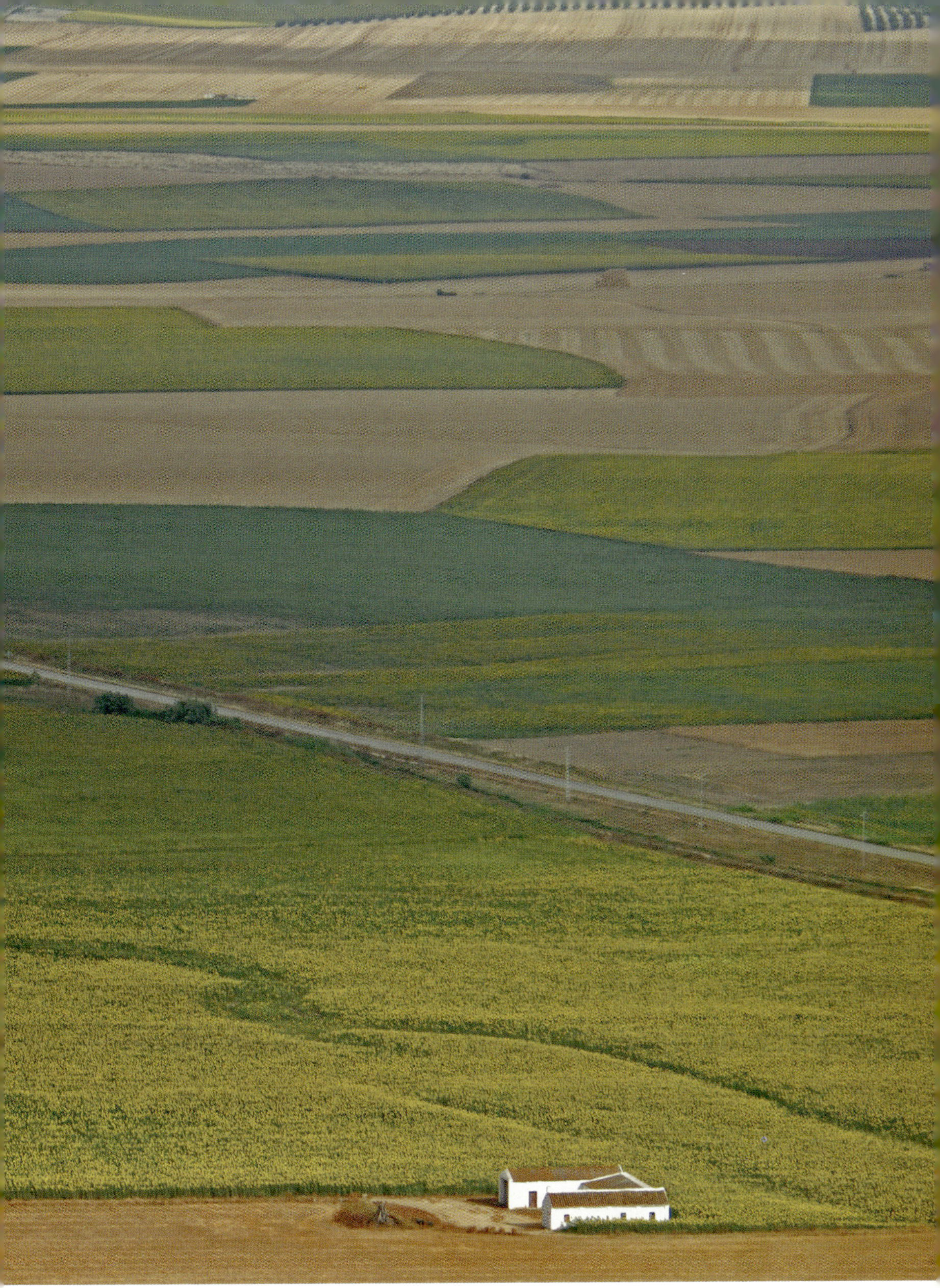

Olive monoculture in Jaén Province

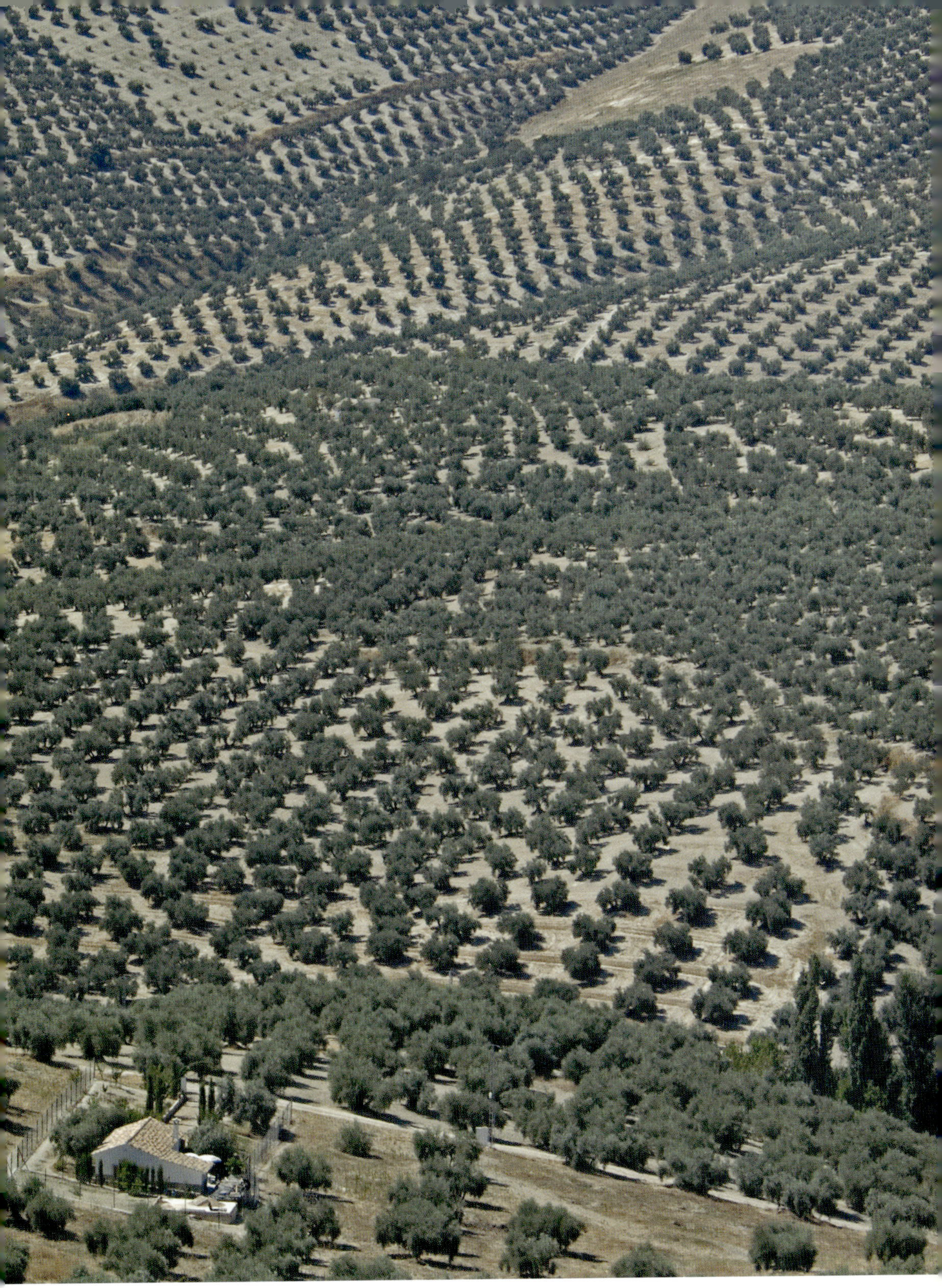

Traditional, low-intensity, olive grove near Velez Rubio, Almería.

These olive groves are ecologically much richer than the intensive and ecologically sterile large-scale practices that have become dominant over huge areas.

during the cold winter nights, we can still hear the haunting wail of the wolf. In those where their existence has been taken away from us we remain orphans of nature...

I have used the wolf as an indicator of the degree to which the apparently pristine wilds of al-Andalus have been ravaged by our voracious appetite for land. Travel along the main motorway from Despeñaperros, the boundary between Andalusia and La Mancha, down towards Córdoba, then Écija and then Sevilla, and you will be overcome by the desolation. We have turned the valley of the great river into a natural wasteland, a land of monoculture where even a single tree that was not an olive, let alone a forest, was an inconvenience. The mountains on either side appear to have saved themselves from the onslaught, only because our technology has not found a way of dealing with the vertical. Look closer and you will see endless rows of olive cultivation creeping up the slopes towards the heights of Cazorla. Look for bearded vultures in the skies of Sierra Nevada or the Serranía de Ronda. There are none. Wherever we look we find that we have been left without the magic of the wolf.

How does a land go from having an abundance of wolves to almost none? In other words, how is it that a land can deteriorate to such a degree that the very indicators of its good health vanish? The elements that can help us answer these questions are all in the following chapters. They include climate, geology and, particularly, human history. Rarely are all these factors considered together when trying to understand the changing ecological fortunes of a region.

I start with a paradox. Ecologically, al-Andalus has no rival in Europe today. It also has a rich and diverse history, one which has contributed above all else to the deterioration of that very ecological diversity. So how can a place be so rich and yet so poor? To us, with our 21st-century eyes, a flock of a few hundred black kites flying across the Strait of Gibraltar leaves us in awe. We never knew the flocks of tens of thousands of an age gone by. To the fishermen of the almadrabas a catch of 1,000 tuna in a season is success because they never knew the catches of 100,000 or more of the Duke of Medina Sidonia's men. We travel long distances into high sierras to catch a glimpse of the bearded vulture because the largest population in Europe is in the Pyrenees, and we marvel at the sight of the solitary bird. We cannot fathom a land in which every sierra had its pair of bearded vultures. We climb the peaks of Gredos, Sierra Nevada or Cazorla to see the wonderful sight of a herd of mountain goats, the Spanish ibex, except that they are only "mountain" goats today because we have wiped them from the coastal cliffs and screes that were once also their home.

My intention is that each of the chapters in this book can be read in isolation. Each tells a story that adds to the very essence of the land that was once known as al-Andalus. It covered practically the whole of the Iberian peninsula. In the final two chapters I will attempt to bring the strands together to answer the questions that I have posed at the start.

The chapters are not arranged in chronological order but there is a sense in the links

CHAPTER ONE *Dances without wolves*

The wolf was once widespread across al-Andalus. Sabiñanigo Reserve, Pyrenees

"In a few places, during the cold winter nights, we can still hear the haunting wail of the wolf. In those where their existence has been taken away from us we remain orphans of nature..."

between one chapter and the next. Some have a largely natural history focus while others are historical. Yet others combine the two. This arrangement reflects my own thinking that we cannot understand life from isolated threads. All is history. Today's landscapes and ecosystems have been woven into a complex fabric by the passage of time. Humans started as, and still are, components of this world. As time went on we also became agents that were able to change that world. We also became agents that affected one another's lives to an increasing degree.

As I write these lines, a heat wave and forest fires are raging across Eastern Europe. Oxford is under water as a great flood has hit the British Isles. A dam threatens to burst somewhere in Siberia as unusual rains hit this land. The news is full of spin about doom and gloom. Climate change has become a term in vogue, a conversation piece at dinner parties and cocktails – as if climate had never changed in the past. Meanwhile people are killing each other in Iraq while celebrating a victory in football. Poor and desperate people, no longer news, are risking their lives each day to cross from North Africa to the beaches of the Costa del Sol, where oblivious tourists are sunning themselves. Many of them never make it across, and drown, just as we sip our gin and tonic with the sun setting over our idyllic beach. Gangs of unscrupulous gangsters plot the next run of illegal immigrants or drugs in some quiet bar not far from the beach, while nearby businessmen plan another urbanisation that will strangle the last shred of natural coast. Scenes from times long past appear to repeat themselves daily on the beaches of 21st-century al-Andalus. It seems as if the human mind has remained unchanged in 10,000 years.

What can the story of al-Andalus tell us about ourselves and the way we have created the situation we face today? This is what I will be exploring throughout this book. It is a personal journey across a wonderful land that I have dedicated my whole life to. The book is not a travel guide, but a journey across the places that I have chosen to include will, if the reader chooses to make it, capture the very nature of the land of al-Andalus and its rich history.

I am an Iberian. I was born in Gibraltar of Scottish, English, Portuguese and Spanish descent. I have lived all my life in the lands of al-Andalus so my approach, unlike many of the accounts that have been written in the past by outsiders, is from the inside. Much of it is first-hand, based on my own studies of ecology, excavations with archaeologists and working with some wonderful people who have dedicated their lives to the history and ecology of this magnificent land. This is the mixture responsible for the thoughts and views put forward in this book.

Where the Griffon Still

Chapter Two

Where the griffon still soars

AL-ANDALUS

About a year before the outbreak of the Spanish Civil War in 1936 three young Cambridge undergraduates ventured into the unknown wilds of Spain with a very specific purpose in mind. Not really knowing exactly where they were going, Robert Atkinson, E. F. Allen and J. M. Naish set off across the English Channel in a brand new red-and-chrome sports car, an anticipated 21st birthday gift, intending to obtain the first close-up photographs of a griffon vulture at its nest. They had just passed their driving tests, which consisted of driving the car 100 yards along a main road, thus qualifying them to do what they liked on a continental road. With the small car crammed with tents and photographic equipment, and with a smattering of Spanish for comfort, they excitedly left Cambridge one March morning no sooner had term ended.

Information on the griffon was scant. The works of the great Victorian naturalists and explorers, Abel Chapman and Willoughby Verner, whom we will meet many times in this book, took them as far as 1914 but nothing had been written on Spain since. The young undergraduates crossed France, from Boulogne to the Spanish border in 24 hours and made straight for southern Spain, through the Basque country, Burgos, Valladolid, across the Sierra de Gredos and down into Extremadura towards Mérida and on to Sevilla, Jerez and from there to Tarifa. These are all places that will appear in this book. Throughout the journey they kept a steady watch for the large vultures which they only knew from stuffed specimens in the Cambridge museum. Although they sighted some vultures along the way, they were no more than specks on the horizon.

However, as they came to the plains of the Laguna de La Janda between Vejer and Tarifa, they hit the jackpot: "The road crossed the river (the Barbate) and opened into a big plain (La Janda), surrounded by mountains. This looked like real griffon country — wide open grasslands, prairies almost, supporting cattle and pack animals, only a few scattered trees. And encircling the plain, the jagged heights of the sierras. Soon we saw a griffon sailing in the blue sky on unmoving wings, round and round; then two more, closer; then a couple of Neophrons (Egyptian vultures), one of which pitched and watched. Far away from the road a jagged ridge of rock was silhouetted against the sky. A few griffons, distant specks only, were circling above it."

They were almost certainly watching the griffons circling above one of their breeding colonies in southern Spain, the Laja de La Zarga on the coastal Sierra de La Plata. Laja is a local term that describes sheer outcrops of sandstone, usually surrounded by oak woodland. They make ideal nesting sites for the big birds and this colony was well known to the Victorian naturalists based in nearby Gibraltar. Atkinson and his friends had rediscovered the stronghold of the griffon.

Today, Spain is home to 23,000 breeding pairs of griffon vultures: that represents more than 80 per cent of the European population of the species. This may sound incredible to the non-ornithologist who probably associates vultures with lions and hyaenas in the Serengeti. The vastness of the wild spaces of al-Andalus, its big mountain ranges and

CHAPTER TWO *Where the griffon still soars*

plentiful food are the secret of this vulture's success in southern Europe. It is a recent success though. When Atkinson and friends visited the breeding colonies in the 1930s, the Spanish population of these vultures would have been on the decline, one that would continue throughout the first half of the 20th century up to the 1960s. The causes are all too familiar: the use of poison in animal carcasses and direct persecution.

Yet, in a world too often dominated by stories of ecological doom, the griffon vulture's recovery in recent decades is a marked source of optimism. Like humans, in Spain vultures are counted every 10 years. The first census undertaken by Spanish ornithologists in 1979 gave a figure of 3,249 breeding pairs for the country; 10 years later the estimate had risen to 8,064 pairs but part of the improvement was due to improved cover of remote regions; in 1999, the figure had risen dramatically to 22,455 even though the coverage was similar to 1989.

It is no coincidence that the use of poisons was made illegal in Spain in 1984. The vultures got a reprieve. Protection of nesting sites also improved with awareness of the country's rich natural treasures. The icing on the cake was an increase in cattle farmed in many regions of Spain. Today griffons feed almost exclusively on livestock carcasses and the combination of plentiful food and reduced disturbance produced rapid dividends. In the southwest of the Iberian peninsula, especially in Cádiz province, griffon vultures roam freely over vast landscapes of cork oak woodland and open plains (the campiña). They find shelter and protection and locate their nests in the lajas that emerge from the canopy of the cork oak forests. These lajas can be cryptically hidden within the dense forest. I recall one occasion when I was in the heart of a pristine cork forest in the mountains north of Jimena de la Frontera. A group of us had spent the night with a local goatherd, having arrived after dark via several kilometres of muddy track. A combination of first light, dawn chorus and inquisitive goats soon got us up. We had slept at the base of a laja. Now, with the first rays of morning sun, the towering wall of sandstone rose above the tallest trees. Whitewashed ledges gave away that griffons were about. The whitewashing was from countless vulture droppings, always a clear sign of nests. We scanned the cliff with our binoculars. The first sight of these huge birds, casually perched on narrow ledges with outstretched wings spanning three metres catching the morning sun, made the heart skip a beat.

What followed was a typical day in the life of a European vulture colony. The temperature rose sharply in the middle of the morning and, as if some magical degree Celsius had been reached, one bird stirred and effortlessly dropped on outstretched wings from a ledge. Without beating once it picked up an up-draught and was off beyond the line of trees. Within seconds others were repeating the operation until we had 50 of these majestic birds circling over us, inquisitively looking down, so close that we could easily see their eyes inspecting us – we made eye-to-eye contact. The big birds effortlessly became specks in the blue sky as, one by one, they entered glide mode and headed off for the plains to the west. Minutes after the first one had taken off the laja was silent.

During the day vultures came and went from the colony, bringing food in their stomachs that they regurgitated to the single youngster in each nest and relieving the partner which would fly off in search of some vulturine gastronomic delight. A mid-afternoon shower brought the birds in early, one by one lowering undercarriage like heavy Lancaster bombers, and we retreated into the goatherd's shelter. I shall never forget what happened next.

The strong evening Andalusian sun broke through the last of the thunderclouds. Everything was crisp. We sat outside on some wet rocks. The scents of moist earth and myriad Mediterranean flowers and herbs were all-pervading. I brought out my telescope which I mounted on the tripod. We could see every detail of the vultures' plumage as they opened their soaked wings to dry them out with the last rays of sun. Then a movement among the low shrubs on the cliff caught my eye. I zoomed in to pick up a pair of horns. This was not a goat, it was substantially larger, the size of a small deer. Other pairs of horns stirred in the vicinity. One stood up from the afternoon siesta – it was an impressive male Spanish ibex. The herd, some 20 strong, had been sleeping through the afternoon rain and were now stirring. Soon we could see them, sure-footed, wandering down the wet ledges. There were several males, one dominant, females and young. As the sun went down a fox appeared out of its daytime shelter. The scene was complete when bats started to come out of a cave in the laja; we identified four different species flying above our heads. This really had been a wonderful day in the midst of a vulture colony.

The cork oak woods in which the lajas are set are rich in plants and animals. It was no coincidence that we had seen such a diversity of life that evening. Walking through the forest surrounding the cliff, we also saw wild boar, red and roe deer. Woodpeckers drummed while Bonelli's warblers, newly arrived from tropical African winter sojourns, pursued tiny insects in the canopy. Nightingales sang loudly near the watercourses. At night, eagle owls patrolled the cliffs of the laja while tawny owls hooted incessantly in the forest. Tracks revealed that genet, mongoose and wild cat had been about that night. The cork oak forests of Cádiz are a unique reservoir of wonderful animals and plants, a treasure that has thankfully managed to survive the ravages of civilisation. Their survival has not been due to some philanthropic human gesture; it has instead been purely and simply the casual outcome of economic exploitation and our insatiable appetite for wine. The cork oak is adapted to resisting Mediterranean fires and it has done so successfully for millions of years thanks to the protection that the outer layer of cork gives to the tree.

For a long time the fate of the cork oak forests of southern Europe, mainly in Spain and Portugal, with smaller populations in southern France and Italy, had seemed highly tenuous. It was not until the second half of the 18th century that cork stopper manufacture took off but the conservation and management of the cork oak forests

CHAPTER TWO *Where the griffon still soars*

gained economic importance much later. By the time such interests moved in favour of the conservation of the cork oaks, huge tracts of forest had already been cleared. As far back as the 14th century cork oaks in Portugal were being exploited for the tanning industry. It was not the cork but the inner layers of the tree that were valued and this meant that huge numbers of trees were cut down, causing extensive devastation of the forests. The practice often went parallel with charcoal production. The exploitation of the cork oak for tanning reached its height in the second half of the 19th century. One major reason was the decline, through over-exploitation, of wild plants that had been traditionally used in the process. Sumac and myrtle had become scarce in Andalusia and Extremadura and the cork oak's tanbark was a natural and plentiful substitute.

I found a clear signal of the rise and fall of the sumac market for the tanning industry while wading through the logs of the Port of Gibraltar for the 19th century. I looked at several years to compare how this product had fared during the century. The number of ships carrying sumac went from six in 1818, to 14 in 1820, 11 in 1830, peaking at 28 in 1840, then declining to 15 in 1850 and only two in 1865. The vast majority of these ships were coming from Italy, especially Sicily and Trieste, and they were supplying markets in Britain (especially Liverpool, London and Glasgow), the United States, Germany and Belgium. The rapid decline by 1865 may have been due to a combination of over-exploitation in Italy, as happened in Spain, and the alternative use of tanbark. The latter product was being shipped from the main source in Portugal and so would not have passed through the Gibraltar port.

So the demand for tanbark created havoc in the landscape. Much of the late 19th-century impact was in the Serranía de Ronda where 25,000 hectares of cork oak woodland were cleared in a 21-year period. Other areas of Andalusia suffered from deforestation, this time for a different purpose — fuel. Charcoal was the traditional fuel in the Mediterranean and the process of making charcoal from wood was commonplace. The impact of logging for fuel was felt most in the Sierra Morena as it was linked to industry. Mining for quicksilver, silver, iron and copper generated a demand for fuel and the forests were cut down. At the western end of the Sierra Morena, the operations in the Río Tinto mines practically wiped out the cork and holm oaks from the area. Even the cork woods around the Coto Doñana, the national park that we nowadays think of as the epitome of wilderness, were described by Henri Cavailles in 1905 as "once the site of a noble forest of cork trees, now laid waste by the axe of the charcoal-burner".

Even though the Romans were aware of the value of cork stoppers for wine amphorae and other uses including shoes, the regular exploitation of the cork itself dates back to medieval times when the Portuguese began exporting cork to Flanders early in the 15th century. The cork was probably used for fishing floats and related maritime activities. It was also used to make shoes, with soles made of several layers of bark six inches thick, that became the fashion among upper class women in the 14th and 15th centuries in

Cork oak woodland. Almoraima, Cádiz.

The trees have been stripped of the bark for much of the lower trunk

Cork bark

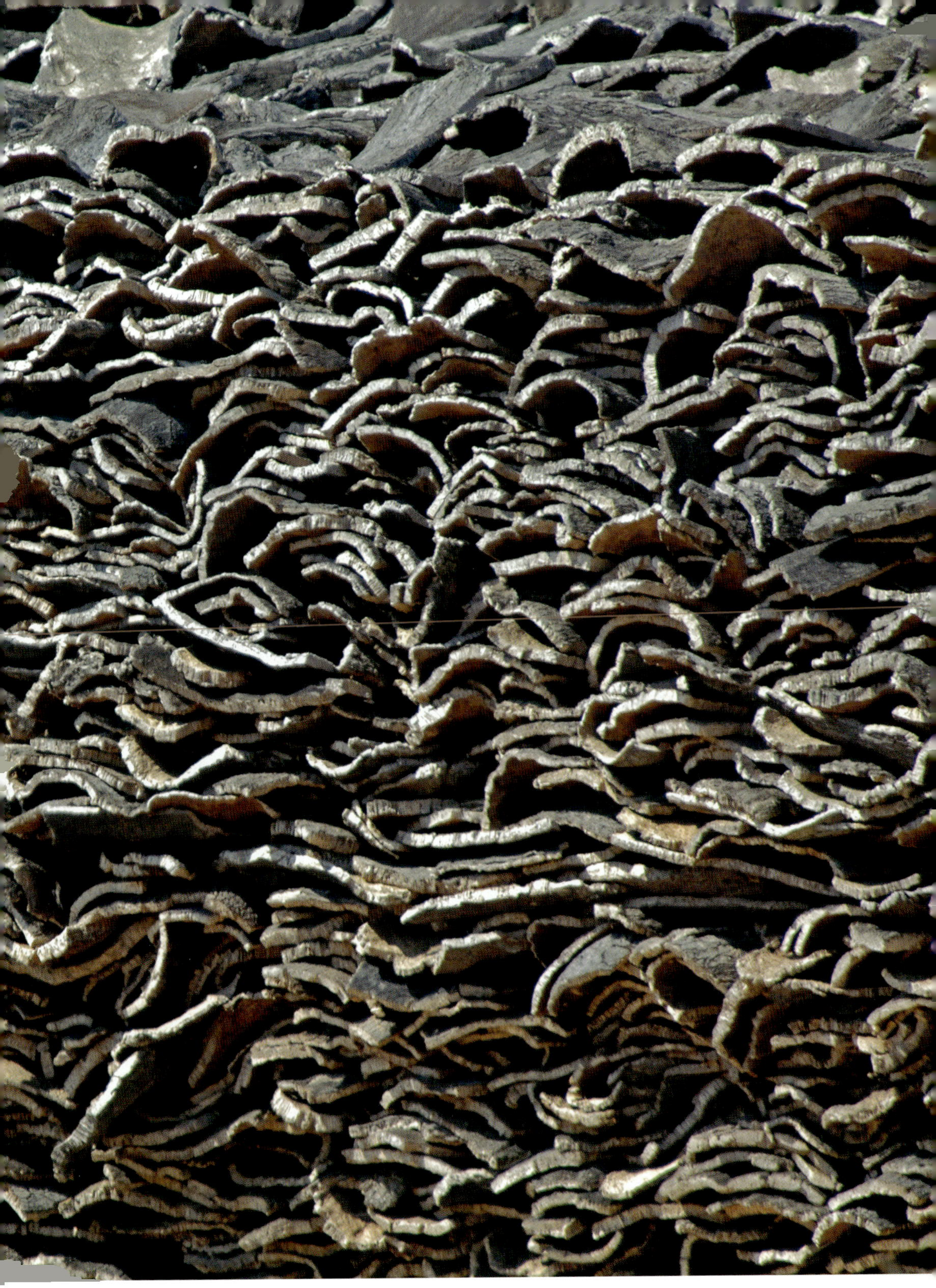

Spain. The muslims called these early platform shoes qorq or al-qorq, so the English cork and the Spanish corcho (cork) and alcornoque (cork oak tree) may well have their origins in a shoe.

Not until the mid-18th century did the commercial exploitation of cork for stoppers begin. It followed the first use of cork stoppers for champagne by the Benedictine monks in Hautvillers, France, in the 17th century. The limited extent of the French forests and the poor quality of their cork soon turned attention to the northern Catalan ones around Girona. Cork stoppers were first manufactured in the border village of Agullana in 1750. The industry grew rapidly and spread within the Catalan region in a decade. Shortages in raw materials in the first quarter of the 19th century widened the horizon of the Catalan entrepreneurs who had moved into Extremadura by the 1830s and into Andalusia in the 1840s. With the increasing economic importance of the cork stopper industry the conservation of the remaining forests began and thanks to this industry I was able to share the joy of the woodland wilderness among the vultures.

Today, cork oak forests cover around 2.7 million hectares of the western Mediterranean, providing income for around 100,000 people. Fifteen billion cork stoppers are produced annually. No trees are cut in the process. The outer bark, the cork, of the tree is removed and this starts to regenerate quickly. Nine years later the bark is removed once more. The cork industry is truly a unique case of sustainable economic exploitation.

On another occasion in the territory of the griffon, I recall visiting the Laja de Aciscar. This laja lies close to the Laguna de La Janda and within the area visited by the Cambridge undergraduates in the 1930s. Aciscar was well known to the 19th century naturalists, military officers like Howard Irby and Willoughby Verner who climbed the cliffs in search of griffons' nests. I too was climbing the laja for a similar reason, except that my purpose was to help place metal rings on the young vultures that were on the nests. I was with Fernando Barrios, naturalist and photographer from Algeciras.

We had spent the morning climbing precariously across ledges and getting up to the nests. My first experience with a young griffon was exactly as Verner had described it 100 years earlier. The young vulture feigns to be dead when approached. Once it realises the deception has not worked it goes to Plan B. This was vividly described by Verner: "...for, after recovering consciousness as quickly as it had pretended to lose it, it makes a series of bows accompanied by a regurgitating process which quickly ends in the rejection of the whole of its last meal! When one considers what this must have been, it is best left to the imagination what it is like when thus presented to the too importunate naturalist."

Danger from the adults may be insignificant, they mostly fly away when the nest is approached, but the child more than compensates for its parents' spinelessness.

The site of Aciscar is quite different from the earlier one I described. The laja is set alongside a stream that gives it its name. A deep canyon traverses the rocky outcrop. To reach the clifftop from where you descend perilously to the nests, you have to spend

CHAPTER TWO *Where the griffon still soars*

some time penetrating the tangle of thicket growing around the river. The cliff was a favourite of other raptors too. Here nested Egyptian vulture, Bonelli's eagle and the eagle owl, a raptor community typical of these outcrops. Unlike the previous laja, which was well set in the forest, this one lay on the edge and faced the large plain of La Janda. It was an ideal location for the raptors, safe on the cliffs and with the open plains, their favourite hunting grounds, next door.

After a long, hard, hot day we descended from the top of the laja, through the mesh of undergrowth. When we paused for a few seconds, the thicket behind us started to shake as though with a movement of its own. The shaking became decidedly agitated until out of the greenery emerged a large cow and her calf, followed by several others and, finally, a bull. They brushed past us and proceeded to stampede down towards the valley. Luckily, they were not fighting bulls. Their reddish-brown colour and long horns gave them away as Retinto cattle, a breed I knew well from previous encounters, with the habit of skulking in the undergrowth in the woods when the heat of the sun forces them away from the open pastures.

Typical of southern and southwestern Spain where they originate and known to Roman, Visigoth and Muslim, Retinto cattle are good for their meat and working capacity. To the west of the sandstone hills and the cork oak forests are vast plains and rolling hills that are perfect grazing grounds for these animals. I cannot resist quoting Verner once again as he gives us a colourful image of the meadows (vegas) in the spring:

"To see the vega at its best, it should be visited in the month of May when the vivid green of the herbage is almost blotted out by the brilliancy of the masses of spring flowers. Nothing is more striking to the eye than the lavish manner in which Nature applies her colours in such districts. Riding across the vega, at one time you may traverse areas of golden marigold, perhaps half a mile to the right the land is pink for hundreds of yards with a beautiful large madder or again, crimson with tre-foil, whilst to the left, maybe, it is as white as snow with waving camomile. As you leave the grasslands and traverse the lower spurs of the fallows, whole hillsides are covered with bright yellow mustard or big white daisies. Perhaps one of the most remarkable effects is that produced by the small blue, yellow and white convolvulus (Convolvulus tricolor) with which the ground is carpeted so closely as to make the hillsides at a short distance appear cobalt blue. In addition to these great masses of colour the whole plain abounds with other flowers which astonish and delight the traveller. Large purple iris and the diminutive pale-coloured one abound as does the crimson gladiolus and a hundred other brilliant blossoms of all shades and colours."

The Retintos, along with fighting bulls descendants of the prehistoric aurochs — from the Celtic aur (wild), orch (bull), are the main grazers of these open lands. The close proximity of the plains and the herds of grazers to the secure cliffs have made this region a veritable vultures' paradise. Ironically, the bullfighting tradition has made a significant contribution to habitat conservation through the maintenance of large tracts of grassland and dehesa which would otherwise have been cleared or ploughed. Distance is not a problem for vultures, however, and, if they have to, they will move across vast tracts of land in search of food. My good friend Dr Juan Plegezuelos, a biologist at Granada University, once told me a chilling story. We have to go back to August, 1921. Forests were being cut back to make way for new railway tracks through the mountainous country around the Sierra de Cazorla in eastern Andalusia. On the ground below the perches of griffon vultures a forester found many buttons from the jackets of Spanish soldiers. The buttons belonged to the Regulares, a regiment that was exclusively based in the Spanish colonies in North Africa and had been involved in a military disaster known as the Desastre de Annual that occurred on July 21 of that year. Between 14 and 16,000 Spanish soldiers had been massacred at Annual, which is situated between Al Hoceima and Melilla on the Mediterranean coast. The inescapable and amazing conclusion was that the vultures from Cazorla had crossed to North Africa to feed on the corpses of the poor Spanish soldiers killed in battle.

In contrast, the Cádiz plains are only a short flight away from the vultures' nests and the vultures spend hours on the wing there patrolling for the carcasses of dead cattle. It is a millennial story that repeats itself each day in the skies of Cádiz. The story may, however, be about to take a turn for the worse. An upsurge in recent years in the use of poisons, especially in private hunting estates, poses new risks to the vultures. New legislation, aimed at controlling the spread of animal-borne diseases, is placing strict controls on how farmers dispose of carcasses. The downside is less food for the vultures. Progress may, once more, take its toll. The cork stopper industry is also suffering from the use of plastic stoppers and aluminium screw-tops by the wine industry and this may pose new threats to the cork oak forests. A recent report revealed that Portuguese cork stopper exports to the United States were cut by 30 million euros between 2000 and 2004. Corresponding exports to Australia were cut by 24 million euros. The future for the vultures and the cork oak forests of southern Spain is far from secure.

Since 1991 I have been directing an excavation project in Gorham's Cave on the east side of the Rock of Gibraltar. The cave is unique in that it has archaeological deposits that go back 120,000 years. They are full of fossilised bones of animals and they are rich in pollen. If you look out of the cave today, all you observe is the Mediterranean lapping the shore close to the cave. For most of those 120,000 years the climate of the Earth was cooler than today. In these days of global warming it is hard to think of a cooler planet but that is how it was for a long time. Much water was trapped as ice in polar ice sheets and glaciers and global sea levels dropped. The coastline was five kilometres away from its present location and the vast plains were like a Serengeti in the Mediterranean. Large herds of red deer, horses and aurochs roamed and were hunted by lions, leopards

Young griffon vulture in nest on ledge at Laja de Acíscar, Cádiz

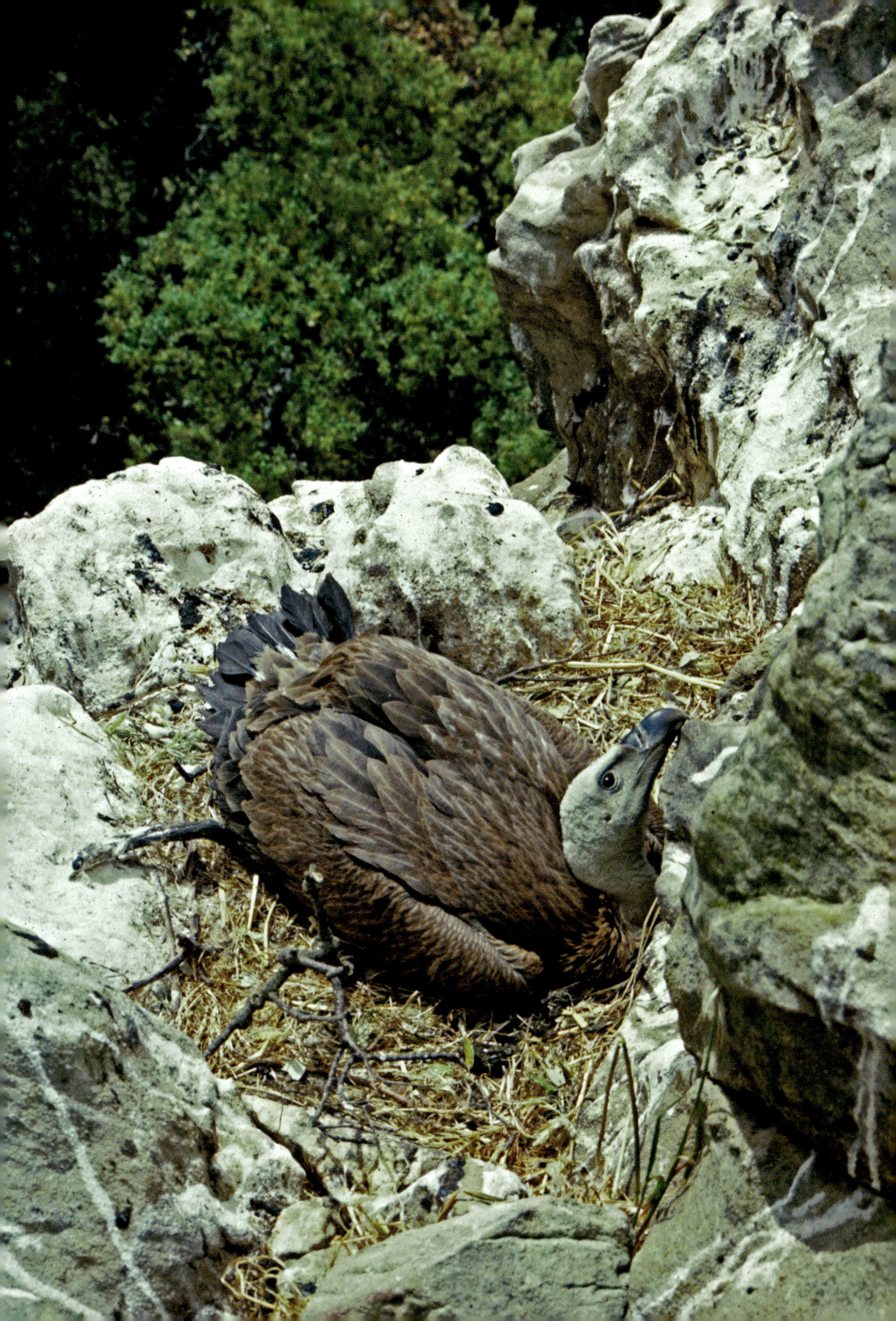

Young fighting bulls in la Janda, Cádiz

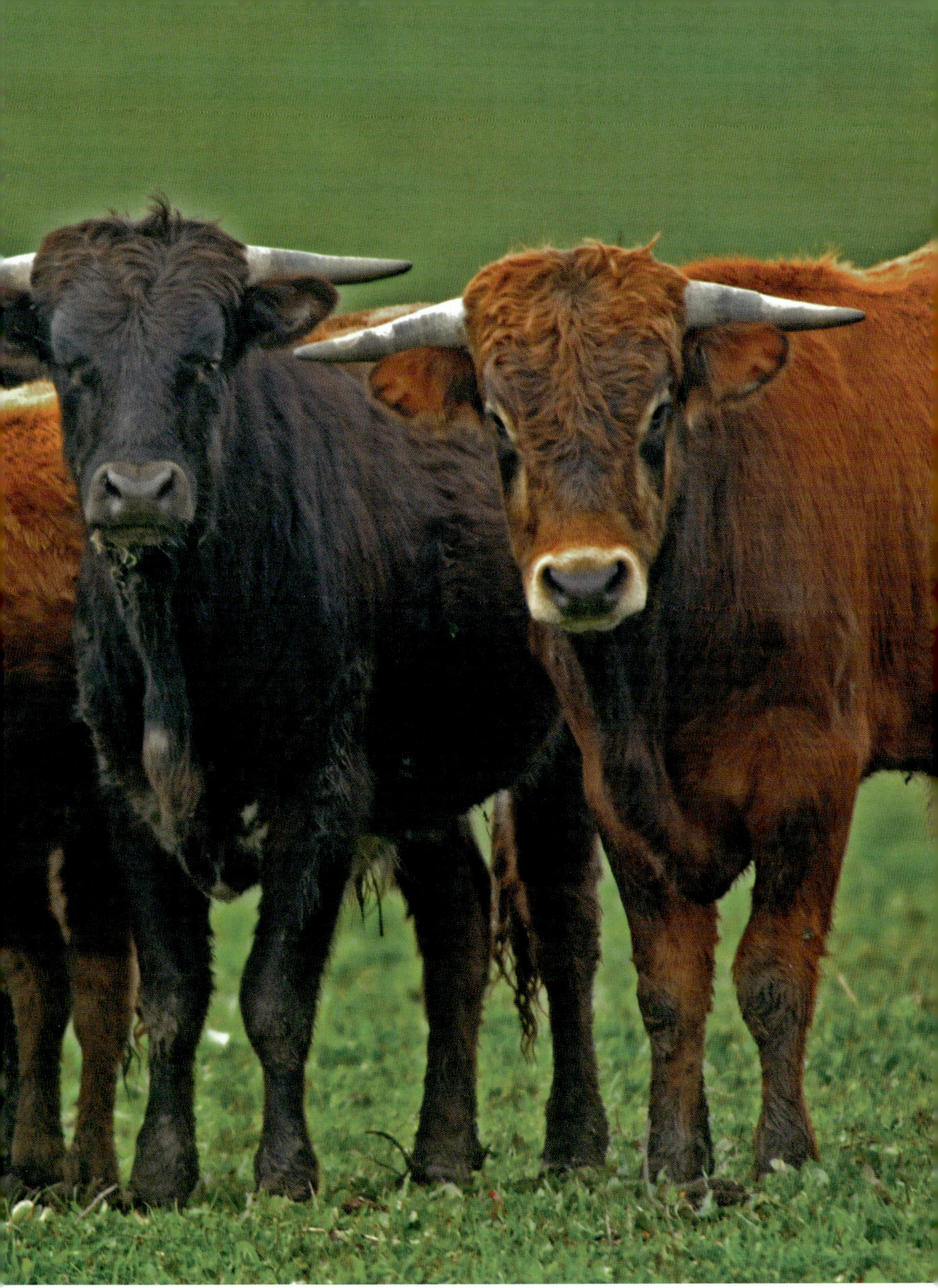

and hyaenas. Apart from the deer, the other species have gone. We transformed wild horses and cattle into domesticates and we drove the predators away altogether. Some animals did manage to survive our ravages. Fossilised with the other bones are remains of griffon vultures, some so large that scientists consider they may belong to a separate species. With the griffons were black, Egyptian and bearded vultures. This was a thriving community of scavengers that lived off the carcasses of wild cattle and other grazers. Much later they managed to adapt and live off the animals that we domesticated and survived. The griffons did particularly well. The others have been less fortunate.

The bearded vulture is now restricted to northern Spain where an estimated 81 pairs are left. This is a sad reflection of our activities when we consider that Verner could find these birds on most of the Andalusian sierras 100 years ago although, even then, he bemoaned their disappearance from many sites within his lifetime. We systematically poisoned and shot them out of al-Andalus. The reason was pure prejudice. This bird, like the griffon, was a harmless scavenger, but it was tainted by an unfair reputation as Verner informs us:

"…in the regions where it originally became known to the world, Switzerland and the Tyrol, it has been since mediaeval times invested with almost supernatural powers, from killing adventurous chamois-hunters or boys who sought to rob their nests by knocking them off cliffs, to carrying off infants and, in its milder moments, preying upon chamois and sheep which it slew and carried off in mid-air to its eyrie in some appalling cliff, many thousands of feet high."

The smaller Egyptian vulture is heading in the same direction. It has been in clear decline in the last 20 years and there are now fewer than 1,500 pairs left in Spain. The Andalusian population has plummeted from 81 pairs in 1987 to 34 in 2006 and all because of poisoning, persecution, habitat loss and electric pylons. The black vulture, the only tree-nesting vulture, is confined to its forest strongholds in central Spain where some 1,400 pairs survive.

Not all is bleak, however. Bearded and black vultures have a low reproductive output, but protection has meant a sluggish recovery in recent years. Despite current threats, the griffon vulture population is healthier than it has been in decades. Nowhere is this better seen than on the shores of the Strait of Gibraltar. Each spring and autumn thousands of griffons cross to and from Africa. It is a spectacle that was unknown three decades ago when I started watching birds. These are mostly young birds from northern Spanish populations and they are driven south by competition from other vultures. It is a reflection of the large numbers of griffons now in Iberia. Many of these birds fly across the Sahara desert to spend the winter months in tropical Africa. The return in the spring has not been without its surprises.

For some years now we have been seeing a new species of vulture on the European shores of the Strait. It is another kind of griffon, an African one known as Ruppell's

CHAPTER TWO *Where the griffon still soars*

Griffon Vulture in flight against cliff nest site. Salto del Gitano, Extremadura

Peñon de Zaframagón. A limestone outcrop near Olvera, Cádiz. It holds one of the largest griffon vulture colonies in the Iberian Peninsula

griffon. The 19th-century naturalists never saw them and they are not present in the fossil record either so this is truly a new phenomenon. The reason seems clear. European griffons are mixing with their African counterparts in the winter quarters. Some of the African birds are getting caught up in the migratory frenzy and are following the griffons back to Europe. Such is the magic of the lands above which the griffon still soars.

A rare sight. An African Ruppell's Griffon over Gibraltar

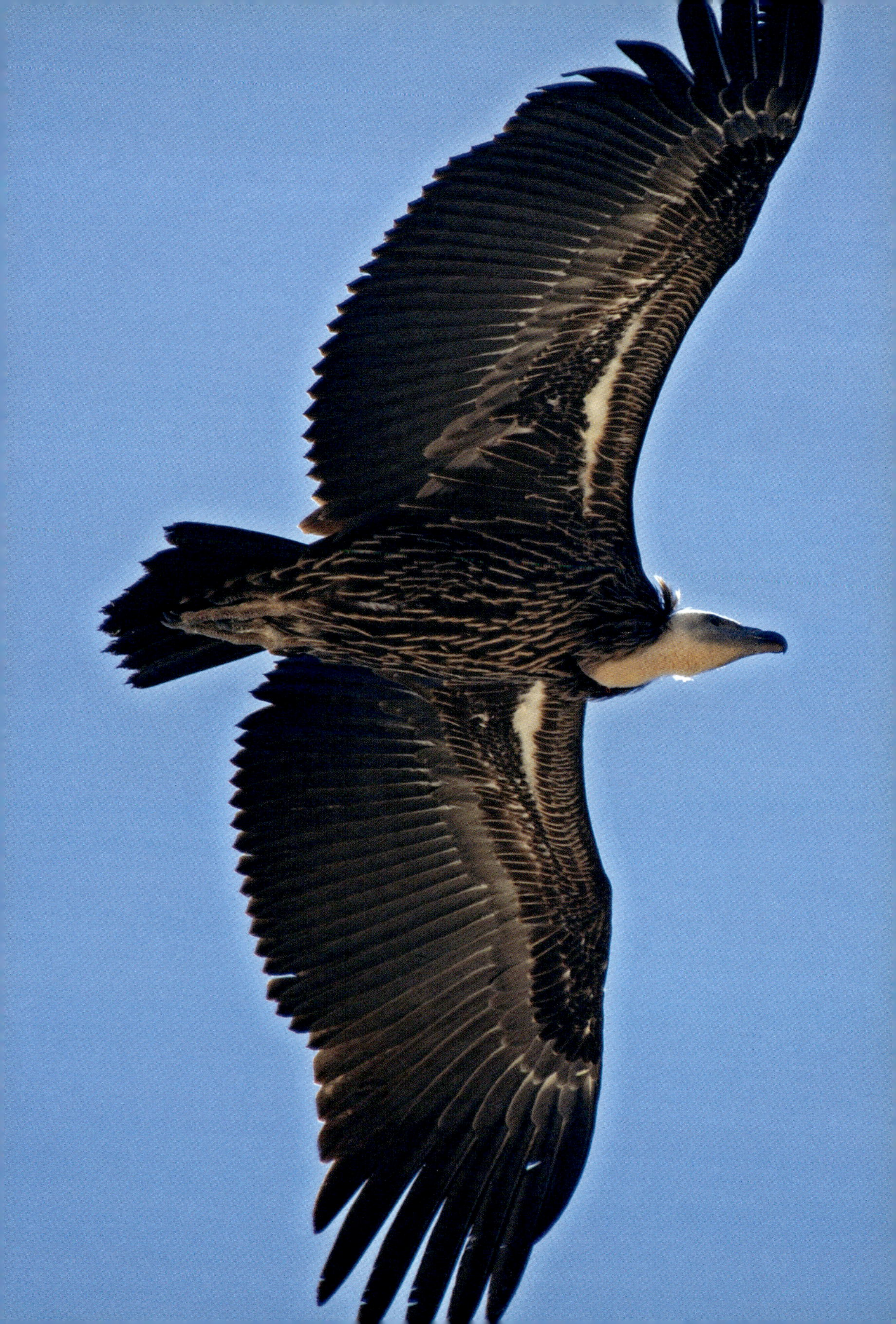

A young Griffon Vulture arrives in Europe and is greeted by mobbing gulls. Europa Point, Gibraltar

A May Day in the Strait of Gibraltar

CHAPTER THREE

A May day in the Strait of Gibraltar

AL-ANDALUS

It was a warm afternoon in early May. The wind was blowing stiffly from the west as I sat at the base of a limestone cliff near the southernmost tip of Gibraltar. I had binoculars set on the opposite coast, the Barbary coast of the pirates of old, waiting to pick up tiny specks that would signal an impending wave of birds of prey on the move towards Europe. Before I could settle to scanning the horizon in detail, the local gulls went into a noisy frenzy that signalled the presence of raptors nearby. There they were, like a squadron of heavy bombers, a dozen griffon vultures coming in from the African sojourn and quickly trying to escape the waves below only to meet the annoying cackle of gulls. The agitation was over almost as quickly as it had started as the vultures pressed on north.

I sat on a rock, exhilarated, taking it all in while checking the photographs I had taken. I too needed to calm down from the excitement. After all had settled down, there was a lull in the migration. This sometimes happens even during peak season. It is as if the birds have also decided to have a rest. The pause allowed me to take in the scenery. The Strait of Gibraltar was choppy as the westerly wind upset the surface of the incoming Atlantic water. Behind stood the Jebel Musa, an 800-metre mountain apparently rising straight from the sea. It was another continent yet you felt you could touch it. The Strait resembled a river separating the two mighty continents of Africa and Europe, but had it always been this way?

Legend has it that when Hercules reached this part of the world, searching for the cattle of Geryon during the course of his 10th labour, he pushed the continents apart creating an opening that allowed the Atlantic to rush in. In the process he created two mountains, Mons Abyla (nowadays the Jebel Musa that I was contemplating) in Africa and Mons Calpe (the Gibraltar one on which I was sitting) which came to be known as the Pillars of Heracles.

This is all in the realm of mythology of course, but the reality of what happened here is not that different from the legend. It happened more than 5,000,000 years ago, so no human could have experienced it. In fact it happened as our remote African ancestors were starting a journey of their own, away from the ape lineage in a direction that would in some remote future produce someone who would write these lines and others who would read them.

The development of the theory of plate tectonics in the late 1960s revolutionised the world. It revealed a dynamic world in which the continents were not static but moved around the planet; sometimes they collided with each other and other times they pulled away. The implications were huge and shaped our view of the history of the Earth for ever. Some changes were so massive that they altered the climate. When the Indian plate crashed into Asia, for example, something had to give. Land was pushed five kilometres into the skies, creating the Himalayas and the Tibetan plateau, an area almost the size of half the United States.

To the west of India, Africa was also on the move. An ancient ocean, the Tethys, in

The Strait of Gibraltar: the African hills are in the background and are separated from the beach on the European side by the narrow Strait. Tarifa, Cádiz

which marine dinosaurs had once roamed, had started to become landlocked when the movement northwards of Africa and the Arabian peninsula cut it off. The old ocean was beginning to resemble the Mediterranean that we know. Water continued to enter from the west along two channels. One was over present-day Morocco and the other near the present-day Guadalquivir river. Scientists have called these the Rif and the Betic Straits. The incessant thrust of Africa into Europe, apart from forming mountain chains such as the Alps, eventually closed off the two channels. The event created huge changes in the climate of the planet.

Even today the Mediterranean Sea survives because of the Atlantic waters that enter daily past the Strait of Gibraltar. If it were not for the Atlantic water the Mediterranean would soon start to dry up because more water evaporates from it than it receives from river and rain water alone. It was not that different more than 5,000,000 years ago when the closing of the Atlantic water input caused the Mediterranean to begin to dry up. It is hard for us to conceive a picture of a dry Mediterranean, allowing you to walk from Europe to North Africa and back without having to cross the sea. Yet, that is how it was in certain parts. The Alborán Sea, the western sea separating Málaga from Morocco, was land. To the east the deeper parts of the Mediterranean were a series of shallow, salty, lakes. Deep canyons formed as the great rivers like the Nile or the Rhone had to cascade down thousands of metres to reach these lake basins. Mediterranean islands, such as the Balearics and Sardinia, stood above this landscape as tall mountains.

In the same way that the great rivers were cutting down through newly exposed rocks to reach the floor of the Mediterranean, new ones were dissecting recently emerged lands. For a long time scientists thought that the re-opening of the Strait of Gibraltar was caused by new tectonic movements of the plates, perhaps as massive earthquakes that opened up a gap for the Atlantic to rush in. Others considered that sea level rise caused by global warming had allowed the Atlantic to spill in. A different picture has emerged only recently as a deep east-west canyon has been identified running along the length of the Strait and on to the Atlantic shelf.

It now seems that the Alborán land area was capturing river water from North Africa, Europe and the exposed land along the Atlantic coasts. The rivers from this watershed were draining eastwards into the deep western Mediterranean Basin, creating giant cascades that plummeted down into the depths of the drying bowl. This main east-west river kept cutting into the exposed land areas of Alborán, eroding and capturing the head waters of its tributaries. As it did so, it eroded westwards until one day its head broke through and connected with the Atlantic. The results were catastrophic and hard to imagine. We think of geological processes as operating over huge timescales even though tragic events, such as the southeast Asian tsunami of 2005, show us that it is not always so. Similarly, the re-opening of the Mediterranean was not a slow process but was, instead, a rapid and spectacular event.

It now seems that at first the entry of Atlantic water was slow. Scientists have calculated that for the first 26 years water trickled in. Then, the process accelerated with astonishing speed. Thirty-three years after the breach, the western Mediterranean Basin had filled and water started to spill over into the eastern basin. After one or two years the eastern basin had filled and the Mediterranean Sea was fully restored 36 years after the breakthrough. It is amazing to think that such a major event would have taken place within a human generation timescale and much of it in a mere decade. Imagine the impact such a catastrophic event would have had on the animals and plants of the Mediterranean. Of course there were no humans around that far back but we can perhaps, in a time when global warming and sea level rise are such topical issues, think about the consequences of such an event today. The lesson is important: dramatic events of global dimensions have been a regular feature of the history of our planet. These have been very rapid and, more often than not, occurred without warning. You just do not see them coming.

To see some of the effects of these major geological changes there is no better place than the Rock of Gibraltar. It is a truly unique place in the western Mediterranean as it has trapped in its rocks much of the history of collisions, uplift and sea level changes.

A Black Kite arrives over the sea to reach Europe from Africa in the spring.
Europa Point, Gibraltar

Much of this information has only come to light in recent years as we studied the detail of the Rock's geological record. Geology may seem a rather dry subject to write about. However, if we take time to reflect on the implications of what we observe, we will soon be awestruck by the sheer scale of the events that have affected this part of the world. Imagine the following. The Rock of Gibraltar rises to 426 metres above sea level. Its main component is limestone from the Jurassic period, a time we are familiar with thanks to Steven Spielberg's movies. Think about what this means. What is limestone? Imagine the warm tropical, shallow seas of the Jurassic. Huge colonies of corals and other small marine life thrive in it. They do well in shallow waters where sunlight penetrates and allows them to make a living. As these small creatures die, they sink to the sea bed. Others follow and settle above the previous ones. In time, the hard parts of these animals, made up of calcium carbonate, become settled and compacted. The product, millions of years later, is limestone. When next you walk on limestone in places like the Rock or many of the high mountains of southeastern Spain, think that you are treading on an ancient sea bed. You will then understand the power behind events that can propel the sea floor hundreds, and even thousands, of metres up into the heavens.

The uplifting of this land was not gradual but took place in a series of events. The cause is all too familiar: Africa kept on coming north and crashing into Europe. On the Rock, where the two continents are closest to each other, we have found evidence of at least five episodes in which the land was pushed up. The evidence comes from many sources but the most striking are the raised beaches. As you walk along the paths of the Mediterranean Steps on the eastern side of Gibraltar, you come across fossilised beaches. The grains of beach sand have become compacted and hardened into sandstone and they contain fossil marine shells. With the blue Mediterranean 200 metres below where you are standing, you begin to grasp the scale of the uplift.

There has been no land connection between Europe and Africa in the western Mediterranean since the Strait re-opened just over 5,000,000 years ago. As sea levels dropped during the ice ages, areas of coastal shelf became exposed and small islands appeared in the middle of the channel. These became stepping stones between Africa and Europe, each separated by no more than six or seven kilometres of sea. There has been much debate regarding the possibility that prehistoric humans entered Europe from Africa across the Strait of Gibraltar. If we consider the long history of humans in Africa, going back 2,000,000 years, it would seem likely that at some stage some may have crossed the sea here. After all, people reached the island of Flores in southeast Asia nearly a million years ago, and Australia was colonised around 50,000 years ago. In both cases sea crossings longer than the Strait were required and people made it. The problem lies in finding the evidence, something which is not easy.

Working against the idea are the Neanderthals. These people were, as far as we know, uniquely European and Asian. They lived on the Rock in full view of the African mountains. There were people on the other side of the Strait when the Neanderthals were around on the Rock and they must have seen the smoke from each other's camp fires. Yet, nobody has ever found a Neanderthal skeleton in Morocco. Maybe they were able to get across but the populations on either shore kept the others from settling. For now it remains an enigma.

It does seem as though the Strait of Gibraltar has been a major biological barrier. With modern techniques for analysing DNA, a number of studies have looked at populations of many land animals that are found on both sides of the Strait. Overall it seems that, with some exceptions, populations of lizards, snakes, frogs and mammals became separated when the Strait re-opened. Since then the DNA suggests that these populations have had no contact and have continued along separate evolutionary trajectories on either side. So the notoriously strong currents of the Strait may have really been a barrier for movement between Africa and Europe.

The raucous gulls interrupted my thoughts. A large bird of prey was fast approaching. This time it was a short-toed eagle, a large snake-eating raptor that spends the winter months in the tropical African savannahs and returns to Europe in the spring. The adult birds return early in the year. In fact most of them do so in the last days of February

CHAPTER THREE *A May day in the Strait of Gibraltar*

Two griffon vultures rest on the Rock of Gibraltar during their autumn migration into Africa

When next you walk on limestone in places like the Rock or many of the high mountains of southeastern Spain, think that you are treading on an ancient sea bed.

and the first half of March. This precision timing allows them enough room to build a nest (or repair last year's), mate, lay eggs, rear the young and move south once again in September. Any later and the departure south would be perilously close to the snake-free winter. The time of the spring arrival is critical: too early and it will not be warm enough for snakes and large lizards to be about, too late and all the good territories will have been occupied by other eagles. The early warmth of these southerly latitudes allows them to come in early in the year.

The eagle that was now poised to make the European landfall was doing so in May. Was it too late to breed? Short-toed eagles have almost pure white undersides. The plumage gets darker with age as the birds develop a most handsome dark chocolate barring on the underside of the wings and body which is accompanied by a dark head and throat. It takes the birds a few years to reach this condition so you can get a rough idea of an eagle's age by the amount of dark colouration. The incoming bird was extremely white. It was an immature (last year's) bird. Many of them came in at this time of the year. They had no intention of breeding, which raised the question of why bother coming back at all?

The journey to and from the African winter quarters is hazardous. The eagles have to cross the width of the Sahara Desert, a minimum distance of 1,500 kilometres without chance of food or water. They have to cross the sea; even the short distance of the 14-kilometre wide Strait is a risk and I have seen more than one exhausted bird sink and drown, tantalisingly close to the shore. It is possible that conditions in the African grounds become inhospitable and the young eagles are forced north. It could also be that they are returning to gain experience of the trip and their future breeding territories. The eagle was now flapping hard and heading towards me, flying very low as it tried to recover height lost over the sea. The gulls were not helping. At this time of the year these yellow-legged gulls have chicks on the nest and they defend their space from any perceived danger, and that includes humans. The eagle, like the vulture, is no threat to the gulls but the sinister shape of the eagle triggers a frenzied response that ends up with several hundred gulls giving chase. It is a case of mistaken identity that is repeated in the skies above Gibraltar many times each day in the month of May.

This eagle was in serious difficulty. I could see it was losing height as more gulls kept diving at it. In a second it had disappeared. I scrambled down the rocks to where it had gone down. I had last seen it close to an old military wall built to fortify the Rock centuries earlier. I could not see it but half a dozen gulls gave its position away as they kept stooping, this time at a fixed point on the ground. I peered over the wall and there it was. A pair of terrified yellow eyes stared at me. Its beak was gaping with exhaustion. We stood facing each other in mutual awe. Only a narrow ditch separated us, but I could see it perfectly through my binoculars. I kept watch over it for over an hour after which it decided it was time to run the gauntlet. It disappeared over the Rock with a trail of pesky gulls in pursuit. This one, at least, had made it so far.

CHAPTER THREE *A May day in the Strait of Gibraltar*

A Honey Buzzard on migration over the Strait of Gibraltar, on its way to breeding grounds in Scandinavia from winter quarters in tropical Africa. Rock of Gibraltar

The Strait of Gibraltar is one of two major European hubs for raptors and other soaring birds, like the storks. The other is the Bosphorus in Turkey. Each year tens of thousands of raptors cross the channel, south into Africa between late July and November and back north into Europe between late February and mid-June. For eight months in the year you can see one species or another of raptor on the move. Why should narrow straits like Gibraltar and the Bosphorus, and to a lesser extent Messina in Sicily, be so crucial for these birds?

The answer lies in the way these birds fly. Most of them are so large that they find sustained flapping flight very energy-demanding. If required to flap their wings for a long time, a raptor like our poor eagle soon becomes exhausted. That limits the distances that can be covered over water. So raptors went green. To minimise the energy spent in flight raptors have gone for energy efficiency, abandoning the energy-guzzling big engine option in favour of a solar-driven vehicle. The sun is critical in the operation. It warms the land and produces rising hot air currents. Raptors have learnt to ride these thermals and they are experts at finding them. They watch each other for the tell-tale sign. If a fellow is circling and gaining height it has found one, so others move towards it. In this way many raptors on migration gather and travel in close company, not always the case in species that are otherwise highly territorial. For the period of migration neighbourly disputes are suspended.

Raptors can soar thousands of metres high in this way without beating their wings once. Early September in the Strait of Gibraltar is peak migration time for southbound honey buzzards. These birds arrive here from Russia and Scandinavia and are heading for the forests of the Cameroon and the Congo. More than 10,000 of these large raptors may cross the Strait each day, but if you are not wise to their ways you may not see a single one. Honey buzzards are masters of soaring on thermals to great heights and the hot Andalusian September sun is perfect for them. As the honey buzzards approach the Strait from the Ronda mountains, they climb on thermals then head south. Sitting on the top of the Rock of Gibraltar, at 426 metres above the sea, I have often stared straight up into the sky, seeing nothing with the naked eye. But with the aid of binoculars I have found hundreds of tiny flapping honey buzzards that must have been flying 2,000 or even 3,000 metres above sea level.

Soaring on thermals has a snag though. Thermals do not develop over the sea. This means that raptors migrating between Europe and Africa have to avoid crossing the Mediterranean. If they risked it over the wider parts they would soon lose height and, after a while, fall into the sea, fatigued, and drown. Our short-toed eagle only just made it after crossing the 21 kilometres of sea between Morocco and Gibraltar; imagine if it had had to cross hundreds of kilometres of open sea. This is the reason that so many thousands of raptors gather in the Strait of Gibraltar. The Strait may be hazardous but it is a lot safer than the alternatives. In effect the raptors soar over land on one side and then glide to the other shore. By the time they reach it they have lost most of the height gained and many have to flap for the last few hundred metres, by which time land is within touching distance. Some drown but most, like our eagle, get across.

For the ornithologist the Strait of Gibraltar is a raptor-watching paradise. Not only are there large numbers of raptors but there are many species and, if they have just crossed the water, they fly low allowing wonderful views. It is not unusual to observe 15 or more species in a single day; ospreys, short-toed and booted eagles, griffon and Egyptian vultures, Montagu's, hen and marsh harriers, black kites, honey buzzards and sparrowhawks are among the main ones.

Life before the Strait opened up must have been a lot easier for migrating raptors. Many land animals would have also regularly crossed between the two continents. Then, as the Atlantic poured in, animals had to get used to a new way of life. For the raptors it involved a riskier migration, for many land species it meant isolation. More than a million years ago early humans had reached the southern Iberian peninsula. They may have arrived from the north, having first come out from Africa via the Middle East and

CHAPTER THREE *A May day in the Strait of Gibraltar*

An exhausted Short-toed eagle makes its landing in Europe during its spring migration.
Europa Point, Gibraltar

An exhausted Short-toed Eagle is forced to land after crossing the Strait.
Europa Point, Gibraltar

then traversed Europe from east to west. On the other hand, perhaps they took the short route from Africa and made it across the Strait of Gibraltar. The story of these early Europeans will occupy us in the next chapter.

An adult yellow-legged gull protects its chicks from the intense May sun. Europa Point lighthouse, Gibraltar, is behind. Africa is in the background. These aggressive gulls defend their young from passing migrating raptors.

CHAPTER THREE *A May day in the Strait of Gibraltar*

THE EARLIEST
INHABITANTS
OF AL-ANDALUS

CHAPTER FOUR

The earliest inhabitants of al-Andalus

As you drive east from Granada, past Guadix and Baza, in the direction of Murcia, the motorway runs for kilometre after kilometre of what at first sight appears to be a monotonous and nondescript desert landscape. At around 1,000 metres above sea level, this upland bowl is usually freezing cold in the winter and the Cazorla mountains to the north are often capped with snow. In the summer it is probably best not to move away from the car during the midday sun as temperatures soar above 50 degrees C. In the centre of the easternmost basin, 150 kilometres east of Granada, lies a small town of around 1500 inhabitants. Orce – the name comes from the Muslim Urs referring to a settlement with lands awarded to combatants – owes its fame to a discovery made there in 1982. It is a discovery that has been plagued with controversy ever since.

As you pass the Orce turn-off on the motorway a sign tells you that here lived Los primeros pobladores de Europa, the first inhabitants of Europe. You are left wondering why anyone in their right minds would ever have settled in this inhospitable place, let alone the first people. The 1982 discovery was of a fragment of skull which was interpreted as being human. It was especially important because it was well over a million years old, according to the dated archaeological levels from which it was recovered. Then the storm started. Was this really part of a human skull? The fragment was not one that would allow such a claim with any certainty according to sceptics. Others were harsher in their treatment — they claimed the fragment was from a donkey. The arguments between the adversaries became increasingly acrimonious as the years went by and have continued until today. Most scientists, however, would admit that the skull's identity cannot be determined with confidence.

What now seems certain is that there were people around in this area a long time ago. We do not have human fossils, but there are the stone tools they made and left behind and these have been dated to around 1.2 million years ago which makes them the earliest in western Europe. The discovery of human remains in Atapuerca, Burgos, in June 2007 have also been dated to 1.2 million years ago. Further east we now know that early humans had reached Dmanisi in Georgia, presumably from Africa, around 1.8 million years ago. Did these east Europeans gradually head west into the Iberian peninsula or are the Orce and Atapuerca people a separate arrival from Africa across the Strait of Gibraltar?

We do not have an answer to that, although the evidence would seem to favour that they came from the east — fossil animals of African or Asian origin are also found in the Orce area. The African ones can be linked by fossils across Europe and the Middle East, implying that they used that long route to reach Orce. They would have been joined by Asian animals, also moving west at that time, and the humans would have been part of this movement. We do not know what these humans looked like but, judging from the age, it is likely that they were close to our remote ancestors, Homo erectus. They would have been fully upright, bipedal and of similar stature to us, but they would have had

CHAPTER FOUR *The earliest inhabitants of al-Andalus*

Plains of the Guadix-Baza Depression at Fonelas, Granada

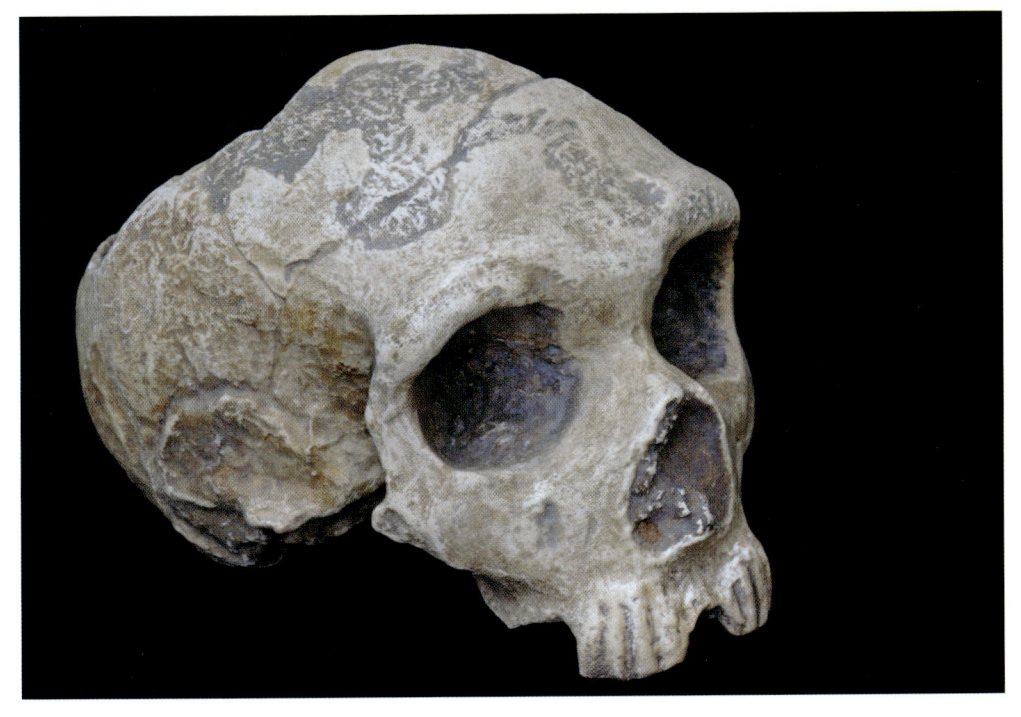

Neanderthal skull discovered in Forbes' Quarry, Gibraltar, in 1848

smaller brains, perhaps in the order of 75 per cent of the volume of our own. With this information we can turn to the question of why people settled here such a long time ago. The answer is in the rocks and the fossils scattered across the huge Guadix-Baza Basin. The oldest deposits with fossils are in the west of the basin, near the small village of Fonelas. Here, recent excavations have revealed huge quantities of animal bones that may be close to 2,000,000 years old. In two field seasons in 2001 and 2002, around 3,000 bones were excavated in 25 square metres. There is no evidence of people at this stage but there were lots of very large mammals. The site was then a lake and the animals were coming to the shore to drink and died naturally or were hunted by hungry predators. The herbivorous mammals included early versions of horse, rhino, mammoth, deer, gazelle and, very unusually for Europe, a kind of giraffe. Clearly conditions were much better then than now and there must have been rich savannahs close to the large lake. All this life attracted large carnivores. There were sabre-tooth cats, hyenas and various types of wolf. It must have been a spectacular sight, from a distance.

Major climate changes affected much of Europe around that time. Conditions got cooler than ever before and sometimes drier too. Many reptiles we now associate with tropical environments, for example large monitor lizards, had lived here but went extinct. It was climate change that triggered immigration as well as extinction and new African and Asian savannah species may have entered as forests gave way to open country. We can pick up the story back near Orce at the site of Venta Micena. The animals of Venta Micena were species of the savannahs and they included some rather fearsome additions to the list. The star of the show was a giant hyena that was the size of a lion. The sabre-tooths were still around, but there was also a large panther and a large relative of today's African hunting dog as well as a huge bear. It is perhaps not surprising that there were still no humans about.

Stone tools signal the arrival of people to the area 1.2 million years ago, almost a million years after Fonelas and Venta Micena. Conditions must have been much wetter than today as we find remains of small shrews and moles that would have been at home in aquatic or damp environments. A remarkable contrast when we consider that this is now one of Spain's driest regions. Many of the earlier large mammals were still around at this time and these early people must have thrived with such a plentiful larder close to the large lake which is now a dust bowl. The competition would have been stiff though and these people must have had to keep a watch out for those hungry mega-hyenas. They could make tools and probably controlled fire by then and that would have given them a great advantage over the carnivores.

The trail runs cold after this. There is no trace of later people for a long time. Perhaps the lake dried up or maybe we simply have not found the evidence yet. People were nevertheless around in other parts of the Iberian peninsula. In Atapuerca there were people around 800,000 years ago, that is over half-a-million years after the Orce clan.

CHAPTER FOUR *The earliest inhabitants of al-Andalus*

Scientists have found sufficient differences in the skeletons of these people compared to their predecessors to warrant the claim of a new species of human: Homo antecessor. This was the immediate ancestor of the Neanderthals and us.

It is with the Neanderthals that we pick up the trail once again in the Guadix-Baza Basin. This time we are back at its western end, near Fonelas where we started. We are at an open air site called La Solana de Zamborino. The time is somewhere around 120,000 years ago, a time of global warming when temperatures were higher than today. The landscape had changed once again. The depression was now a huge savannah, but with scattered pockets of woodland. Groups of Neanderthals had come here to hunt and were making sophisticated tools out of quartzite and flint. These included beautifully carved hand axes and knives for cutting hide and flesh. The large, fierce, animals had gone. There were no giant hyenas any more. Scattered in the plains were groups of rhinos and wild cattle, but the Neanderthals had come to hunt the most abundant prey. Horse remains dominate the archaeological site and these Neanderthals had a taste for horse meat.

For a long time the Neanderthals have been viewed as brutish ape men that eked out a living in the depths of Ice Age Europe. The image still persists and is often the way the Neanderthal is portrayed in television documentaries. Nothing could be further from the truth. Neanderthals were intelligent people who were very successful for more than 300,000 years. They had large brains, often larger than our own. Their behaviour was human in every sense. The unravelling of the Neanderthal story has been largely achieved in the Iberian peninsula. It is here that permanent populations survived, in places like Gorham's Cave back on the Rock of Gibraltar. It is here that we must now return to find the next episode of our story.

On March 3, 1848, Edmund Flint, a British military officer, inspected a quarry at the northern end of the Rock. Convicts had been brought to Gibraltar from Britain to help with these quarrying operations that were designed to extract limestone for the building of new piers. Flint returned later that day to the Garrison Library, an 18 th-century institution built to ensure officers had sufficient reading material in times of siege. If we visit this magnificent building today, we will find many wonderful texts from the Victorian era. Among them is the diary of the Gibraltar Scientific Society. The entry for March 3, 1848, simply reads: "Presented by the Secretary (Flint) to the Society a human skull from Forbes' Quarry". As far as scientific understatements go, this one beats them all.

Eight years later, in 1856, similar human remains excavated in a valley near Düsseldorf in Germany stirred interest among the scientific community of the day. The valley was the Neander Tal and it gave this newly discovered kind of human its name. Today we talk of Neanderthals because the importance of the earlier Gibraltar discovery was not recognised on time.

My good friend Professor Doug Larson, biologist at Guelph University in Canada, on first seeing the line of large caves on the east side of Gibraltar in which Neanderthals had lived exclaimed: "Man, this WAS Neanderthal city!" I had never thought of it in that way, but he was right. Neanderthals never built cities, of course, but the unique accumulation of such large caves indicates that the Rock was a favourite piece of Neanderthal real estate. Here we have now discovered no fewer than 10 caves in which Neanderthals lived. It is the highest density in the world.

Neanderthals were people of Europe and Asia. Nobody has ever found a Neanderthal in Africa. They were toughly built people, shorter than us on average but much more robust. Their skeletons were different from ours in a number of ways. The best-known difference is probably the pronounced brow ridges, whose function we are uncertain about. They also lacked a chin. The skull was less rounded than ours, but this does not mean that they were less brainy. They were certainly not stupid, as we will see from their behaviour.

Much of the hunchback image of the Neanderthal comes from a poorly reconstructed French skeleton, one of the early discoveries known as the old man of La Chapelle. The old man, a 40-year-old, was partially deformed because he had lived his last years riddled with arthritis. Despite more recent discoveries and reconstructions, the old man's image as the archetypal Neanderthal has remained engrained in our culture. Its influence has been so great that many scientists still believe that is was the intellectual superiority of our ancestors, the Cro-Magnons, that dealt the Neanderthals the final blow and sent them to oblivion.

So let me tell you how studies in Gibraltar and elsewhere in the Iberian peninsula are changing this view. I will focus on Gorham's Cave, which is the most important site in the peninsula. The best way to take in the cave is to arrive by boat. As you turn the corner around Europa Point, sheer cliffs overpower the surroundings. Then, as you head northeast into the Mediterranean, a line of huge, cathedral-like caverns appear at the base of the cliffs. The main one is Gorham's Cave, named after the military officer who first entered it in 1907.

The cave was forgotten for a long time until a Captain Alexander found ancient artefacts there just after the Second World War. The findings prompted an excavation in the 1950s which confirmed that Neanderthals had occupied the site in some remote past. Nothing else was done until Dr Chris Stringer, of the Natural History Museum in London, and I revisited the cave in 1989 and started excavations in 1991. These excavations have continued until today.

Gorham's Cave is special because people have been living in it for at least 100,000 years. As these people came and went, they left artefacts, rubbish and spent camp fires. Sand blew in and covered these items. Bat guano accumulated on the floor. All this material built up inside the cave and filled it. In all, 18 metres of deposit, rich in artefacts and fossils, were laid down. What it has left for us is a unique archive, one in which books and documents are replaced by grains of sand, stone tools and bones. It represents a

CHAPTER FOUR *The earliest inhabitants of al-Andalus*

Three Neanderthal caves: Left to right are Bennett's, Gorham's and Vanguard Caves, Gibraltar

once-in-a-lifetime opportunity to reconstruct the lives of the Neanderthals. Nowadays we can put a date on a single grain of sand. The progress technology has made recently allows us to go to sites like Gorham's Cave and obtain a massive amount of detail that would not have been possible even a few years ago. Dating the levels of occupation at the cave has been essential in working out when people lived there, when they were gone and why. As well as dating sand grains, we can obtain dates from radioactive information trapped within cave formations. There is also the traditional radiocarbon method of dating. Even that technology has advanced to the degree that we now only need tiny amounts of charcoal to obtain a date. Putting all the evidence together, we now know that Neanderthals were living in this cave 120,000 years ago. They were the contemporaries of the horse hunters of La Solana de Zamborino. This is the oldest archaeological level in Gorham's Cave, so it is a good place to start. We talk of global warming as something that affects us today, but 120,000 years ago the Earth's climate was even warmer than now. So much ice had melted from ice caps and glaciers that the sea level rose much higher than it is today. In Gorham's Cave an old fossilised beach eight metres above high water mark marks the sea level 120,000 years ago. The Rock would have been an island or a peninsula connected by a tidal land bridge. The Neanderthals were about then, but what where they doing here?

The most surprising discoveries have come from Vanguard Cave, situated next door to Gorham's. Here we excavated a Neanderthal camp site from that early time. There were the usual stone tools and remains of animals that had been hunted and butchered. There were remains of deer and ibex, the wild goat of the cliffs, but some of the fossils were very different from what we were used to seeing. To our amazement we found remains of monk seals which the Neanderthals, it seemed, had been eating. How could we tell? Under the microscope we can still see the tell-tale cut marks on the seal bones made as the Neanderthals sliced the flesh with their stone tools. Their stone knives slipped occasionally and left their imprint on the bones.

Even more exciting was the discovery of dolphin bones, belonging to two species still found in these waters: the common dolphin and the bottle-nose dolphin. Then, looking at the smaller bones, we found fish sea breams. There were also many shells of limpets and mussels that could only have been brought there by people. Many were charred, having been thrown into the fire by the Neanderthals. In an instant our entire understanding of the world of the Neanderthals had changed. Here were intelligent people, capable of adapting to a rise in sea level and the corresponding depletion of land animals by exploiting the products of the ocean. Such behaviour had hitherto been thought of as being the exclusive property of "modern" people, our ancestors.

How were the Neanderthals catching these animals? Did they have boats and nets or were these simply scavenged from the shore? We do not know, but the amounts excavated so far in a small area suggest that this was no accident. Another exciting discovery has been the great diversity of birds recovered from Gorham's and other caves inhabited by the Neanderthals. In all, we have now identified more than 140 different species, which is about a quarter of all the birds of Europe. Gibraltar is on a major migratory route, as we saw in Chapter 3, and many different species pass by the Rock even today. Our findings in the cave suggested that the Neanderthals may have learnt how to tap the seasonal abundance for food though how they did it we do not know. When the excavated materials were sieved, large quantities of smaller bones appeared. These belonged to small rodents, shrews, frogs, snakes and lizards. As with birds they revealed a richness of species that was unique in Europe. These animals were particularly sensitive to climate change so their remains could help us paint the picture of the climate at the time. As we excavated the different archaeological levels in Gorham's Cave we were travelling in time, going from the oldest at the base to the most recent ones near the top. Some levels were occupied by Neanderthals. We knew this, not just from the remains of the food that they ate, but also because the remains of their camp fires were still there. Hearths contained a wealth of information. The charcoal could be sampled for radiocarbon dating which meant that we could work out when the

Gorham's Cave, Gibraltar

CHAPTER FOUR *The earliest inhabitants of al-Andalus*

AL-ANDALUS

Neanderthals had enjoyed their barbecue. We could also look at the charcoal under the microscope and identify the wood that had been used. That told us which trees had been growing near the cave when the Neanderthals were there and that, in turn, told us what the climate and the landscape were like.

Levels that represented times when the Neanderthals were not in the cave could tell us about conditions then and why the cave had been abandoned. What we found was that when Neanderthals were not living in the cave, quite often the site was taken over by hyenas who raised their young here in relative peace. These hyenas were spotted hyenas, the same species that you see in documentaries of the Serengeti or Masai Mara today. They were abundant across many parts of the Iberian peninsula until around 10,000 years ago when they disappeared from the European scene. Hyenas have provided us with a surprising new line of evidence. Along with fossils and artefacts we sometimes find hard, roughly oval, structures in the deposits. Scientists call them coprolites which is a polite term for fossilised dung. Most were produced by the hyenas and amazingly they have been preserved for tens of thousands of years.

My good friend Professor Pepe Carrión at the University of Murcia has developed an incredibly sophisticated technique that allows him to dissect the coprolites and extract microscopic grains of pollen. This technique has enabled us to piece together the vegetation outside the cave and tell the story of how it changed as climate changed. Why should the fossilised droppings of a carnivore contain pollen you may ask? The story goes like this. Let us imagine that we are in the remote past, peering at the landscape from a window inside the cave. A deer is grazing in a small grassy glade unaware that a leopard up a tree is ready to pounce. The deer seeks shade under the tree, giving the big cat the chance to make its kill. However, before it can drag the deer up the tree to keep it away from scavengers, a passing hyena begins to harass the leopard. Soon the leopard is forced to retreat and a group of hyenas tear at the carcass, fending off griffon vultures that have been quick to spot the opportunity. The dominant female hyena goes for the preferred bits of the deer, the intestines, and gorges on these. By eating the gut of the deer the hyena has inadvertently swallowed the deer's last meal and so the pollen in its intestine has been transferred to the carnivore. The hyena, replete, returns to Gorham's Cave and some time later defecates. Forty thousand years later archaeologists dig up the coprolite and my good friend Pepe identifies the pollen in it.

All this material has been assembled by my wife, Geraldine, as part of her doctoral thesis. Her aim was to reconstruct the landscape outside the cave in which the Neanderthals were living. You may ask where this landscape was if, as we saw earlier, the sea was even higher than today. The last time that the sea rose so high was 120,000 years ago when the Neanderthals were hunting seals. Soon after the climate took a downturn and ice began to accumulate, once again, in glaciers and ice sheets. Sea levels dropped worldwide and Europe was heading for an Ice Age. Off Gorham's Cave the

CHAPTER FOUR *The earliest inhabitants of al-Andalus*

The Przewalski's Horse is the closest living relative of the wild horse that Neanderthals hunted. Sabiñanigo Reserve, Pyrenees

drop in sea level, by as much as 120 metres, exposed the coastal shelf and the shoreline was no longer by the cave but five kilometres away. This huge area of exposed land was the hunting ground of the Neanderthals and this is what Geraldine was successfully able to recreate.

If the Neanderthals were living here during the build-up to the last Ice Age, the climate must have been quite severe and life must have been hard for these people. That was the consensus, until we started to look at the evidence. The first surprise came when we found charcoal and pollen from olive trees in abundance. Olives have a strict Mediterranean distribution. They like it warm and do not take too kindly to frosts. Here we had olives, lots of them and they were everywhere and they were always there, in every time period that we looked at. It soon became apparent that climatic conditions in the extreme south of Europe could not have been that bad as we kept finding more plants typical of Mediterranean environments, in fact plants that you can still find in the area today. There were lentiscs and cork oak trees and shrubs that are only found today along the hottest parts of the Mediterranean coast between Gibraltar and Murcia. There were stone pines, trees that love warm, sandy environments.

Sand was to be the next revelation. We started to find huge amounts of bones of western spadefoot toads. These small animals must have been so abundant that the Neanderthals would have had difficulty avoiding trampling them. What is so special about these toads? They live in sandy environments where they burrow deep into the ground to avoid the summer drought. They can live under ground for years if the rains do not come but, when they do, they will emerge in plague proportions, noisily singing to attract mates. So the toads suggested sandy environments outside the cave, seasonal freshwater pools in which to breed, warm climate for their eggs to hatch and periods of drought. Now we were starting to paint the picture.

Other lines of evidence began to open up and point in the same direction. We found many bones of large mammals, the animals that the Neanderthals hunted and those of the predators with which they competed. We looked for animals that would indicate cold conditions. We knew that woolly mammoth, woolly rhinoceros, reindeer, musk ox and bison, had all reached northern Spain during the Ice Age. In fact conditions had become so severe in Europe that they even penetrated the Meseta, the large inland tableland, all the way down to Madrid where fossils of these animals had been recovered. We found nothing. Not a single bone of any of the so-called "cold fauna" was to be found in Gorham's Cave. It was becoming quite clear that conditions had not been that bad down here. The plants and animals of Gorham's Cave, from olive trees to tortoises were typical of warm, Mediterranean-type, climates.

If you visit the east side of Gibraltar today you will see a huge, sandy cone reaching three-quarters of the way to the top of the Rock. This was once covered in metal sheets that trapped rainwater for the population. With the advent of desalination these sheets became redundant and were removed, exposing the sandy slope beneath. From the road below you can see intricate patterns that reveal different moments when the sand was deposited there by the wind. Where did the sand come from? Popular history has it that it is sand blown from the Sahara. Not so. The sand came from much closer, from the plain that was exposed for tens of thousands of years outside Gorham's Cave. The sandy plain where Neanderthals hunted, stone pines grew and toads lived happily. Here we have a fossilised sand dune from the time of the Neanderthals.

Putting the evidence together we realised that the Neanderthals had chosen where to live well. Outside the cave they had an open Mediterranean savannah with seasonal lakes, rivers and scattered patches of woodland. The coast, with its own resources, was never too far away and behind them they had the cliffs with its wild goats. Food was

CHAPTER FOUR *The earliest inhabitants of al-Andalus*

plentiful and the climate was benign which meant that they could stay there the year around.

In September, 2006, Gorham's Cave hit the world news. We had published in the journal Nature our results from the upper levels of Gorham's Cave, where we had found a Neanderthal camp fire, their tools and the remains of their dinner. We had excavated this in 2005 and had sent charcoal samples to a prestigious radiocarbon laboratory in Florida. When the results came back, we were speechless. We checked and rechecked and sent more samples for dating. They all pointed in the same direction. The Neanderthals had been round the camp fire on many occasions and the last time had been 24,000 years ago. Nobody could have suspected that Neanderthals could have survived so late. For most scientists the Neanderthals had disappeared 30,000 or more years ago. Here we had evidence that they held out much longer, by more than 6,000 years. Gorham's Cave was the last place where Neanderthals had lived.

Suddenly it all made sense. Conditions down here had been mild. The world had continued as always. In central Europe Neanderthals had been disappearing fast as the onslaught of the Ice Age buried their traditional territories under ice and permafrost. Here, oblivious of the fate of their northern cousins, they kept on doing what they had always done until they were the last ones left. It is sad to think that one day there would have been a lonely Neanderthal, perhaps a child, sitting on the edge of Gorham's Cave, waiting for others of his kind to return from a hunting trip. That sad day the light switch was turned off and the Neanderthals were no longer.

In 2007 we published new results. We had looked at a detailed record of climate change taken from a deep sea core in the Mediterranean Sea close to the Iberian peninsula. A severe climatic event had hit Iberia around the time of the last Neanderthals at Gorham's. It was the most severe event in the previous quarter-of-a-million years. Nothing could have prepared the remaining Neanderthals for what overcame them: cold and severe drought. It was the final nail in the coffin.

We had succeeded in recreating the way of life of the Neanderthals and as more evidence piled up we realised that their habitat was not that dissimilar to one that we knew very well. Barring the hyenas and leopards, the landscape outside Gorham's Cave had a present-day counterpart: the Coto Doñana. It is there that we shall go to next.

The Rock of Gibraltar from the south-east.

The 300-metre high prehistoric sand dune is clearly visible in the centre. The Neanderthal caves are by the sea towards the left.

IN THE COTO DOÑANA

CHAPTER FIVE

In the Coto Doñana

AL-ANDALUS

A line of cork oak trees was silhouetted against a pastel sky as the sun rose, a red ball over the low and distant horizon. Patches of orange water glistened against a dark background of sedge and rush. The nocturnal chorus of frogs sang its encore and went to sleep before the first hungry kites took to the wing in search of breakfast. Raucous calls from within the oaks signalled another day in La Pajarera, as the huge heronry is known in these parts. The tones became harsh as the rising sun shone brightly across the marsh. Serenely sitting on the highest branch of the highest tree was the lord of this scene – the Spanish imperial eagle. This was Doñana.

Between 1993 and 1996 Doñana was our second home. Our aim was to study the birds of the reserve and observe the changes in numbers and distribution over a period of years. To do this we had to visit Doñana once a month and we kept this up for three wonderful years. We would spend three days there on average. The roads were not as good as they are now and the journey from Gibraltar usually took more than three-and-a-half hours. Come gale or scorching sun the monthly pilgrimage was faithfully observed.

Getting to Doñana by road from Gibraltar takes you through a range of landscapes that reveal much of the region's ecological diversity. Once past the industrial pollution along the northern shore of the Bay of Gibraltar, one of General Franco's many legacies, you turn north close to Los Barrios. At the junction you pass on the left what is left of the estuary of the Palmones river, stranded like a green island in a sea of steel and petroleum. With luck an osprey will fly past and there will certainly be storks and cormorants about, but not much more. The road pushes across mountains of sandstone, the domain of griffon vulture and cork oak tree, then after Alcalá de los Gazules gently descends into rolling hills known as the campiña. In April and May the most wonderful riot of colours floods the fields on both sides of the road as the wild flowers come into bloom. Close to Jerez, inland lakes dot the scenery and often, if the water levels are right, they are pink with flamingoes. The motorway between Jerez and Sevilla takes you through monotonous lowlands which are the drained agricultural areas once part of the marshes of Doñana. Black kites, egrets and pratincoles are usually about in the spring. From Sevilla you take the busy motorway towards Huelva and peel off at Bollulos Par del Condado in the direction of El Rocío, and Doñana beyond. The first hint of the changing landscape comes as you approach the town of Almonte. Stone pines, some natural, some planted, begin to dominate the scenery and birds appear. Black kites swoop between the trees and flocks of azure-winged magpies fly low across the road in front of you.

The next village is El Rocío with its bizarre combination of flamingoes, wild-west and Spanish Catholicism. Marsh meets sand in the streets. From the edge of the village you can always observe aquatic birds going about their daily business while men on horseback sip glasses of manzanilla (a local dry sherry) behind you. Lines of pilgrims noisily weave their way through the streets, overseen by kites that whistle and mew in

CHAPTER FIVE *In the Coto Doñana*

Azure-winged Magpie. Doñana, Huelva
(Photo by Stewart Finlayson)

the blue heavens above. In El Rocío medieval scenes are replayed daily in 21st-century clothing.

The village is best known for its annual spring pilgrimage in honour of the Virgin of El Rocío when more than a million people congregate here. In our time working in Doñana it was the week that we always avoided. We were not alone as we found out. Many local people would leave, let their houses for a substantial profit and escape the chaos.

From El Rocío we would drive for another 16 kilometres towards the coastal resort of Matalascañas, but were spared from having to enter this enclave of sun-worshippers just a few hundred metres before reaching it. A small sign indicated a left turning for the Palacio de Doñana. This was our base for three years: a country house with palatial aspirations serving as biological station on the edge of a huge marsh. On turning off the main road we were immediately on an un-asphalted road. Within 100 metres there was a barrier and a small porter's lodge. Once the research permits had been duly examined, the barrier would lift and we were in the most strictly controlled part of the Doñana National Park, the Biological Reserve.

You thought you were there, but there was still a long way to go. This was horse, punt and four-wheel drive country. The road was often so bad that it was easier to drive along tracks on the sand dunes than on it. These tracks (known in Doñana as rayas) were deeply rutted with constant use by park four-wheel-drives, to such an extent that you could take your hands off the steering wheel and the vehicle would follow the trail like a train on its track. After 11 kilometres of this terrain the white buildings of the palace could be seen in the distance in a small wood of eucalypts and poplars. Progress was slow, not only because of the bumpy topography but because deer, boar or lynx could cross in front of you without giving notice. Extra care had to be taken at night when many animals were about.

The palace was a wonderful, old, white Andalusian building. It had a central open courtyard with cobbled floor and beautiful geraniums and carnations hanging in pots around its walls. Inside we had the living quarters, a large kitchen and a hunting lodge-type dining room and lounge. After a long and tiring day in the field it was pleasantly relaxing to sit and read through the day's notes by the fireplace. As the palace was in the middle of the reserve wildlife surrounded it. In September, we would spend many sleepless nights listening to the stags rutting outside our windows. In mid-winter it was the racket of 80,000 Scandinavian greylag geese feeding on the dunes a kilometre or two away. Other times it would be frogs or mosquitoes. In mid-summer, on still nights, it was the suffocating heat. Walking into the courtyard in the middle of the night and staring at the stars, here so far away from city lights, reminded us how much we urbanites had lost touch with nature.

Living within a wilderness and listening to the night sounds revealed how much of the natural world operated under darkness. Red-necked nightjars, tawny owls and Scops owls called all night in the spring. The distant cry of the stone curlew, shy and retiring

CHAPTER FIVE *In the Coto Doñana*

Collared Pratincole. Doñana, Huelva

by day, gave its sandy haunts away. In the autumn you could hear the calls of migratory birds, using the stars to navigate as they headed towards Africa in the blackness above. In the morning the dunes were covered in the prints of deer, lynx, partridge or goose that had wandered this way and that in search of food the previous night.

We would be up before dawn ready to get out into the field before the first rays of light. We followed a fixed route that took us across 20 kilometres of wilderness. As we left the Palacio in the morning in the darkness, we would often see the silhouettes of the last of the park guards returning home after a night's patrol on the lookout for poachers seeking deer and boar. They would wave as we passed them, coming home after a tough night in the open that few of us would regard with such nonchalance. They were marismeños, people of the marshes, and this was their home.

A half-hour drive brought us to the starting point. Many a deer or boar crossed in front of us in the darkness. Our objective was one of the guards' houses, Casa de Martinazo, on the very edge of the marsh. Once at Martinazo we would start our work, painstakingly recording birds and plants, stopping at intervals of a kilometre to repeat the operation. The marshes extended east from us as far as the eye could see. Our only reference point was a solitary and distant tree on the horizon, traditional nesting site of a Spanish imperial eagle on a small island.

In wet years the Doñana marshes are impassable except in shallow boat or on horseback, but during the years of drought we were able to drive across much of it, taking care to avoid treacherous holes and sticky mud. Travelling across the marsh produces a wonderful feeling of solitude and intimate contact with nature. Out here you are alone with the birds. The dramatic changes in environmental conditions that we observed between seasons and years were a clear testimony to the precarious way of life of the hardy animals that inhabited these regions. It all revolved around water.

A local marismeño once explained to me how the marshes changed from blue to green to brown as the spring advanced. In this simple and succinct manner he showed his understanding of the seasons here. The winter rains, when they came, started in October and continued irregularly through the winter and early spring. Old lake-beds began to fill, merging in wet years to create a vast, blue, inland sea. As spring advanced and vegetation sprang up, shallow patches of blue water were engulfed by the verdant splendour of the emerging water plants. Soon blue had been overtaken by green and birds found cover in which to hide their nests. By late June the baking sun had reduced the waters to tiny islands and the mud began to bake in this open-air oven. By July all was parched and brown and you could walk across what a couple of months earlier had been the domain of herons and ducks.

Some years the rains did not come and the marshes stayed brown and caked all winter. When this happened repeatedly, as was the case in the mid-1990s, many animals died. Someone's misfortune was another's gain. In the winter of 1994 the marisma resembled a desert. The geese arrived but food was scarce. It was pitiful to drive across the dry marsh seeing the scattered corpses of geese and deer. Thousands of animals must have died. However, the griffon vultures from our lajas in the sierras, visible on the horizon, were laughing. For them the 100 kilometres from the lajas to the marsh were a short step. So they arrived in numbers, making the most of the bounty. They could only fly a short distance once they had their fill and many improvised by replacing their usual rocky perches, settling instead among the kites on the nearby trees. They would sleep there instead of returning to the safety of the lajas. For the scavenger death is a powerful magnet.

The following year saw relief as powerful fronts brought intense rain from the Atlantic. By January the marsh had been transformed into an azure sea once more. There was so much water that the geese were on this occasion all gathered along the edge of the marsh as the central parts were too deep. Deer were squeezed into tight groups along the narrow boundary of grazing ground, between the marsh and the dry land, that the locals called la vera (literally, the verge). One warden who lived on an island in the

Seasonal freshwater pool. Doñana, Huelva

CHAPTER FIVE *In the Coto Doñana*

Atlantic coastal dunes at Doñana, Huelva

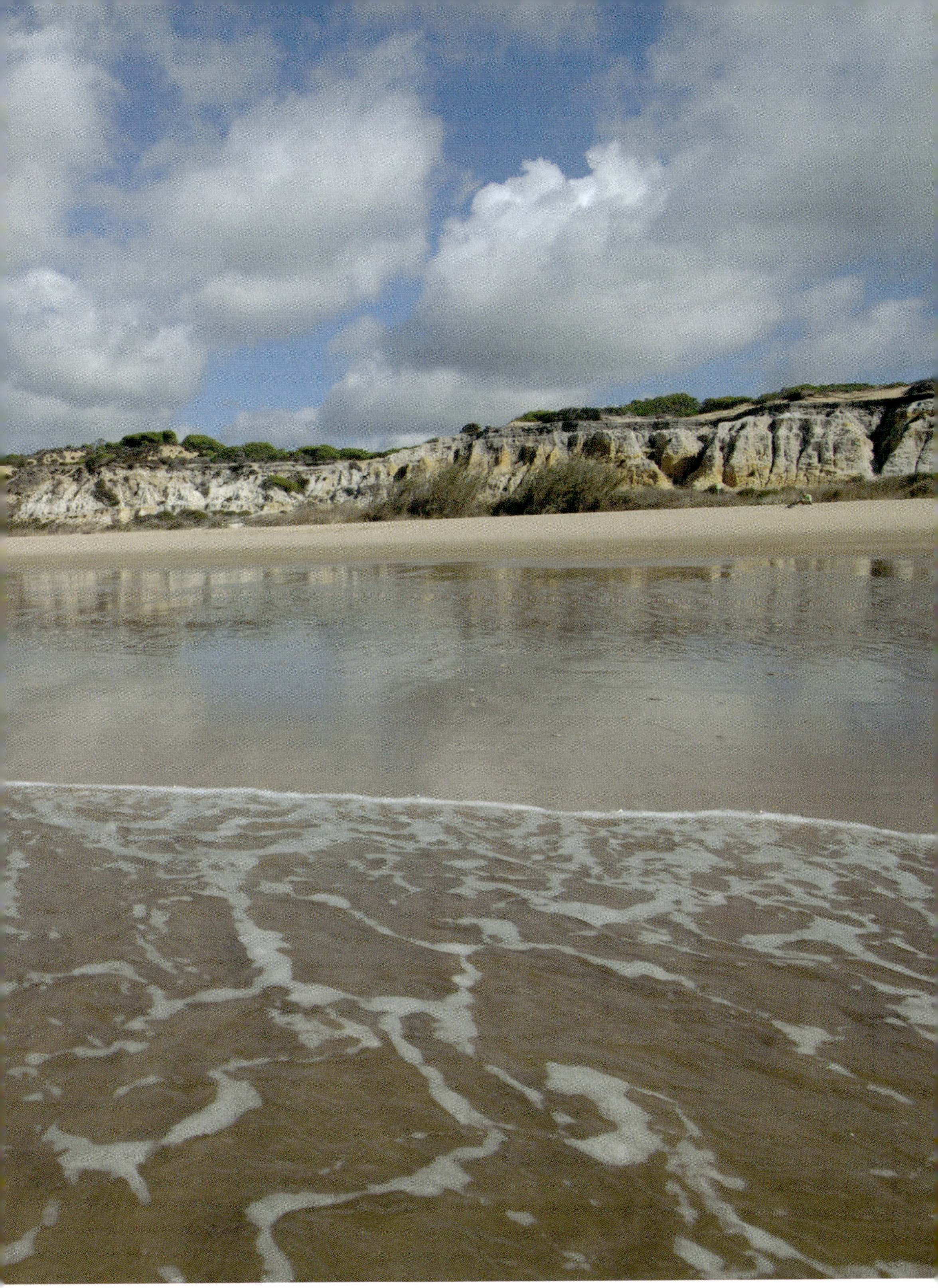

Stone pine woodland. Doñana, Huelva

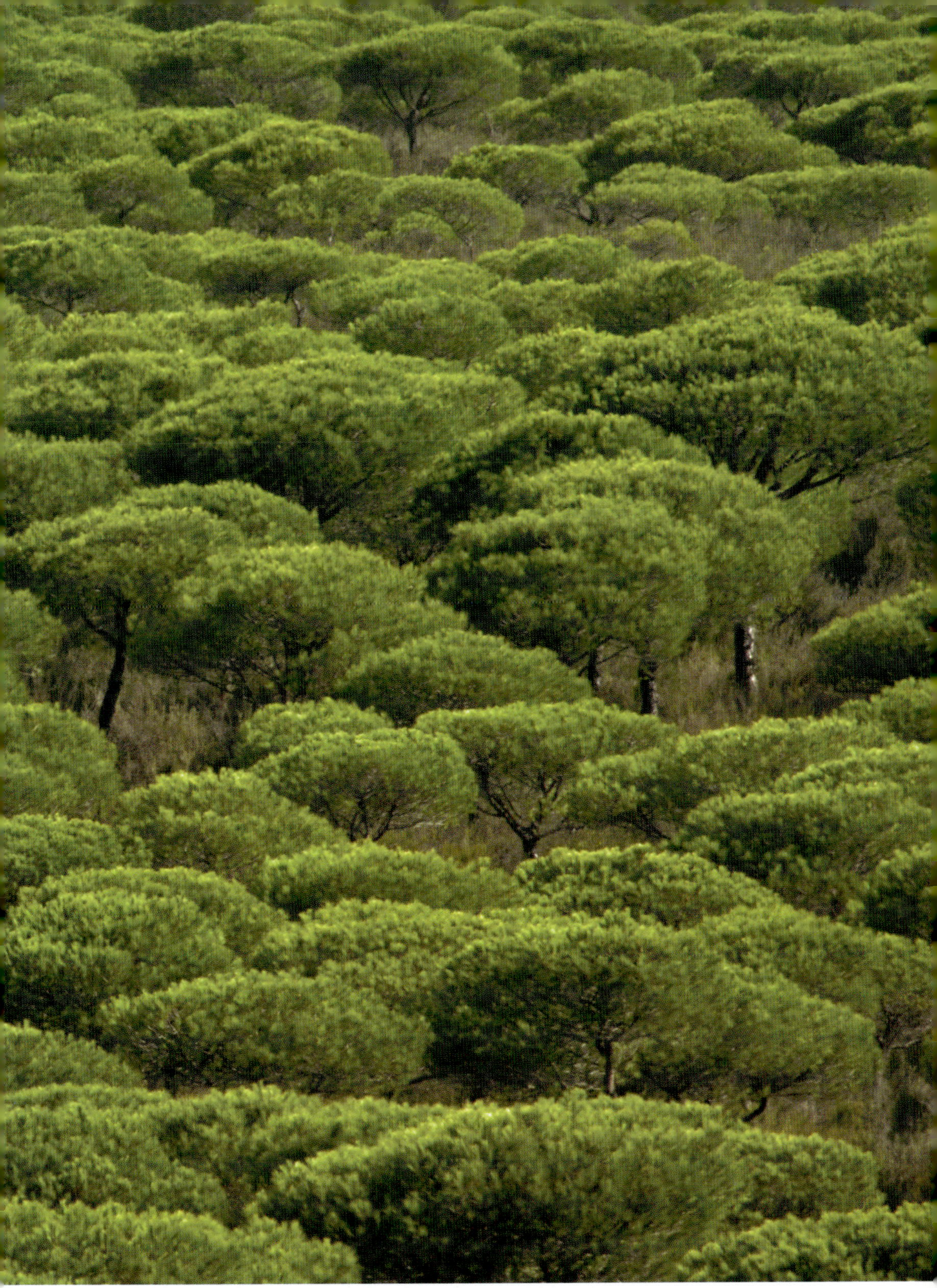

marsh had to be rescued by shallow boat and many cows and horses lay stranded on sandy islets. We sat on the edge of the marsh and wondered whether a year earlier we really had been walking among carcasses where ducks now floated. There were no vultures that year.

The months that followed brought further surprises. The marsh turned green according to plan and the trees became white with egrets and spoonbills. Not only were there many more than on previous years but there was a greater variety. Night herons, squacco herons, little and cattle egrets, grey herons and spoonbills were around in numbers that we had not seen before. They stayed for much longer too. In drought years these birds came in, assessed the dire situation and disappeared. We did not know where they went to, but by early July these birds had vanished. Our suspicion was that they made an early return to Africa where they could enjoy the benefits of the monsoon. With the rains, water and food were plentiful in Doñana and young could be raised successfully. The birds were not tempted away and stayed around all summer. The young made the most of the easy pickings of fish and frog as the pools receded in the August sun. That was the way of these birds. They may not have been able to produce offspring for a number of years, but when food became plentiful they pressed on to raise as many children as possible. The secret of success was to be quick to react to Nature's impromptu generosity.

Some birds were successful no matter what the conditions threw at them. The starting point of our survey was a good place to see some of them. From Martinazo we ventured along la vera, a veritable prairie on soft sand. Here were flocks of magpies and jackdaws. It would have been easy to dismiss these crows amidst such ornithological affluence, but we had only admiration for their resilience. These birds could cope with anything. If the ground was dry, they would probe for larvae and worms underground. If animals died, they would scavenge alongside the vultures. If there was too much water, they would move along on to drier ground and search for insects. Or they could make the short trip to the visitor centres on the outer edges of the park to raid bins for tasty morsels. Here we had a wonderful lesson in ecology. Specialist birds, like the herons or the vultures could do very well some of the time but needed to move on at other times. Jacks-of-all-trades, like our magpies and jackdaws, simply changed lifestyle and stayed put. It made me wonder about our own evolution.

One of our favourite birds here was a colourful crow, the azure-winged magpie. This was a highly intelligent and social bird that lived in large family groups. They were a noisy bunch and we loved spending hours watching their antics, quite reminiscent of our own. These magpies are only found today in Portugal and southwestern Spain. There is a second population far away, so far that the Iberian birds are unaware of their existence. This second population is in China, Japan and Korea.

How could this be? How could two populations of the same species be so far apart? When we started our work, the prevalent view was that the Portuguese sailors of

CHAPTER FIVE *In the Coto Doñana*

The Red Kite is one of the most common tree nesting raptors in Doñana

Among the herons that breed in Doñana is the Little Bittern, a migrant from across the Sahara.

centuries gone by had seen these colourful birds in China, captured a few and brought them back home. There, some escaped and spread. Like any good theory, it was waiting to be proved wrong.

The solution came from an unexpected source. Among the fossil bones in Gorham's and Vanguard Caves were some odd-looking ones that had not been seen before. After close examination they turned out to be azure-winged magpie bones and they had been excavated from 40,000 year-old levels. These birds had always been here. The Portuguese sailors had had nothing to do with it.

Since then DNA extracted from birds of the two existing populations has shown that they have been separated for more than a million years. Such has been the violence of climate change that the vast area beween Iberia and China – once hospitable for these birds – became unusable. The birds, which once must have spanned the entire Eurasian land mass, vanished, except those at the two extremes.

Back in Doñana, behind la vera, we entered an extensive area of scrub, so high in places that we could not see over it. This was the Monte Blanco where many shrubby plants had managed to gain a foothold on the shifting dunes. Rock roses, heathers, rosemary and lavender suffocated the air with colour and scent. We were usually here in the first hours of the morning and I shall never forget one such spring morning. It was a beautiful sunny day as we drove slowly between our preset points where we collected our data. The bushes were so tall in places that, to see properly, we had to stand inside the car with our heads sticking out from the vehicle's sun roof. Spiky tree heathers would brush past as we penetrated deeper into the tangled thicket. Red kites were common here and there was usually a buzzard about that would spend hours chasing the kites away from its favourite tree.

On this occasion the place was unusually quiet so we stretched higher to see what was about. We entered a small clearing and we froze, speechless, at the scene that unfolded a few metres in front of our eyes. A large shape emerged from the thicket, paused and regally looked us in the eye, indignant at our intrusion. It stopped in the open and watched us, before disappearing leisurely into the undergrowth. He was master here and was not about to be pushed around by intruders. It had been a few seconds but it had felt like a timeless moment. We had seen our first wild Spanish lynx.

Our long transect across Doñana would take us through all of its major habitats. Once we had reached the Palacio we would turn west towards the sand dunes that formed the precarious interface between land and sea. Before reaching the dunes we would follow, for several kilometres, a route that took us past a series of freshwater lakes, dotted among forests of stone pines. The largest was Santa Olalla, a picturesque and historic place. The dunes backed the lake to the west and the sea was just beyond. The constantly changing magical colours left by the setting sun as it disappeared behind the dunes, the silhouettes of deer coming down to drink on the lake shore and the lines of

CHAPTER FIVE *In the Coto Doñana*

The lynx is the top predator in Doñana.

A family of wild boar in Doñana

flamingoes sliding across the sky made this place a favourite haunt of ours. Other, more distinguished, visitors had also felt the mystery of this place. King Alfonso X of Castile (1252-1284) – El Sabio (the wise one) – hunted in the Coto which he established as royal hunting ground in 1262 shortly after the conquest of the county of Niebla, in which it was included, in 1261. A devotee of the Virgin Mary, he erected a hermitage to Santa Eulalia on the shores of the lake. The Arabs referred to it phonetically as Shant Ulaya, a variant reaching us as Santa Olalla. The holy building had long since been engulfed by the sands of Doñana, but the location retained its special mood. How wonderful that it was still possible, in the dying days of an overpopulated 20th-century Europe, to find peace here. Alfonso truly was a wise man.

CHAPTER FIVE *In the Coto Doñana*

Ancient cork oak in Doñana, Huelva. Note this tree has never had its bark removed.

The author in field work at Doñana

AFRICA IN EUROPE

CHAPTER SIX

Africa in Europe

AL-ANDALUS

"To us, this same Coto Doñana had always appeared as if it were a fragment of some savage African solitude, detached and specially dumped down for our personal benefit in this remote corner of Europe."

This is how Abel Chapman, the 19th-century naturalist, described Doñana. Chapman first visited Doñana on April 8, 1872, when he was 21, and was immediately captivated by its magic. He returned on numerous occasions over the following 40 years and his colourful accounts of Doñana are recorded in Wild Spain, Unexplored Spain and his subsequent Retrospect and Memories. The first two were co-written with Walter Buck, who was British Vice-Consul in Jerez. Buck was also a keen naturalist and hunter and founded the first pigeon-shooting club in Spain in 1869. Chapman, a Durham man, became partner in the family brewing and wine merchant business in 1875. His connection with the wine business must have introduced him to Jerez and its sherry industry where he met and became a close friend of Don Guillermo Garvey. Garvey later bought the Doñana property and rented it out to Chapman, Buck, Pedro González de Soto and Alexander Williams for hunting. Guillermo was the grandson of an Irishman, William Garvey Power, who had arrived in Jerez in 1778 with the dream of building the largest bodega in town. He prayed and promised St Patrick that if he achieved the dream he would name the bodega after the saint. It was his son, Patricio, who successfully completed the enterprise and made St Patrick's bodega the biggest in Jerez. Patricio's son Guillermo, a kind-hearted gentleman, inherited the family business and bought Doñana and so the late 19th-century discovery of one of Europe's greatest wildernesses owed much to the arrival of an enterprising Irishman in Jerez 100 years earlier.

Chapman and Buck were the first to provide detailed descriptions of the Coto Doñana and its wildlife, but others had been enthusing about its natural wonders for centuries. King Alfonso XI, great-grandson of Alfonso X, whom we met in the previous chapter, gave an early description of Doñana in his Book of Hunting written between 1342 and 1348: "Near the village of Niebla there is a place called Las Rocinas, which is flat and wooded, and where there are always wild boars – one cannot hunt there except in the spring – winter is too rainy and summer is too dry and hot."

When we started our work in Doñana we did not realise how closely the lands of this remote wilderness and the Rock of Gibraltar had been connected throughout history, nor indeed how much this part of the world really had been a piece of Africa in Europe. Chapman's link with Africa was ecological but, perhaps because of its similitude with the southern shores of the Strait of Gibraltar, the association had also been heavily political. Alfonso XI lost Gibraltar in 1333 to a North African Muslim dynasty known as the Merinids. In his effort to regain possession of the Rock, shortly after writing the Book of Hunting, he laid siege in 1350 and died in the attempt on March 26 — not from battle wounds but from the plague. He was the only European monarch to have died

CHAPTER SIX *Africa in Europe*

from the Black Death.

The closest and longest-lasting link between Doñana, Gibraltar and North Africa is provided by a powerful medieval dynasty – Medina Sidonia – which emerged on the back of the tussle between Christian and Muslim, at the time of Alfonso's great-grandfather, King Alfonso X. In 1278 there emerged a character central to the lineage of interest to us. He was the 20-year-old Alonso Pérez de Guzmán, a mercenary who had been working for the sultan Yusuf in Morocco. Traditionally, Guzmán's origins have been traced back to Christian strongholds in the mountains of León in northern Spain, but the current Duchess of Medina Sidonia has contested this interpretation on the basis of original documents in the family archive. It now seems that originally Guzmán may well have been a Muslim from Morocco who later converted to Christianity. Much later, in the staunchly Christian Spain of 1544, the sixth Duke of Medina Sidonia paid for politically and religiously correct ancestors to be procured.

In this ruthless world of medieval war lords, unholy alliances were often struck between unlikely partners. King Alfonso wanted to quash his own son's rebellion so he made a pact with Yusuf. The mercenary Guzmán fought for both monarchs. His prize for loyalty to Alfonso was a wife, María Alphon (a Jewish surname later Christianised to Alonso Coronel as part of the sixth duke's historical revision), and the tenancy of Alcalá Sidonia, present-day Alcalá de los Gazules. He thus gained a foothold on European soil but, when King Alfonso died, the rebellious Prince Sancho claimed the throne of Castile and Guzmán was forced into exile to Morocco. There he continued in the service of the sultan of Fez and amassed a fortune.

With these funds Guzmán bought land in al-Andalus. The future geographical sphere of influence of the Guzmán lineage – in the coastal lowlands of southwestern Iberia, the border regions of Huelva with Portugal and the lower valleys of the Guadalete and Guadalquivir – was already being shaped at this early stage.

Life continued to improve for Guzmán. Undoubtedly aware of the need to have men of his ability on his side at a time when much of the land was thinly populated and control from central authority difficult, Sancho (now king) summoned Guzmán and gave him the tenancy and defence of Tarifa, captured from the North Africans in 1292. Eight years after his exile Guzmán was back and on friendly terms with his former enemy.

The next Castilian political confrontation was between King Sancho and the supporters of his nephew who also claimed the throne. Sancho's brother Prince Juan had visited the court in Fez where he conspired to overthrow Sancho. His carrot to the North Africans was Tarifa and the trump card was Guzmán's eldest son. Prince Juan, with a large force of North African soldiers, laid siege to Tarifa in 1294. Once more Christian and Muslim joined forces against a third party, illustrating the complexity of the long Christian conquest of the Iberian peninsula, which was not the simple Christian versus Muslim picture so often painted. Instead, what drove much of the long-drawn-out process were scrambles and squabbles for land by warmongers who received royal support in

Guzman's chapel
(Photo by Stewart Finlayson)

*Chapel where the remains of Enrique de Guzman were buried by his son.
Tower of Homage, Gibraltar.*

exchange for their loyalty.

Some noble acts punctuated this free-for-all and the events of Tarifa have shone through with legendary dimensions. Imagine the city of Tarifa with its walls and banners. Christian troops were inside the fortress under the command of Guzmán, sworn to allegiance to King Sancho, his former enemy. Outside were massed troops from Fez, with support from Granada, and their unlikely leader, the Christian Prince Juan. Before an arrow was fired Juan displayed Guzmán's eldest son and offered to exchange him for Tarifa. If Guzmán refused, his son would be killed. Guzmán, in an extreme act of medieval chivalry, threw his own knife to Don Juan, signifying his refusal to surrender. Guzmán's son was killed in full view. But Tarifa still resisted and the disillusioned North Africans finally cut their losses and left. Alonso became known as Guzmán El Bueno (the Good) for his heroic defence.

The incident is important because it gave Guzmán the town that was to become his lineage's seat of power for centuries to come. As a reward for his defence of Tarifa, Guzmán gained the estate of Sanlúcar de Barrameda on the east bank of the Guadalquivir estuary. He also secured the lands on the estuary's west bank, later known as the Coto Doñana, and the tuna fishing fleet (almadraba) at Conil. Doñana would remain the property of the Guzmáns until 1900.

In 1309, the Christians renewed their crusading spirit and besieged Algeciras. The town, despite being encircled, continued to receive supplies from Gibraltar which enraged the attackers. Guzmán was despatched to attack the Rock. It was the first encounter between Guzmán and Gibraltar and the first of 14 sieges of the Rock. Guzmán took the place for the Castilians in just over a month. Shortly after, during the follow-up of this campaign, Guzmán was killed in battle in the Sierra de Gaucín. Some sources have suggested that Guzmán had connections with the Knights Templar who at this time were suffering persecution across Europe and that his death, in unclear circumstances, may have been linked to the political situation at the time and not to fighting Muslims in al-Andalus. Sixty years later the Guzmáns were involved in yet another struggle for power, between Pedro (the Cruel) of Castile, son of King Alfonso XI, and his half-brother, Enrique of Trastámara, the illegitimate son of Alfonso. The long and bitter feud at one point even involved Edward the Black Prince fighting on Pedro's side. Enrique killed Pedro and took the throne in 1369, becoming King Enrique II (the Bastard) of Castile. For supporting Enrique the Guzmáns received the title of Count of Niebla and gained substantial territory in the neighbourhood of Doñana.

The connection between the Guzmáns and Gibraltar was renewed in violent fashion in 1436. Tired of constant raids on his border lands between Tarifa and Cádiz by Muslims from Gibraltar (then controlled by the sultans of Granada), the second Count of Niebla attempted an amphibious landing on the Rock. Apparently unaware that the North Africans had built a defensive wall, he and his knights were trapped on the beach as the tide rose. The count and 40 knights drowned. The Muslims beheaded the count's body,

CHAPTER SIX *Africa in Europe*

placed it in a basket and hung it over the city walls, where it remained for 26 years. The count's son obtained the town of Medina Sidonia by an exchange of properties in 1440 and five years later his support of the king in another dynastic struggle earned him the title of Duke of Medina Sidonia. He participated in the siege and capture of Gibraltar in 1462. A new conflict, over ownership of Gibraltar, now raised its head. The duke had just established himself there by right of capture when the king declared it Crown property. Medina Sidonia reluctantly withdrew, but not before retrieving his father's remains hanging from the fortress walls. He buried the bones in a chapel inside the Tower of Homage.

Medina Sidonia's loyalty to the new queen of Castile, Isabel, was rewarded in 1488 when he was made first Marquis of Gibraltar. He fought alongside the Catholic monarchs in the conquest of Granada in 1492 but died in Sanlúcar in August the same year. His successor sought confirmation of his titles from the queen, but she would only agree provided Gibraltar was handed back to the Crown. The duke argued that Gibraltar was his by right of conquest and inheritance and Isabel, conscious that she needed his support in her next campaign against the Muslims in North Africa, conceded, for the moment.

The process of expulsion of the Jews and some Muslims from al-Andalus started in 1492 and was a long-drawn process. Initially, the Sephardic Jews, those originating in the Iberian peninsula, suffered most. The Catholic monarchs, Fernando and Isabel, decreed that they should all leave the country and later King Manuel I of Portugal did the same in his country. Estimates of the number of Jews expelled vary from 250 to 800,000 within a few months.

When the Jews were about to strike a deal to allow them to stay in return for paying a large sum of money to the Crown, Tomás de Torquemada, the fanatical Grand Inquisitor and Isabel's personal confessor, allegedly stormed into the royal palace, holding a crucifix high and shouting: "Judas Iscariot sold Christ for 30 pieces of silver; Your Highness is about to sell him for 300,000 ducats; here He is; take Him and sell Him." The deal collapsed in an instant and the long suffering of the Spanish Jews began.

Gibraltar was used as a military base for Isabel's invasion of North Africa in 1497 when the third Duke of Medina Sidonia captured Melilla. Gibraltar had prospered under the duke, partly because he had received a royal concession allowing him to retain rent in order to pay for a mayor, garrison and supplies. This was important to the queen as it guaranteed Gibraltar would remain in safe hands. A measure of the importance she attached to Gibraltar was that the sums waived were a third higher than those agreed for Antequera which was right on the border with Granada. Once Granada had fallen, the concession lapsed, but the duke successfully negotiated its transfer to the newly acquired garrison of Melilla.

Conscious of Gibraltar's strategic importance in the invasion of North Africa, Isabel determined that it should be under Crown control. Medina Sidonia — probably on

Palacio de Doñana, Huelva

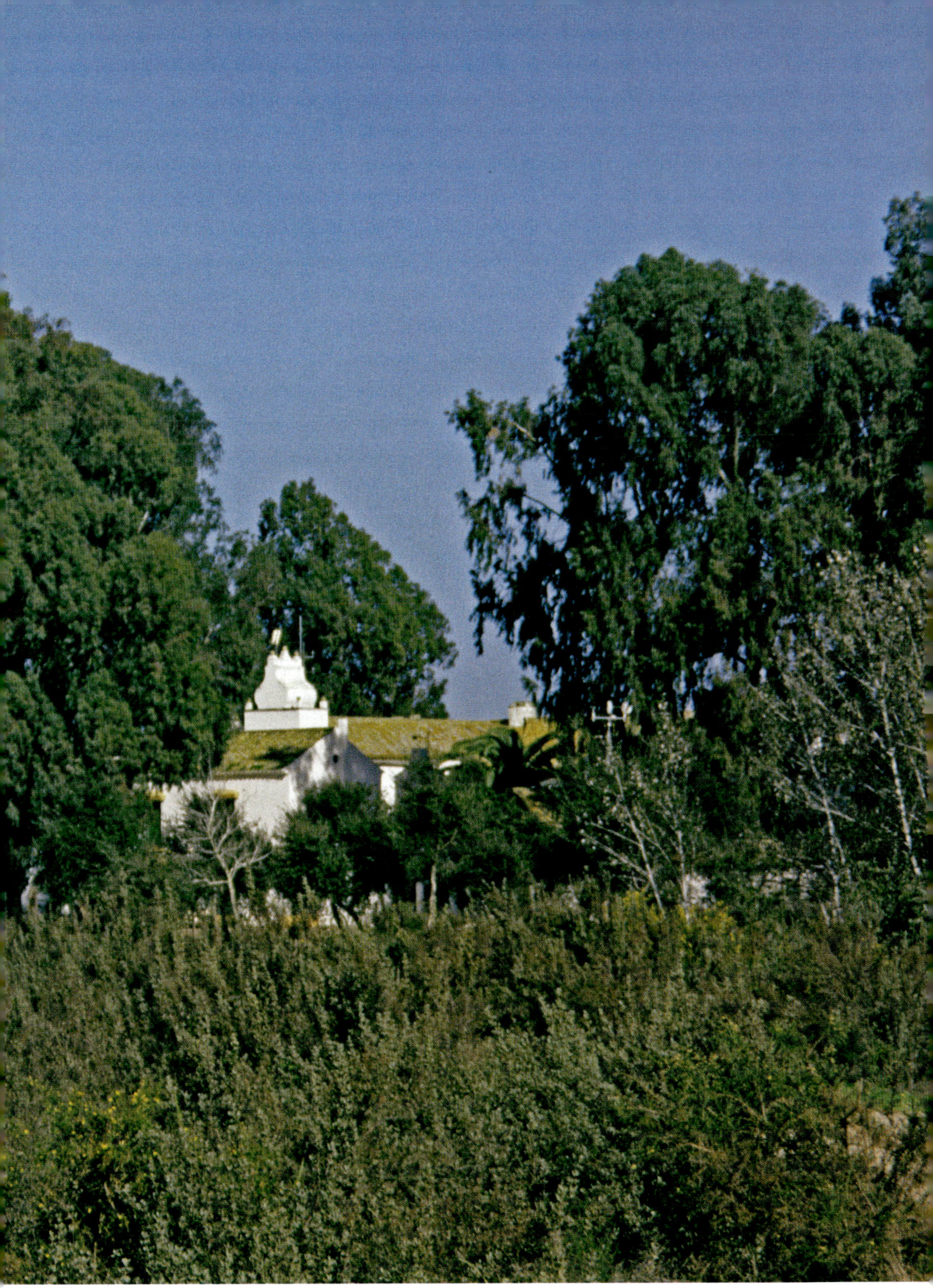

account of the privileges obtained from Melilla and his need for royal approval for the integration of towns in the Serranía de Ronda into the dukedom – yielded without apparent resistance. A royal decree on December 22, 1501, made Gibraltar Crown property and its new governor arrived to take command 11 days later. There would be no third Marquis of Gibraltar.

One territory that Medina Sidonia did retain was the hunting ground on the west bank of the Guadalquivir. In 1495, in the "quiet" moment between the fall of Granada and the conquest of Melilla, the third duke decided to make the forests productive and introduced the red deer as an animal for the hunt. He also organised wolf hunts, designed to reduce their numbers and allow the breeding of cattle on the estate. The estate retained its character as a cork oak forest with junipers and Mediterranean scrub, used exclusively for hunting for another 130 years.

In the intervening period some of the land in the north of the estate had been lost in a legal battle with the municipalities bordering the marsh. In 1585, the seventh duke bought this land back from the town of Almonte. The duke, another Alonso Pérez de Guzmán, following family tradition, would become famous in a completely different context. When the Spanish Admiral and Commander of the Galleys, the Marquis of Santa Cruz, died in 1588, King Felipe II gave the command of the Spanish navy to the duke, making him Captain General of the Ocean Sea. At the time the duke was Captain General of the coasts of Andalusia, from the Portuguese border to Gibraltar, so his promotion may not have been too unexpected. His first task was to complete the plans of his predecessor, to command the Invincible Armada and conquer England. Despite his pleas to the king against the endeavour, Medina Sidonia was forced to set sail, with the well-known disastrous consequences.

Medina Sidonia was married to Ana de Silva y Mendoza, daughter of the infamous Princess of Eboli. The princess's intrigues in court and licentious life were notorious and it was rumoured that she was mistress of the king. Her subsequent disloyalty to the Crown led King Felipe II to have her imprisoned. Ana, a shy, withdrawn woman, was deeply affected by her mother's behaviour, which seemed to have coloured her whole life. She persuaded the duke to leave the family home in Sanlúcar to live in the solitude of the forest across the river. It was then that the duke purchased back the lands from Almonte. Shortly afterwards, the estate became known as the Forest of Doñana (Doña Ana), a name that has endured and become renowned. A house, where the couple lived their later years, was built in the forest and came to be known as the Palace of Doñana. Ana died in 1610, the duke died five years later, and their remains were buried together in the palace in accordance, it is said, with their wishes.

The middle of the 17th century saw the progressive deforestation of Doñana as pastures were created for sheep and cattle and shepherds were permitted to cut wood. The density of the forest cover is said to have dropped from 45 per cent in 1636 to

CHAPTER SIX *Africa in Europe*

27 per cent in 1652. Burning of the scrub became a regular practice. Although the stone pine was native to the region, its large-scale introduction as plantations was first recorded in 1737. The practice became widespread in the dunes until the end of the 19th century. Vineyards, designed to cater to the demand for wine, were first planted in 1773, but the enterprise declined and was abandoned by 1785. This was around the time that Irishman William Garvey Power arrived in Jerez, on the opposite side of the Guadalquivir river.

Many years later, in 1900, Joaquín Álvarez de Toledo Caro, 19th Duke of Medina Sidonia, was in financial difficulty, owing substantial sums related to his title and lands. The most urgent debts were paid by the sale of the properties of Jimena and the Coto Doñana, the latter being sold to Don Guillermo de Garvey, which brings us full circle back to Chapman and Buck at the beginning of this chapter. The Medina Sidonias, descendants of the North African mercenary who gallantly defended Tarifa, played a central role in the affairs of the southwestern lowlands of al-Andalus for many centuries. Their economic interests were diverse. One of these is said to have provided a third of the entire annual revenue of the Medina Sidonia estate. It is the subject of the next chapter.

Fish processing vats in Roman town of Baelo Claudia. Bolonia, Cádiz

ON THE ROAD

CHAPTER SEVEN

On the road to Tarifa

Bronze Age human remains at Bray's Cave, Gibraltar

In the excitement of obtaining photographs of griffons on the nest, a Herculean task bearing in mind the kind of photographic equipment available to them at the time, Atkinson and friends (we met them in Chapter 2) overlooked or chose to ignore the context of their site. The Sierra de La Plata formed, with the Sierra de San Bartolomé to its east, a mountainous arc that separated the hinterland from a protected bay within the Strait of Gibraltar. Close to the beach lay the ruins of a Roman town where archaeologists had been digging since 1917. We can forgive Atkinson & Co. for the omission because it would take the archaeological world another 30 or so years to fully appreciate the significance of the site: here was the most complete Roman urban complex in the Iberian peninsula, with a basilica, theatre, market and temple dedicated to the goddess Isis. This was Baelo Claudia, established at the end of the second century BC and reaching its heyday during the reign of the emperor Claudius (41-54 AD), who gave the town the status of Roman Municipium.

Walking among the ruins of Baelo gives the visitor a clear impression of the scale and organisation that the Romans achieved. The grand public buildings do not, however, capture the essence of Baelo. Instead, less presumptuous vats, hollowed from rock in the

Bronze Age ships painted on the walls of Laja Alta. Jimena, Cádiz

ground, give meaning to this place. The town grew here for one very specific purpose and that was fishing. The Roman period pales into insignificance when we cast our mind back to the days of the first people to take advantage of the rich waters around the Strait of Gibraltar, where the cold Atlantic meets the warm Mediterranean.

Only in 1997 was the full impact of the long relationship between people and the sea in the Strait brought home to me with the discovery that Neanderthals had lived off seals, dolphins and other marine animals. The close relationship between the inhabitants around the Strait and its approaches and the rich marine life has apparently always been a feature of these lands. The modern human hunters that came after the Neanderthals fished regularly, judging from the large numbers of fish bones excavated from sites like the Cueva de Nerja. The climatic improvement from 10,000 years ago, which led to the origins of agriculture in the Middle East and its spread across Europe, does not seem to have changed the way of life of the Strait's coastal people very much. Around 5,400 years BC, the Neolithic people living in caves inside the Rock of Gibraltar were fishing and cooking tuna. We know because we have found many burnt tuna bones in the caves they inhabited. It shows us that the exploitation of the seasonal migrations of this large

fish, into and out of the Mediterranean, was deeply rooted in prehistory.
Long before the Romans arrived in the shallow bay of Baelo Claudia, at the end of the third century BC, others had seized the commercial opportunity provided by the large fish of the Strait. They were the Phoenicians, ancient mariners from the shores of the eastern Mediterranean, present-day Lebanon. Their arrival, or perhaps that of even earlier Greek mariners, was captured forever in a cave in the hills close to the Strait.
To get to the cave of Laja Alta you have to ascend into the cork woods behind Jimena de la Frontera, first in four-wheel-drive vehicles, then on mule. Eventually you reach a precipitous cliff (the Laja) and descend into a series of small rock shelters carved out of the sandstone by wind and rain. The views are stunning, across the valley of the Hozgarganta river and down towards the distant Strait. The rock shelters were painted in some ancient time, not unusual around here where there are many painted caves. The uniqueness lies in what was depicted: splendid sailing ships, readily identifiable as belonging to the ancient world of the mariners of the eastern Mediterranean. Some paintings show the craft following one other, as if representing the movement of a small fleet. They were painted by the local Bronze Age indigenous people of these hills, at least 2,500 years ago and probably much earlier than that.
Imagine what the first sight of these distant floating objects would have done to the minds of people still immersed in the depths of prehistory. I suppose that it would have been similar to the arrival of a spaceship on Earth today. Although the first contact between the eastern mariners and the people of Iberia has been established archaeologically at around the eighth century BC (around 2,700 years ago), tantalising clues suggest such contact may have been much earlier. Certainly the ships painted in Laja Alta are reminiscent of those of the ancient Mycenaean Greeks of the Homeric battles for Troy, but that would place them another 800 years – almost a whole millennium – before the Phoenicians. The discovery of Mycenaean ceramics inland, in Montoro on the upper Guadalquivir valley, would seem to provide some support. Excavating in a Gibraltar cave a Bronze Age burial from between 2,265 and 1,505 BC produced another hint. Here we found, as part of the burial goods, a delicate bead made from amber. Since the closest sources of amber would have been either the central or eastern Mediterranean or the Baltic Sea, the discovery suggests there had been contact with people from afar, presumably mariners, which would have been contemporary with the Mycenaean Greeks. The references to the Pillars of Heracles in ancient Greek legends may therefore reflect a knowledge that went back much further than the classical Greek or Phoenician periods.
The first solid evidence of a sustained presence in the Strait of Gibraltar and adjacent coasts, as opposed to these possible pioneering voyages, is from the eighth century BC

Calpe on the east coast of Spain, bearing the same name as the ancient name for Gibraltar. These prominent rocks were guiding features to ancient mariners.

CHAPTER SEVEN *On the road to Tarifa*

onwards and is mainly by Phoenicians. In Gorham's Cave in Gibraltar, they prayed and made offerings to the gods for safe passage into the open ocean, the Atlantic. Here an archaeological level, reliably radiocarbon-dated, indicates use of the cave as a coastal shrine between 800 and 410 BC, and this use probably continued until the arrival of the Romans in the third century BC. From their first arrival in the Strait, the Phoenicians took part in religious rites at what was then the end of the known world.

Commercial reasons lay behind their arrival. They were a nomadic sea-faring people who made their ships from the cedars that grew in the mountains near Phoenicia. They survived the pressure from the Assyrian Empire by acting as go-betweens and providing silver, tin and other vital metals that kept their vast armies supplied. Their knowledge of the sea, keeping their sources of supplies carefully guarded secrets, made them indispensable and this guaranteed their survival. After crossing the Strait, they ventured along the coasts of present-day Cádiz and Huelva, where they met and traded with the legendary peoples of Tartessos, a Bronze Age Iberian kingdom. The main Phoenician interest was minerals and there was a plentiful supply here. Gradually, they established colonies along the coast and a network of harbours to protect their ships, which arrived in the west during the summer with the easterly trade winds and returned home across the Mediterranean with the spring westerlies.

It was probably the Phoenicians who started marking the end of the world at the Pillars of Heracles (or their equivalent god Melkart, Gorham's Cave very likely being the temple to Melkart) in the Strait of Gibraltar. Since we know that the Phoenicians passed by the Pillars to reach the mineral-rich Atlantic coasts, we can but wonder whether creating the myth that the world ended at the Pillars had something to do with cornering a new-found market.

Although minerals were the prime reason for venturing into the western Mediterranean and beyond, the Phoenicians were quick to realise the wealth of the seas in this area. It had been exploited for thousands of years by local peoples but the Phoenicians took the exploitation a step further. They were the first to exploit commercially the migration of red tuna into the Mediterranean in spring and their return to the Atlantic in early summer, building factories to process and salt the fish which were then sealed in amphorae for export. This industrial development seems to have taken off around the Atlantic coast near the Strait around the fifth century BC and continued at least until the second century. A number of well-preserved fish-salting factories from this period have recently been excavated around El Puerto de Santa María in Cádiz province. The tradition is unknown from archaeological sites in Phoenicia, which is not surprising as it is not on the tuna's migratory route. In ancient times – less so nowadays when over-exploitation has decimated numbers – the tuna would migrate past the coast of Sicily, Carthage (in present-day Tunisia), along the coast of Tripolitania (Libya) and into the Black Sea via the Bosphorus and Dardanelles. As early as the eighth century the Greeks had established colonies in the Black Sea area that produced salted tuna for Athens. The

CHAPTER SEVEN *On the road to Tarifa*

Ceuta almadraba fishing for tuna and other migratory fish

Phoenicians very likely learned the fishing and conserving techniques from the Greeks and, eventually, salted tuna from the Strait of Gibraltar also found its way to Athens, where it competed with the products from the Black Sea and adjacent areas. The boom in factories from the fifth century coincides with the dominance of the Iberian coast by the Carthaginians, who were descended from the Phoenicians and had established colonies in the western Mediterranean. Since the migratory tuna passed their capital, Carthage, the Carthaginians may have picked up the Greek tradition, developed it and brought it west to the Strait and Atlantic.

The Iberian peninsula was largely under the control of the Carthaginians in the year 219 BC. When the inhabitants of Saguntum, near present-day Valencia, assaulted Carthaginian towns and killed their allies within the city, Hannibal, the Carthaginian general, was provoked to attack. Since Saguntum was an ally of Rome, this led to the second Punic war between Rome and Carthage, which lasted from 218 to 201 BC. The Romans referred to the Carthaginians as Punici (from Poenici, Phoenician), a direct reference to their eastern Mediterranean ancestry. It was in this war that Hannibal made a daring surprise attack over the Alps with his elephants.

Hannibal's younger brother Hasdrubal defended Hispania but he finally had to retreat and Carthage lost Hispania for ever. The Roman general Scipio Africanus took the war to African soil and defeated the Carthaginians in the Battle of Zama. To leave no trace of the civilisation, the Romans are said to have levelled Carthage and covered it with salt so that nothing would ever grow there again – an early case of mass ethnic cleansing. The contact with Hispania during the war made Rome aware of the peninsula's strategic value and of the wealth of its natural resources and it set out to conquer it. In 195 BC, six years after the end of the second Punic war, they divided the conquered territory into two provinces: Hispania Citerior on the Mediterranean coast and Hispania Ulterior, covering roughly present-day Andalusia. The complete control over the whole peninsula would take them another 176 years.

This brings us back full circle to Baelo Claudia, the Roman fishing city on the shores of the Strait of Gibraltar. With Rome's arrival the industrial exploitation of the marine resources of the Strait and adjacent coasts reached an unprecedented scale, one which would characterise the area until the end of the 20th century. The Romans exploited the vast richness of local marine resources: squid, octopus, spider crab, lobster, oyster, clam, urchin and ray. The tuna and related migratory species, however, were the main focus of attention, particularly the red tuna though also preferred were Atlantic mackerel, Atlantic bonito and the bullet tuna.

The Romans used a variety of fishing techniques, single animals with hooks, others with trawl or circling nets, but the preferred method was the fixed net. They even learned to attract fish at night with lights. Opianus in the second Century AD describes the range of techniques that were in use: "Four methods have been devised by fishermen for capturing from the sea. Some take delight using fish hooks, and of these some use long rods to which they have tied a well-braided line of horse mane hair. Others simply throw a linen cord with their hands, and others amuse themselves with lead lines or lines with many hanging fish hooks."

Fixed net fishing produced the greatest dividends, however. Nets were placed in places where tuna were known to pass close to the coast and the tradition continued for centuries after Rome's fall. Opianus also described how tuna were caught in this way once migratory shoals had been sighted from the observation point (thynnoscopion): "They spread all the nets like a city among the waves, because the net has its porters, and interior doors and secret enclosures. The tunas advance quickly in lines, as human phalanxes marching in tribes, some younger, others older, others of medium age. They pour into the nets in infinite numbers, all the time that they (the fishermen) wish and the capacity that the net will admit. And the fishing is rich and excellent."

During Rome's domination, the Strait became the hub of fishing in the Mediterranean and the commercial enterprise was on a pan-Mediterranean scale. Conservation of fish by salting reached its heyday and allied commodities were also produced in great quantities for export, one of the most favoured products being garum. This was a kind of sauce made from the salted soft parts (intestines and the like) of the tuna, to which were added whole small fish (such as anchovies and red mullet). The mix was left in solution in large vats, macerating in the sun for two months, after which it was stored in

CHAPTER SEVEN *On the road to Tarifa*

Common dolphins in the Bay of Gibraltar

amphorae.
Salt extraction, a vital allied production, went hand-in-hand with fishing. Although several methods were employed in Roman times, including mining, the geography of southwest Iberia lent itself to the exploitation of salt pans along the littoral plains. A network of channels led sea water at high tide to the pans where the water was evaporated by the sun and the salt extracted. In some fishing towns it appears that the process was accelerated in ovens. The importance of salt has reached us even in our language, salarium being the salt ration given to the Roman soldier. The salt extraction business guaranteed a monopoly to the Carthaginian kings, not just of the salt but of the fish-salting and allied industries. With the Roman takeover the industry was put in the public domain, under state control and exploited by societas, opening the door for large-scale commercial expansion.
At least five cities around the Strait lived off fish produce: Baelo Claudia, Mellaria (near Tarifa), Iulia Traducta and Caetaria (in Algeciras) and Carteia (near Gibraltar). Baelo Claudia became the prototype of the large fish-salting factories. Since at least the second century BC, the Republican period, the city centred around exploiting marine resources. The industrial district, covering 20,000 square metres, developed during the Augustine period and typified the expansion that followed peace within the empire at the end of the first century BC. Another large fish industry which started at this time in Iulia Traducta

AL-ANDALUS

covered 90,000 square metres. Carteia, founded as early as 171 BC, became Rome's first colony, the Colonia Libertinorum Carteia. It was created to give Roman status to the children of Roman soldiers with local wives and became the most important Roman city of the entire Strait area. Coins from Carteia, depicting fishermen, Neptune, boat rudders and dolphins, show the close relation the city had with the sea. These major industrial sites functioned until the first decades of the sixth century AD, close to six centuries. Shortly after, in 533/534 AD, the coasts of the Strait were conquered by the Byzantines under the Emperor Justinian.

The industry did not disappear altogether though. Fishing was habitual in the Islamic period (711 to 1492 AD) of al-Andalus when fish was the staple of coastal populations, especially the poorer people. Many Spanish fishing terms currently in use are derived from Arabic and illustrate the importance of the fishing tradition at that time. The fixed fish net practice of catching tuna that had been in use since at least Roman times was continued by the Muslims who called the nets the al-madraba, literally the place where you wrestle with and club the fish. It was a direct reference to the process of killing the tuna, with large wooden cudgels, as the nets were lifted. The name almadraba is still used in Spanish today. The Spanish names of a number of fish are also derived from the Arabic: for example al-surel for jurel (the Atlantic mackerel), al-sardin for sardina (the sardine) or al-qamarun for camaron (or shrimp). Almoceros were the people who were in charge of taking food to the fishermen, from which almuerzo (lunch) is derived.

The Muslims practised two methods of tuna capture. One was the long net or shoot-trap net (sabaka) from which the Spanish name jábega is derived. The other was the al-madraba (fixed net) itself. Al-Idrisi, the 12th-century geographer born in Ceuta, described the fishing in this area: "There exist near Ceuta places dedicated to fishing. No coast produces or exports more. There are more than 100 different species of fish, but the main species captured is the tuna which is very abundant there. It is fished with lances, with tips in the form of open wings with which the fish is hooked and cannot escape. Attached to the end of the shaft are long twines. These fishermen are so experienced and skilled in their work that they do not have rival in the world."

The fish caught were not all for local consumption. Some of it was dried and, according to al-Zuhri (12th century), exported as mojama to all places on Earth.

As the Muslims were pushed back during the long period of Christian conquest, the latter took over, expanding the tuna-fishing tradition to the extent that boats from as far as the Catalan coast started to arrive in the Strait. We meet an old friend from the previous chapter, Guzmán El Bueno. Following the capture of Tarifa by King Sancho IV in 1292, the king gave Alonso the virtual monopoly of the tuna fishing in waters of the Atlantic and the Strait. The Royal Privilege, ratified by King Fernando IV in 1295, read as follows: "You are given the present and future almadrabas, from where the river Guadiana (marking the boundary between Spain and Portugal) enters the sea to the coast of the Kingdom of Granada (at that time the western boundary of the kingdom

CHAPTER SEVEN *On the road to Tarifa*

Sandwich Tern over the Strait of Gibraltar

was Gibraltar). And also if you conquer any place with an almadraba, it cannot be exploited by any person but you, Don Alonso de Guzmán, El Bueno, and those coming with you."

The exploitation of the almadrabas became the mainstay of the Dukes of Medina Sidonia, generating a third of their revenue. The privilege was only abolished in 1817 by King Fernando VII. In the intervening five centuries the Medina Sidonias monopolised the tuna along the whole coastline between Portugal and Gibraltar. The operations started each year on St Mark's day (April 25) and ended on the feast of St Peter and St Paul (June 29). Between 1525 and 1740 they caught around 10 million tunas, averaging 46,000 per year. The annual figures varied widely. As an example, the Conil almadraba alone captured 82,074 in 1540 but only 20,424 in 1544. In 1558, the duke's combined almadrabas captured 110,052 tunas, generating a return of 80,000 ducats. In the mid-18th century the duke paid the Crown 300,000 ducats for the continuing fishing rights in the Strait so the investment was clearly worthwhile. It is perhaps not surprising that the Medina Sidonias were so reluctant to return possession of Gibraltar to the Crown in 1501.

The start of the tuna season was marked each year by the duke sending out a drummer

Isla de las palomas, Tarifa, Cádiz. Africa in the background.

to signal the recruitment of personnel, as if for an army. The duke personally attended the almadrabas in Conil and Zahara, often taking his family with him. His children played on the beaches as if on holiday but, at the same time, mixed with the crews and learned the skills of the trade that would serve them when it became their turn to run the family business.

Buyers would come to the almadrabas from far and wide to purchase the tuna. This provided hard cash for the dukes who would pay off debts accumulated through the year. During the 15th century, in the last throes of the Christian conquest, the first duke introduced a system by which at the end of the season part of the money raised from the tuna was used to pay ransom for the release of two Christian hostages in Muslim hands. In his will he left funds for the extraordinary rescue of 30 captives. Alms were also passed each year to holy orders, the Monastery of Guadalupe in Extremadura benefiting the most.

No sooner had the almadrabas closed each year than preparations started for the next season. Supplies were replenished over the winter across the duke's estate. Nets were made in the county of Niebla and carpenters repaired boats in Sanlúcar, using oak and

The Strait of Gibraltar has a rich marine life that has attracted fishermen since prehistory. Seven Sisters reef, Gibraltar. (Photo by Geraldine Finlayson)

willow from the estates around Doñana. Wheat to make bread and hay for horses was bought during the harvest and stored in granaries in Sanlucár for the following season. At the beginning of the 16th century the only permanent staff was that of the factory (la chanca) which was in charge of preparing and conserving the fish for export. A crew of local professionals initially controlled catching the fish which were then sold to the duke, but later, in order to cope with the workload, workers had to be hired from outside. They were each given a ration of a quart of wine and a loaf of bread per day and a pound-and-a-half of beef a week during the season. The crew captains were given double ration. The almadraba employed its own bakery and butcher, separate from that of the town itself, laundry, barbers and water suppliers. The whole operation was indeed run like an army.

As the beach was regarded as sanctuary and exempt from royal jurisdiction, all kinds of unsavoury characters could escape the law while working the tuna. Rogues and scoundrels mixed with people from far and wide. The men responsible for pulling the ropes were usually lazy delinquents in search of adventure who were hired on the basis of name and town of origin without need of further proof. Order was established

The waters of the Strait have always posed a threat to shipping. Europa Point, Gibraltar. Gorham's Cave is on the left. (Photo by Geraldine Finlayson)

when the watch tower, as in Roman times, signalled the arrival of a shoal and crews assembled.

The duke appointed a captain, usually a long-serving and trusted member of his household, to patrol the beach on horseback directing operations and, aided by agents infiltrated among the rabble, keeping an eye on the daily problems that arose among the men. The beach was not a safe place. Theft, gambling, going off with women and stabbings were common. Those who stole tuna invented all kinds of ingenious tricks to evade detection, from concealing fish underwater until nightfall to dressing a fish in clothing so that it appeared to be a drunk when it was dragged away from the beach. In the second half of the 16th century Jesuits discovered the almadrabas as a place of mission. A Father León, chaplain of the prison of Sevilla, took the missionary fervour a stage further by contracting prisoners to go and work on the almadrabas while still in jail. As such bands could cause problems in every town and village they passed through, they were transported directly to the almadrabas in boats. Father León would accompany the prisoners with the express mission of stopping blasphemy and removing women from the almadrabas. Both aims failed; the constant swearing made it

Storm at Europa Point showing the violence of the seas of the Strait.

impractical to deny work to so many men and it was impossible to keep them away from the prostitutes. Commercial and spiritual interests clashed on the Atlantic beaches of southwest al-Andalus – and as usual business won.

Rogues in search of easy money frequented the chain of almadrabas established along the Atlantic coast from Cabo de Roche to Tarifa. They called it the Vía de Tarifa (route to Tarifa), an expression that has continued in use to the present, usually meaning to digress or go off at a tangent. The rogues had an ability to play with words and give them multiple meanings, hence the vía in a profoundly religious society had connotations of the road to sanctity or eternal salvation. Pilgrims taking the Vía Jacobea to Santiago de Compostela, for example, received many indulgences. Tarifa, since its early conquest by King Sancho IV, had been a frontier town in a zone of conflict. King Alfonso XI, in desperate need to populate this important coastal town, gave the local population the "privilege" of exempting from punishment murderers who chose to live there. The town gained a bad reputation for harbouring aggressive people given to fighting and lacking respect for authority. Thus, to go by the Vía de Tarifa implied to escape from justice. Rich though the marine life of the waters of the Strait of Gibraltar still is, historical accounts reveal to us how much has been lost. Tourists are taken out into the waters of the Bay of Gibraltar or the Strait nowadays to see dolphins and pilot whales. Sometimes, a larger specimen shows up. This is a rare sight, but it has only become rare in the past century. The monk seal is now confined to refuges in Turkey or remote parts of the Moroccan coast. Once whales too were a regular sight. Francis Carter, living in Gibraltar between 1771 and 1772, looked down on the bay from the upper part of the Rock and described how: "When we had regained sight of the sea, the ladies were alarmed with a phenomenon they never observed before; several fountains appeared playing in the middle of the bay, and throwing up jets d'eau to a considerable height. I smiled at their surprise, and informed them they were grampuses (whales) who frequently amuse themselves in that manner in fine weather."

Much later, between 1918 and 1923, the Governor of Gibraltar, Sir Horace Smith-Dorrien, recalled: "There was one sport to be had from the Rock, which I believe is little known, and that is 'whaling'. A company just after the war established a station close to Algeciras and opposite the Rock. Their success was remarkable – four and five whales a day very often, and that close by in the Straits. The company were good enough to take me out twice, and I can thoroughly recommend it as an exciting sport, especially being towed by the whale until he is played out. The skill of the man who fired the harpoon was marvellous. He never missed."

Picture the scene today, more than 700 years after Guzmán obtained his concession on the tuna. A satellite orbits the Earth, spying on the blue waters of the Mediterranean. An alarm scrambles the crew of an aircraft. It locates a shoal of tuna as they are about to lay their eggs and hovers over them. Guided by satellite and plane, a fleet of boats encircles the animals, capturing thousands in a single go. While the sushi restaurants of Tokyo and New York prepare their menus, the animals are fattened in "farms" before being killed and transported by air to maintain their freshness. These are not farms but killing grounds on a massive scale.

Meanwhile the traditional almadraba fishermen in the Strait of Gibraltar are reporting a disaster. The catch for the 1906 season was 80 per cent down on six years earlier. The traditional sustainable method that employs 500 families is being put out of business and the tuna are heading for extinction. Fish of all ages and sizes are being taken in the Mediterranean while breeding and approved quotas are being dodged. The price of a single good red tuna in the Japanese market is 50,000 euros. It is the end of an era. It is the end of the road to Tarifa...

Moonrise over Trujillo castle, Extremadura

Chapter Eight

In the land of knights and conquistadores

AL-ANDALUS

The sun rises over the lake, casting a golden hue over its flat, calm waters. Life is already stirring everywhere. Three great bustards are startled by my presence and laboriously take off, like giant turkeys, towards some distant field where they can resume feeding in peace. A Montagu's harrier sits on the ground, still half asleep, resisting having to fly at this unearthly hour. A short-eared owl silently glides over the horizon. Its day is coming to an end as the sun gets higher in the sky. It has six well-fed chicks that have just mastered flight. The presence of the harrier makes the adult owl uncomfortable and a chase ensues, driving the sleepy harrier along to a safe distance from the owlets. Quails call incessantly their familiar "wet-my-lips" notes from deep in the uncut wheat. Three break with the skulking tradition and fly low to the next field. There are bird sounds all around: calandra, crested and skylarks compete with the musical chatter of the wheatear and the whistle of a little bustard's wings as it flies past. It lands on the edge of a ploughed field where a dozen great bustards are nervously feeding. Gull-billed terns arrive from the lake and join the army of lesser kestrels in sorting out the day's first contingent of swarming crickets, as if in some perpetually repeating skirmish on a long lost battlefield. The sun is now high as black kites and buzzards ride the thermals. The owls are asleep in the tall grass. Another day has ended for some, just as it is starting for others.

I am in the vast treeless expanses of the tableland (meseta), northwest of Madrid. This is old territory, one that was taken by the Christians very early from the Muslims to become the pivot of the later southward expansions that came to be known as the Reconquest. The area was part of the old Kingdom of León and was taken by King Alfonso III (El Magno, i.e. the Great) who reigned from 866 to 910. León united with Castile early in the 11th century to form the western prong of the southward advance of the forces fighting the Muslims. The other point of attack, led by the rulers of Aragón, proceeded in parallel along the Mediterranean coast.

In the distance, across the large lake, I can see the church tower rising above the houses of the town of Villafáfila. These farmland areas have seen a massive population exodus from the 1950s onwards. Villafáfila is the largest town in the district with around 650 inhabitants. Yet, in 1950, its population was 1,784. So what brought people here in the first place? It may seem surprising that here, in the middle of the country and well away from any coast, the main reason should have been salt. There were no tuna or other fish to attract people but, for a young and expanding landlocked kingdom, salt was a priceless commodity that was hard to find. The water of the lakes here was salty and could be extracted from wells and cisterns, then placed in pans where the sun would do the work. These were the only salt pans of the entire Kingdom of León so this place was hugely important.

Four hundred years later King Alfonso XI, whom we have met previously in connection with the Book of Hunting and Doñana, established a royal monopoly over the exploitation of salt. His decree remained in force for more than 200 years, into the 16th

Statue of Francisco Pizarro in Trujillo

century, when commerce with the Kingdom of Portugal intensified. The high quality and competitive price of the salt imported from the Portuguese coast forced these inland salt works out of business. There was a brief attempt at reviving the industry around the lakes in the 18th century but it was short-lived.

The area around Villafáfila and its lakes became well known during the 19th century for its cereal and wine production as well as for the good hunting, especially hares, partridges and ducks on the lakes. The mechanisation of agriculture in the second half of the 20th century led to emigration, leaving today's population at the level it was at the beginning of the 19th century. Mechanisation was favoured by laws passed during Franco's régime that amalgamated small parcels of land into larger fields. The move also caused the almost total removal of vines, leaving the open, cereal-dominated, landscape we see today. Wheat and barley occupy between 70 and 90 per cent of the fields depending on the year, with the remainder left fallow or dedicated to alfalfa.

This system seems to have favoured the great bustards, of which Spain has 75 per cent of the European population. These large birds are found in very large numbers here, with concentrations up to 2,800 birds, representing 11 per cent of the European total. These spectacular birds were once widespread across the plains of Iberia right down to the shores of the Strait of Gibraltar. Nineteenth-century naturalists, like Willoughby Verner, Howard Irby or even Abel Chapman himself reported huge flocks roaming freely across the open spaces surrounding the Laguna de La Janda, northeast of the town of Vejer, in the plains south of Jerez and north towards Sevilla. The 20th century saw their mass annihilation, through changing agricultural practices, widespread use of pesticides and even from the practice of shooting the birds from light aircraft.

Such is Man's power of destruction that at the turn of the new century there were just a handful of great bustards left in the entire province of Cádiz. On April 10, 2006, the last survivor in the province — in the plains of La Janda where there had once been so many — was killed. The cause of its death appears to have been electrocution after colliding with an electric pylon. It is sadly ironic that the fate of the species in this area was sealed not by the gun but by our voracious appetite for growth and expansion into the last wildernesses of the planet. Wild places, like La Janda, are being swamped by forests of modern windmills. Those who advocated these as a source of green energy are to blame. In the shallow search for supposedly environmentally friendly energy we have overlooked the damage to countryside and species. It is best that the 19th-century naturalists cannot see what we have done in the name of ecology.

To find the magnificent great bustards our best bet is the plains of Castile y León, as around Villafáfila, or our next destination: the forgotten, western region of Extremadura. Above the city of Trujillo the sun filters through the snow-white cumulus clouds, casting a sheen on the earthen blanket of roof tiles. The clapping of storks' bills mixes with the shrieks of jackdaws, interrupted only by the occasional tolling of bells from some medieval church or remote monastery. Hundreds, probably thousands, of swifts busily scream past, avoiding mid-air collision as they collect insects. Storks and lesser kestrels fly to and fro between this bastion and the parched, insect-rich plains below. Sparrows still chirp and squabble here – 21st-century over-sanitation has not got them just yet. The clatter over the cobbles of a ghostly knight on horseback mixes with the chant of the imam and Sephardic songs from the synagogue. It is difficult to distinguish dream from reality in this ancient roof-top scene. As the clouds break a line of vultures, black and griffon, purposefully flies over the fortress. Once more the storks clap and their young joyfully launch themselves into the air, rehearsing for future flight – in another month they will be somewhere in tropical Africa. The west wind howls along narrow streets between monastery and palace. A black kite takes advantage as it glides past, forked tail rudder rotating this way and that, always in search of an opportunity. It swoops down to catch a scrap from a sandwich left by a tourist, or perhaps the entrails of some poor mortal killed fighting to take the fortress, or maybe even the left-overs from Pizarro's return banquet last night...it is hard to disentangle the threads of time above the roof-tops of medieval Trujillo.

If you visit Extremadura, Trujillo has to be your base. Perched high on a 170-metre-high island-hill of granite, its castle dominates the vast surrounding plains. Muslims

CHAPTER EIGHT *In the land of knights and conquistadores*

One of the most colourful African migrants is the bee-eater

The black stork is a rare migrant from Africa that breeds in Monfragüe, Extremadura

Holm oak dehesa near Trujillo, Extremadura

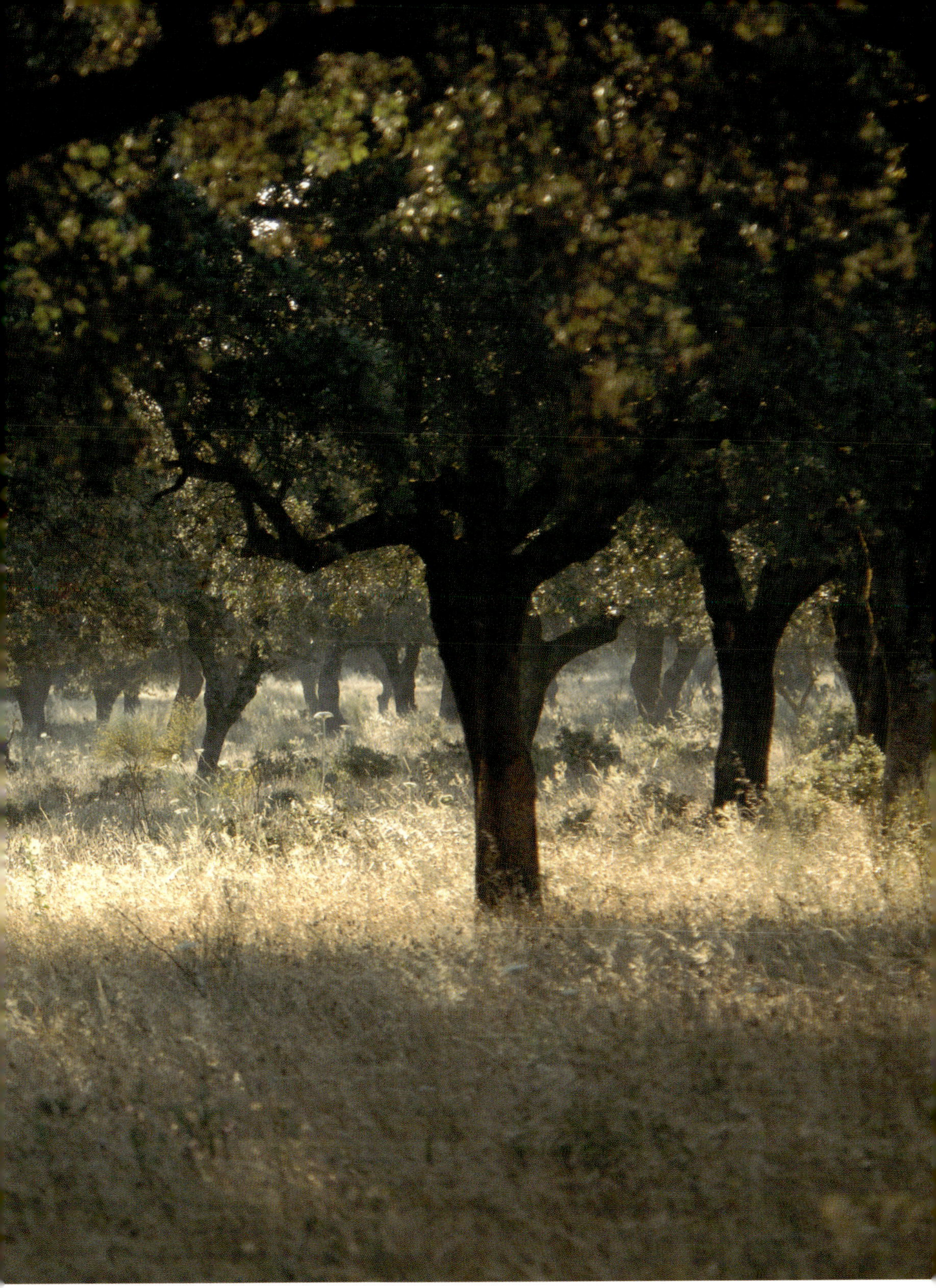

built the castle in the 10th century and occupied it until 1233. Trujillo's origins may lie in the Roman period when a settlement known as Turgalium appears to have existed here. Under Muslim rule it only began to gain importance with the southward advance of the Christians from Castile and León. These plains, a natural corridor to Andalusia in the south, formed the frontier zone between Christian and Muslim for a while. The knights, who controlled the plains to the north including the lands around Villafáfila, had long cast their greedy eyes on this region.

The Castilians aimed to establish a series of advance positions in the towns from which they could secure the largely unpopulated landscape. Having secured these strategic points, they would then sweep south across a land free of major natural barriers and therefore ideal for cavalry to reach the Guadiana river. This large river flows westwards across the flat lands of southern Extremadura then turns south to open into the Atlantic near Huelva. It has traditionally marked the boundary between Spain and Portugal.

For the Muslims, on the other hand, securing this vast area and protecting it with castles and towers on the hills that marked the higher ground provided them with a buffer that protected its major cities to the south, most notably Sevilla and Córdoba. Each of their outposts had to be individually conquered before the territory could be controlled. Thus, any Christian advance was seriously slowed down. Indeed, the conquest of these territories took the Christians roughly 350 years, from the first incursions by King Alfonso III in 881 practically to the fall of Trujillo in 1233. During this period the territory was subjected to constant raids and counter-raids.

The Muslim geographer al-Idrisi visited Trujillo in the 12th century and left us this first hand account: "This town is large and resembles a fortress. Its walls are solidly constructed and there are well-stocked bazaars. Its inhabitants, both cavalry and infantry, make continuous raids into the country of the Christians. Ordinarily, they live from prowling and subterfuge."

Of the towns of the plains, Trujillo was the last to fall. It was surrounded by Christian-dominated land for Cáceres had capitulated in 1229, Badajoz, Mérida and Montánchez in 1230. Once Trujillo fell, in 1233, the southward advance was very rapid. A year later Medellín, Santa Cruz and Alanje were taken and the Christians dominated the lands north of the Guadiana. Córdoba, to the south, fell in 1236; Sevilla followed in 1248. Tarifa, in the extreme south and facing the North African lands, fell in 1292. Such was the speed of the Castilian onslaught across the plains and valleys of southwest Spain. As the frontier moved south, Trujillo lost strategic importance although it became embroiled for a while in the dynastic struggles of the petty nobility. Christian military orders of knights played a key role in the conquest of Extremadura. Their use was the most appropriate in the defence of unpopulated areas and the orders, in turn, capitalised by exploiting the local riches. Three prominent orders cut up the spoils between them. The Order of Santiago controlled the area from Montánchez (south of Trujillo) south to the limits of today's Sevilla province. The Order of Alcántara controlled the area to

CHAPTER EIGHT *In the land of knights and conquistadores*

The Hoopoe is another elegant African migrant

A male Lesser kestrel brings food back to the nest. Otero de Sariegos, Zamora

the north, to the limits of Salamanca. The international Order of the Knights Templar held specific outposts in this territory. Jerez de los Caballeros (caballeros referring to the Knights Templars) and Fregenal de la Sierra were enclaves of this order within the territory of the knights of the Order of Santiago.

When Trujillo fell, the Grand Master of the Order of Alcántara requested it for the order, but the king refused and kept it for the Crown. Great efforts were made to encourage repopulation of the land, but as it was a veritable desert the process was slow. Special privileges and lands were given to knights and lesser nobles to stimulate settlement. Trujillo became the main population centre of the vast territory which it controlled. Scattered villages and hamlets, depending on the agriculture the poor land could support, emerged across the landscape. Its jurisdiction covered an area of 300,000 hectares, 78 kilometres from east to west and 98 kilometres from north to south, and its limits were marked by rivers and isolated mountains. More often than not in a largely flat landscape, trees, rocks and tracks marked internal territorial limits. Such vague markers were the cause of constant conflict among nobles.

Some disputes involved conflict between adjacent towns. The two principal towns of the area were Trujillo and Talavera to the northeast. In 1338, King Alfonso XI created the monastery of Guadalupe on lands that belonged to Trujillo and Talavera. It was a way of populating and controlling empty land. In subsequent years the power of the church and the monastery's increasing territorial influence were a source of conflict with its neighbours (a century later this same monastery was supported by the Duke of Medina Sidonia's tuna industry).

The resources that were exploited across the granite and slate lands around Trujillo remain similar today and account for the state of relative wilderness of this thinly populated country. Cattle, pigs and sheep have been the main animals. The natural production of acorns from the vast holm oak woods, managed in estates known as dehesas (montados in nearby Portugal), was a major source of sustenance for the pigs. This resource was also exploited by tens of thousands of cranes and wood pigeons arriving here from northern Europe in the winter. The dehesas of Extremadura are still the major wintering ground of the northern European cranes.

Traditional land uses were the cutting and burning of wood for charcoal (the only source of energy for the inhabitants as across much of Spain), small-scale game hunting and the exploitation of the abundant sources of fresh running water. Water mills were placed along many rivers and streams which operated with the winter rains, grinding the wheat from the previous harvest. The use of the land around Trujillo has been the sustainable exploitation of the rich Mediterranean forest and it has maintained a diverse range of species now hard to find anywhere else in Europe.

The forest and its wildlife are best preserved in the 17,852-hectare Monfragüe National Park (its status was upgraded from Natural to National Park in 2007), less than an hour's drive north of Trujillo. This is one of Europe's main refuges for large birds of

CHAPTER EIGHT *In the land of knights and conquistadores*

The Montagu's Harrier, a trans-saharan migrant, is a typical ground nesting raptor of the Extremaduran plains

Along with Bee-eater and Hoopoe, the Roller forms the colourful trio of African migrants that breed in Extremadura (Photo by Geraldine Finlayson)

prey that can be seen with relative ease at close quarters. Here we find a combination of cliff-nesting species, most notable being griffon and Egyptian vultures, golden eagles and eagle owls along with raptors that nest in the canopy of the oak tree forests. Among these is a major population of the black vulture and the Spanish imperial eagle. Monfragüe is also home for a population of the rare black stork, a species that arrives from tropical Africa, across the Strait of Gibraltar, in February to nest in ledges and small caverns among the vultures.

Many of these raptors regularly fly from their mountain refuge to seek food in the rich dehesas to the south, in the direction of Trujillo. The dehesas and open plains are home to many of the birds we met in Villafáfila, bustards, quail, harriers. Although Villafáfila is the stronghold of the great bustard, the plains between Trujillo and Cáceres to the west are arguably richer in species and numbers. In spring the fields, free from pesticide and other chemical treatment, are swarming with locusts and bush crickets which attract spectacular concentrations of predators, all keen to take part in the bonanza. Among these are Montagu's harriers, black kites and lesser kestrels.

The lesser kestrel, a tropical migrant from West Africa, arrives here in February and uses the old buildings and walls of Trujillo to nest and rear its young. For lesser kestrels settlements with isolated and abandoned farm buildings are havens in which they can raise their young. They live in islands of human construction surrounded by seas of plenty. The depopulation of the Castilian countryside has favoured these birds perhaps even more than in Extremadura. Otero de Sariegos and its hinterland, near Villafáfila, holds Castile y León's largest colony with 345 pairs censused in 2004. The village itself had 119 inhabitants in 1940. Nobody has lived there since the mid-1980s.

The lesser kestrels of Otero are doing well because they are exploiting a recent explosion in the number of voles in this region. While birds of the Trujillo colony hunt large insects almost exclusively, much of the prey brought back to the Otero nests are field voles. The large numbers of voles has also been good for barn and short-eared owls. Short-eared owls used to visit these fields in winter but would not stay to breed in the spring; in fact, the species did not breed in Spain at all. The first attempts at breeding were observed in 1990 and there are now several pairs regularly nesting here.

These success stories mask an underlying malignant disease that is affecting many species of birds and other animals. The loss of vines that provided cover, over-hunting, the merging of small fields and the intensification of agriculture, aided by European Union funds, with mechanisation and massive use of chemicals in fields is swiftly killing a community of animals that have survived here since before the days of King Alfonso III in the ninth century. Many of the birds of the open fields are in serious decline: Montagu's harrier, red-legged partridge, quail, little bustard, stone curlew, black-bellied sandgrouse and turtle dove are jewels on the way out unless the situation is soon remedied...

A stork stares down from its lofty nest on the top of the medieval church of Otero

The Turtle Dove is the only migratory pigeon that crosses the Sahara. They breed in the open plains of Extremadura and the meseta

de Sariegos. Its bells no longer toll. The village is devoid of human life. The wind howls through the abandoned streets, lifting dust and plumes, carrying seeds to some unknown, destination. Yet, I have the feeling I am being carefully watched from the shadows. A splash of orange, red and blue catches the corner of my eye — it is a spectacular male lesser kestrel. There is life amid this desolation. The collapsed roofs, broken-down doors, shattered tiles, glassless windows, mud-and-straw pigeon coops, all provide opportunities for life to thrive here. The constant chattering of lesser kestrels arriving from the nearby fields transforms the scene and suddenly makes this place feel like a London train station at rush hour. The downy young are hidden under roof tiles and in holes in the ruins. They scream incessantly when they hear the parents returning with a juicy vole or crunchy bush cricket. Swallows flit by, flying into old houses which they share with little and barn owls. House sparrows and spotless starlings participate in the insect bonanza, returning with beak-loads to feed hungry young lodged in cracks and spaces of the decaying buildings. A black redstart angrily scolds in defence of its own progeny. In the background the rusty chatter of agitated black-winged stilts reminds us that the old lake is just down the road. Avocets take to the air to chase off

Plains at Villafáfila at dawn with Short-eared owl hunting

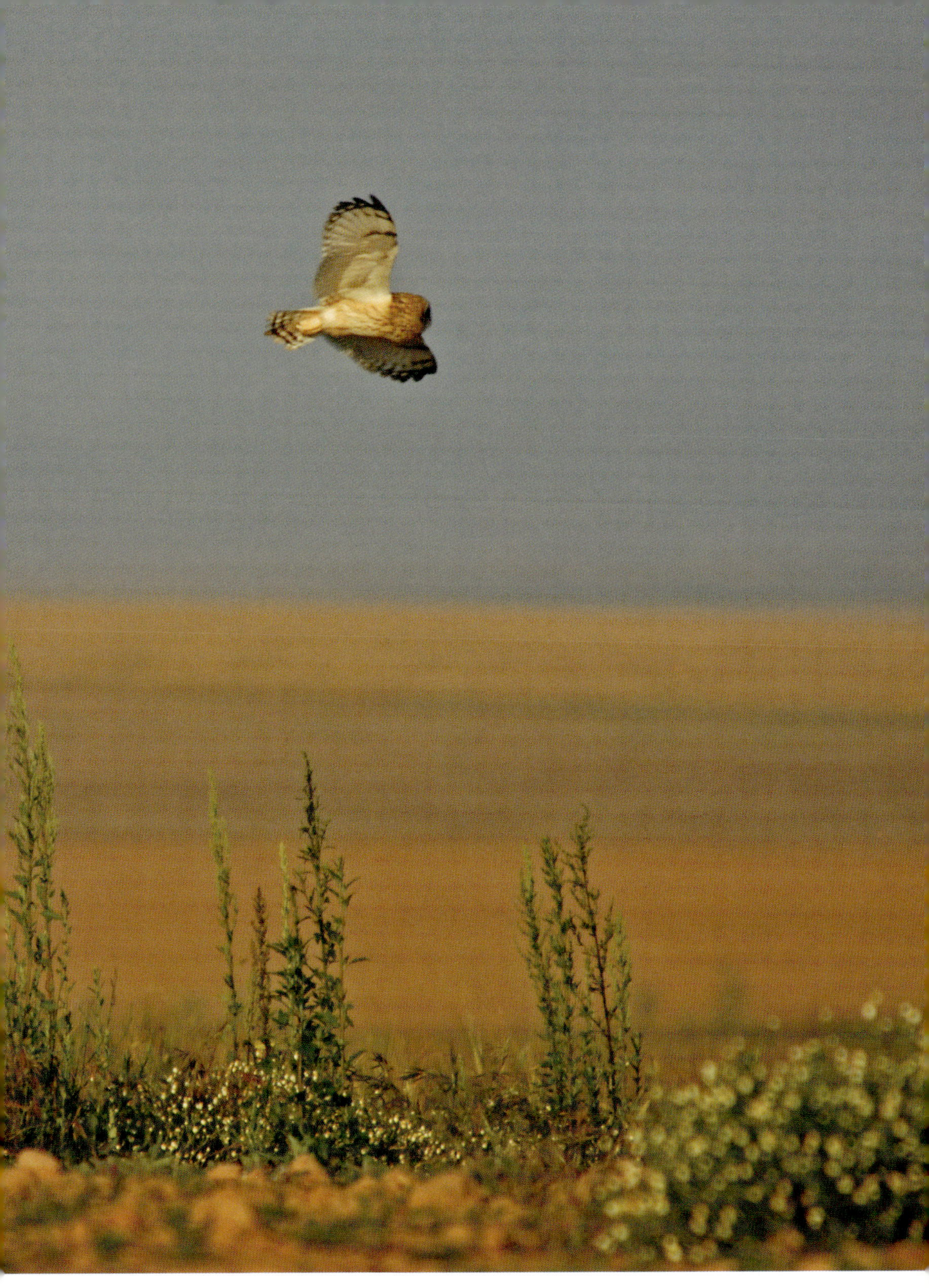

a black kite that got too close to their own youngsters. The sun starts to descend. A hungry short-toed eagle patiently sits on an old pylon, hopefully waiting for some unsuspecting snake below. Gull-billed terns perform acrobatic manoeuvres over the ditches, catching beetles and crickets for their hungry young. A fluffy lapwing chick, watched by neurotic parents, takes its first footsteps across a muddy pond margin where it has just been born. Great bustards stir and resume vespertine feeding, stealthily hidden among the swaying wheat. Time stands still in the salty lakes, wheat fields and ghost villages of Old Castile. But for how much longer?

Epilogue
In 1532, with a handful of men, Francisco Pizarro, an illiterate former swineherd from Trujillo, captured the most powerful leader in the New World, Atahualpa, King of the Incas. Like his second cousin Hernán Cortés Pizarro, from Medellín in the south of Extremadura, Pizarro was perpetuating the land and treasure-grabbing experience of his ancestors against the Muslims. Al-Andalus had been taken across the Atlantic. Despite the difficult terrain of the Andes, the conquest of Peru was rapid compared with that of the mountainous Kingdom of Granada. The reason: the huge technological differential between the opposing forces.
The conquest of Peru, Mexico and much of America was the natural consequence of the Christian conquest of Spain. Once that had ended in 1492, nobles, knights and soldiers had to find ways to continue the warring lifestyle that had produced such dividends in the name of religion. America presented itself as the land of opportunity and the warlords, most of them from the lands around Trujillo, got their reprieve. Their departure quite accidentally ensured the survival of the wilderness at home. Destruction was delayed while it was transferred to the new lands of the Indies.

Short-eared owl at Villafáfila, Zamora

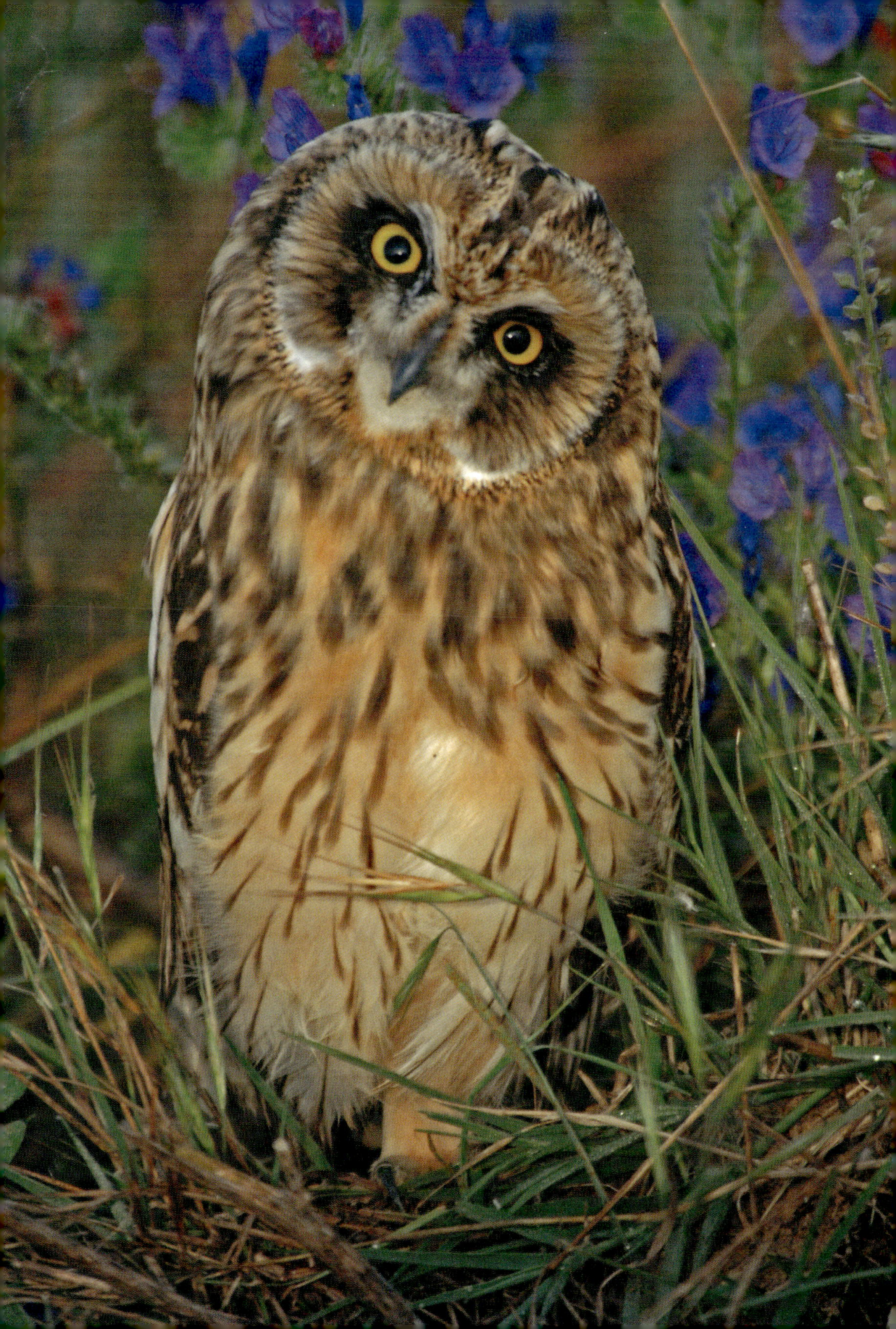

The colourful vega of La Janda

JANDA

CHAPTER NINE

Janda

Cattle Egret roost, La Janda, Cádiz

"Amid the marshes of southern Spain a great variety of birds find suitable nesting-places. The size and exact locality of these swamps vary from year to year and depend upon the amount and time of the rainfall during the winter months. But there are certain low-lying portions which usually remain flooded for months after the shallows around have become expanses of sun-baked mud."

This is how Willoughby Verner described the wetlands of southern Spain. He was almost certainly describing the old lake of La Janda, northeast of the town of Vejer on the shores of the Strait of Gibraltar. This was Spain's largest lake with a surface area of 3,700 hectares. Unfortunately, a process of drainage started as early as 1825 but not fully completed until 1967, destroyed this wetland paradise once on a par with Doñana in terms of ecological importance. The plains of the former lake are taken up by agricultural land today but still retain important natural values that are enhanced when unusually heavy winter rains temporarily flood the basin. Forty years after its final death as a natural wetland, La Janda retains natural vegetation along the drainage canals and, because of its strategic geographical location, attracts thousands of birds migrating across the Strait. In the supposedly green and enlightened days of the

Cranes over Gallocanta, Teruel

21st century, the recovery of La Janda is achievable but remains a distant dream.
To picture what La Janda was like prior to its drainage we must rely on descriptions, photographs and maps. The wetland consisted of a complex of lakes of varying sizes. In years of heavy rainfall they all coalesced to form a veritable inland sea. In drier years, or towards the summer when water evaporated, the levels receded and the individual lakes became discernible. La Janda was not a body of open water. It was closer to the marisma of the Guadalquivir described in Chapter 5.
When the British naturalist G. K. Yeates visited it early in the 1940s he noted: "The lagoon is certainly a surprise. On the map it is marked as a big expanse of water, but as one views it from the edge of the cork oaks the land falls away over a flat level (vega is the technical name) on to what looks like a vast plain. Beyond, the sierras rise in rugged mass. At first I thought the place dry, but a closer inspection showed that in fact the whole area was flooded to a depth of about two feet, the water being hidden by the density of reed growth."
Verner knew this well, being a regular visitor to his favourite haunt, into which he waded in search of birds: "Between the months of April and June they (the lakes) are densely overgrown with enormously strong and tall bullrush, which make all movement

Cranes going to roost at Gallocanta

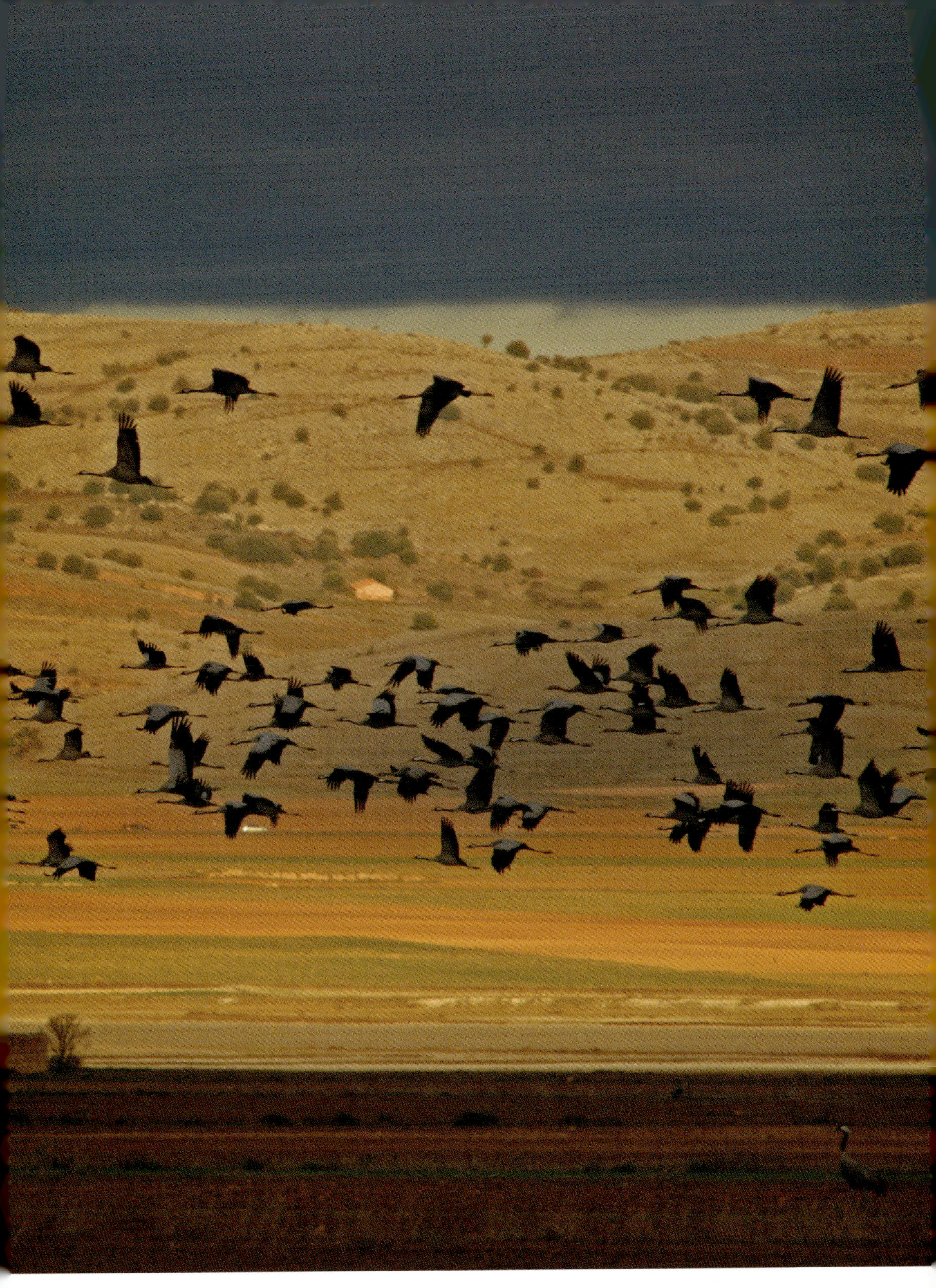

Flooded fields in La Janda

through them a continuous struggle."
Despite, and probably because of, the difficulties of access, La Janda was an absolute wilderness teeming with birds. The Neolithic people who populated these plains around 5,000 BC may not have known the lake in its pre-drainage shape, but they were clearly living on the edges of a wetland and they recorded what they saw. In the 1990s I was privileged to work with Martí Mas Cornellá, an archaeologist specialising in prehistoric rock paintings, at a site known as the Tajo de las Figuras. This was a small rock shelter, a few kilometres north of La Janda and the people who painted its walls chose to depict the animals of the surroundings. Unlike most caves with rock art that I was used to, which depicted large mammals like bison, horse or mammoth, this one featured birds. Here we found hundreds of beautiful paintings showing flocks of cranes, bustards and waterfowl. The numbers of large birds living in the lake and its surroundings must have been spectacular 7,000 or so years ago and, although deer were also painted on the walls, it is clear that the birds were the dominant resource for the people of the wetland.

The first description that we have of migration across the Strait, probably over La Janda judging from the species described, dates to the 14th century when Pedro López de Ayala wrote the Book of Bird Hunting: "I saw by the Strait of Morocco, which is

Sunset over Gallocanta lake and town

---

between Ceuta and Tarifa, the passage of storks at the end of the summer, as they turned towards Africa; there were so many that no man could count them, and they spent a long time in the sky, so large was the flock. The same happens with the herons and other birds and they say that the quails also do so, because very often, when it is windy, many are found and when the wind changes they depart, when many are seen leaving."

The earliest specific reference to La Janda was written as far back as 1794 by A. Ponz in his Voyage across Spain: "...Later I waded across the Barbate river, and a little further on another stream called Celemín, which flows into the Strait via the Lake of Xanda. This lake is much larger than the one I mentioned to you between Xeréz and Medina-Sidonia: an infinite number of birds of diverse kinds visit this lake, as with the previous one, that naturally cross the Strait at will and are flying inhabitants of two parts of the globe."
The link between La Janda and migratory birds, given its proximity to the Strait, has been the source of the delight of many naturalists who were lucky to reach this district. The large and noisy cranes – a flock of around a thousand birds still visits La Janda every winter – did not escape attention. The Neolithic people painted them in the Tajo de las Figuras and the migration was beautifully described by Howard Irby in his

AL-ANDALUS

Ornithology of the Straits of Gibraltar written in 1895:
"On the 11th of that month (March) in 1874, Mr Stark and myself had the pleasure of seeing them (the Cranes) on passage, and a grand sight it was, as flock after flock passed over at a height of about two hundred yards — some in a single line, some in a V-shape, others in a Y-formation, all from time to time trumpeting loudly. We watched them for about an hour as they passed, during which time we calculated that at least 4,000 must have flown by. This was early in the morning, and we were obliged to continue our journey, but when we lost sight of the vega of Casas Viejas (now known as Benalup on the northern end of La Janda), over which the cranes were passing in a due northerly direction, there appeared to be no diminution in their numbers, and, as my friend remarked 'one would not have believed there were so many cranes in all Europe'."
I first read these lines as a boy of 11 when my father showed me Irby's wonderful book that he had borrowed for me from the Gibraltar Garrison Library. The year was 1966. Since then the image of cranes flying in lines and V-formation, trumpeting as they migrated, had remained deeply etched in my mind. I saw cranes many times, the odd small group over the Rock or the relatively small gatherings in La Janda, but not the spectacle described so vividly by Irby. Then, in 2003, I resolved to put this right. Cranes no longer migrated in such large numbers this far south, but I knew that Scandinavian cranes flew south in autumn to the north of Spain, resting in the lake of Gallocanta in Aragón, before dispersing to their wintering grounds in the dehesas of Extremadura. In late November of 2003, I drove north with two ornithologist friends who were up to the challenge. The drive took all day, crossing the meseta in torrential rain. Near sunset we reached the village of Gallocanta, with its 80 souls, which was to be our base of operations. The rain had stopped but there were menacing grey clouds approaching from the west. Though tired and wet, we did not opt for a warm room but went straight to where our research told us the migratory cranes would come to roost. We opened the car door and stood in the cold. All we could hear was silence. It was rapidly getting dark and we were coming to the conclusion that this was a battle best fought another day. Our faces showed our disppointment as we prepared to leave this desolate lakeside.
Just as I was about to get into the car a distant sound caught my attention. Yes, it was the trumpeting of the cranes. Binoculars came out in a flash as we scanned the skies, but there was nothing to be seen. The sound came closer. Then I realised that we were looking too high. There, just above the horizon, a "V" of some 50 cranes was coming straight towards us. The trumpeting grew louder and intermingled with more distant sounds as flight after flight of cranes, in lines and V and Y formations — as described by Irby — came over our heads and down to the marshy ground on the lake edge. In the 15 minutes before total darkness 14,000 migratory cranes arrived, from the north

Sunrise over La Janda

Donkeys are bred in La Janda's dehesas

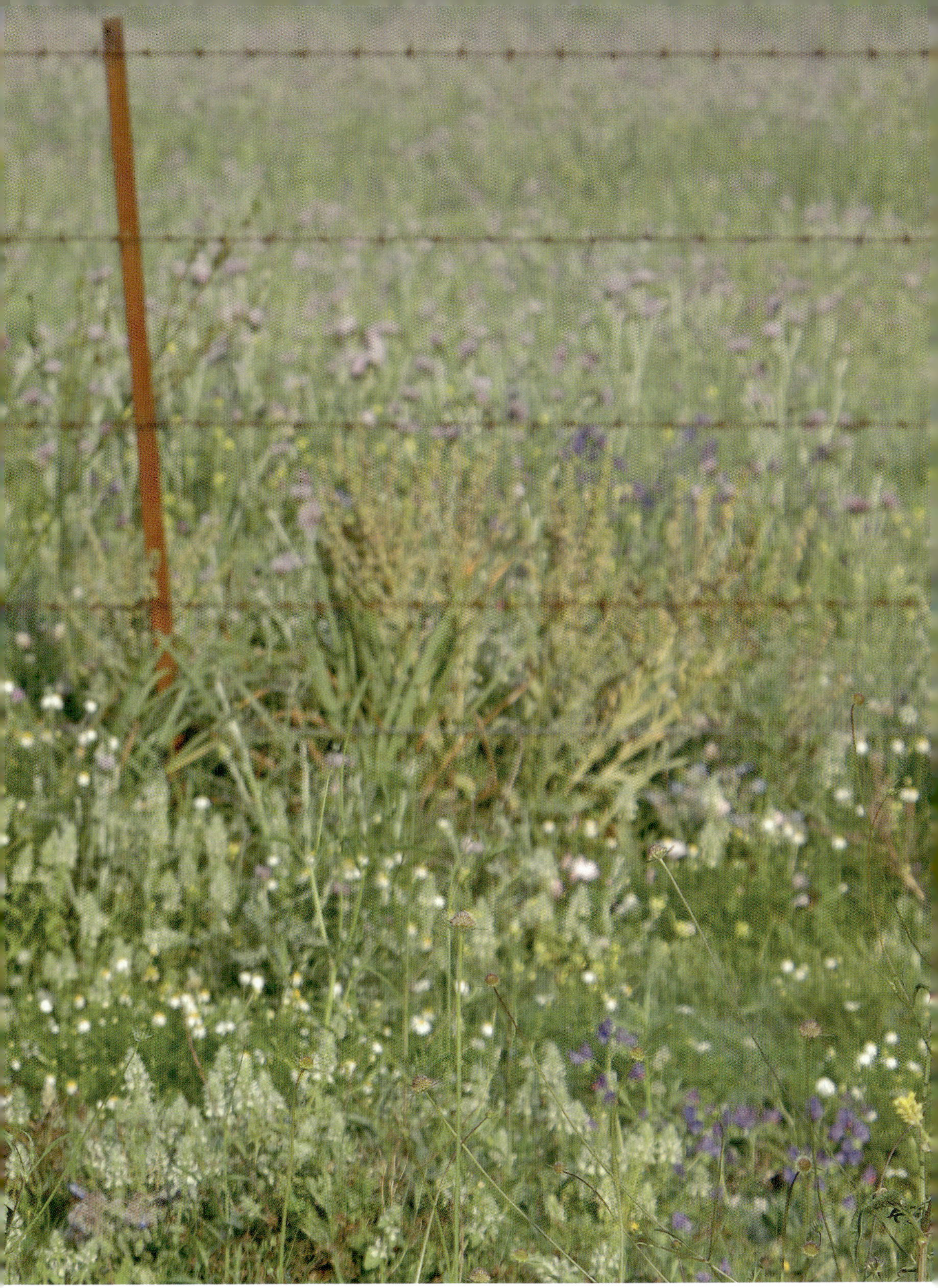

and west, to roost in their traditional stop-over. As the tired birds settled to sleep and the trumpeting noise subsided, I emotionally turned to my friends and remarked "today I have touched Irby", and I remembered my late father. I do not think they fully understood my sentiment. I did not sleep a wink that night. I was up before dawn, in a frosty temperature of minus seven degrees C, to catch the departure of the cranes at daybreak. Since that day I have returned each year to see the spectacle of the cranes. With the draining of La Janda, Gallocanta, 7.7 kilometres long and 2.8 kilometres wide, is now Spain's largest lake. Like La Janda and the Villafáfila lakes of the previous chapter, it is shallow with a maximum depth of 1.5 metres. Unlike La Janda, its surface is water and is not covered by dense aquatic vegetation. Apart from the cranes the lake attracts a range of wildfowl, although poor in comparison to La Janda. All the same it is worth the visit, between October and March, just to see the crane festival. Numbers vary as cranes come and go, but there are usually at least 10,000 in mid-winter. The largest number in recent years was recorded on March 1, 2007, when more than 38,000 cranes descended on the lake on their way back north.

G. K. Yeates, continuing his early 1940s description of La Janda in April, inadvertently gives us another clue why La Janda was so hugely important: "But soon my eyes were wandering on to the vega of La Janda. Here were numerous White Storks standing at rest, and, joy of joys, close to us a pair of Common Cranes were parading with long elegant strides. Their soft grey plumage and their drooping plumes are indeed lovely, and our views of them were perfect. Over the reed beds Marsh Harriers were drifting, and a great flight of Mallard rose from the hidden waters."

The importance of the description is that these cranes were still in La Janda after the migration north and paired. We know from Irby and Verner that cranes nested in La Janda in the 19th century and they were still there in the 1940s. This was their most southerly breeding outpost in Europe. According to Irby: "On the Spanish side (of the Strait of Gibraltar) some 30 to 40 pairs (of cranes) breed in the district (comprising many thousand acres) which extends from Tapatanilla along the Laguna de La Janda to Vejer, and thence eastwards to Casas Viejas."

The last pair of Spanish cranes nested in La Janda in 1954. Shortly afterwards the lake was subjected to the most intense period of drainage, leading to its destruction in just over a decade.

The drainage of La Janda was a drawn-out process and exemplified the incompetence and political wrangling characteristic of the time. It was done in three phases. The first, between 1825 and 1838, was largely unsuccessful. It commenced with a Royal Order awarding an administrative concession to Don José Moret of the "...flooded plain occupied by the waters of the lake of La Janda and demarcated lands".

It appears that the system of channels for draining the waters of the basin was insufficient to cope with the winter volume of water entering from the Barbate and smaller rivers rising in the sierras and the project was eventually abandoned.

CHAPTER NINE *Janda*

A new study for draining La Janda carried out in 1918 led to a Royal Order granting permission in 1929 to the company Colonias Agrícolas to drain "...a total of 4,414 hectares, scattered in the following way: Lake of La Janda with 3,445 hectares, Jandilla 282.5, Espartinas 376.5 and Rehuelga 38 hectares".

The lake had a reprieve as the draining process was halted by the Spanish Civil War, between 1936 and 1939, and did not resume until 1946. A series of drawn-out legal wrangles between owners and developers only served to delay it to the benefit of the lake and its wildlife. A further engineer's report produced in 1948 showed the difficulty of the enterprise of converting the land for valuable agriculture but supported the draining, arguing that it would increase cattle production and, presumably by removing a source of mosquitoes, eradicate yellow fever that was endemic in the area at the time. Colonias Agrícolas lost the concession and Lagunas de Barbate took over in 1954. Drainage carried out by this company led to the final disappearance of the natural wetland by the middle of the 1960s.

Casas Viejas often appears in the Victorian naturalists' accounts of La Janda. It was the closest town to the lake, at its northern end. The town was also known as Benalup, its original name derived from the Arabic. Its name was attributed to the location of a Muslim tower, that of Ben Alup, said to have been related to the 711 conquest of al-Andalus by Muslim forces. In fact, the battle in which Tarik ibn Ziyad, Berber leader of the invaders, defeated the Visigothic King Roderic is said to have taken place on the plains of La Janda itself. Benalup was captured by King Alfonso X in 1264, between the capture of Sevilla in 1248 and Tarifa in 1292, as part of the southward wave of Christian advance. A hermitage was built on the site in the 16th century and gradually a hamlet grew around it. The town currently has a farming community of just under 7,000 inhabitants.

The procrastination in draining La Janda has to be seen in the context of the poor social conditions endured by the country people. While the draining of the lake was an ecological disaster, the need for cultivable land and to feed the poor has to be understood. Nevertheless, the problem of the peasants could have been resolved without such a drastic measure as draining the lakes. Many of the problems in the Andalusian countryside at the end of the 19th century and beginning of the 20th century could arguably be blamed on the lingering of a medieval feudal system of rural management. Incidents at Casas Viejas brought a fame it did not wish for itself and were responsible for the collapse of the Spanish Government of Republican Spain in 1933. The story goes back to the time of the Christian conquest when land-grabbing nobles established huge estates, or latifundia, on conquered land. They were especially common in Extremadura and Andalusia where the Christian conquest had been speedy and huge land incentives were given to nobles in the interests of repopulation of abandoned lands. A latifundium in Roman times was a large agricultural estate which used cheap or slave labour. In medieval Spain, and later in South America, the term was applied to large

The Ocellated Lizard is the largest lizard in Europe. It lives in La Janda where it hunts rabbits among its prey

estates worked by low-paid casual or semi-servile peasants for the benefit of landlords who were largely absent from their estates. The term cacique became synonymous with that of the powerful landlords of the latifundia. There are still some very large estates in Andalusia today, even on the land of the old lake of La Janda.

The conflicts in rural Spain are exemplified by the situation of the peasants of Casas Viejas and its neighbouring town, Medina Sidonia. Queen Isabel II's fall in 1868 led to a series of popular uprisings in Andalusia, and particularly Cádiz province where Casas Viejas is situated. The degree of poverty in the countryside was beyond belief, peasants in Medina Sidonia being reduced to eating the carcasses of cattle that had died in the fields from starvation. The situation created ideal conditions for the development of the anarchist movement, which was much stronger and longer-lasting in Spain than in any other European country.

In 1887 the discontent of the peasants in the district of Medina Sidonia and Casas Viejas exploded. Lands on the large estates were set alight by peasants and Medina's mayor requested more Civil Guards to control the situation. The degree of poverty is best understood when we see the wages of the country people. In 1892 workers in Medina Sidonia earned a peseta for a day's work "from sunrise to sunset" during the

Display of convolvulus in spring at La Janda

harvest and 65 cents during the autumn. They were unemployed the rest of the year. The cost of a pound of bread was 27 cents. By the beginning of the 20th century the people of the countryside had started to organise themselves into unions, with anarchist support, organising a series of general strikes.

Repression by the local caciques, who refused to employ those they considered ringleaders, generated further discontent. The legend of the Mano Negra, the Black Hand, had its origins in this part of the Andalusian countryside. It was supposedly a secret society of anarchists who murdered the rich and others they saw as enemies. In reality, it was an invention of the Jerez police and provided an excuse for the landowners to quash unions in the name of social order (bandoleros, see Chapter 16). All attempts at countryside reform were effectively crushed for a while. In 1915, the Black Hand was used once more by the landowners as an excuse for closing the unions of Medina Sidonia and Casas Viejas.

The peasantry hoped that, with the declaration of the Spanish Republic in April, 1931, the traditional problems of the countryside would be finally over. The people of Casas Viejas came out into the streets and celebrated the new government. Two years later their lot had not improved. If anything it was worse as bureaucracy slowed down reform even further. The following statistics for Casas Viejas in 1933 explain the problem. Of 53,067 hectares of land in the municipality 29 landowners owned 12,585 hectares and another four controlled 7,490 hectares, i.e. 33 persons owned close to 40 per cent of the total. Nearly 30,000 of these hectares were pastures or uncultivated land in latifundia. This mismanagement of the land meant that, in 1932, only 100 of the 500 labourers in the village found some form of employment. Those out of work relied on the archaic alms system, single men receiving one peseta and married men one-and-a-half or two pesetas. In comparison, pay for the day workers oscillated between 6.50 and 11.50 pesetas in summer and between 5.25 and 6.50 pesetas in winter.

It is in this scenario that we have to see the events of 1933 in Casas Viejas. A nationwide anarchist insurrection planned for early January had been suppressed by force, but this news did not reach the anarchist peasantry of Casas Viejas. On the night of January 20 300 peasants, unaware of what was happening in the rest of Spain, decided to proceed with the insurrection and laid siege to the Civil Guard barracks. Shooting ensued in which two guards were mortally wounded. The anarchists cut the telephone lines with Medina Sidonia, the only source of communication with the outside world. Civil Guard reinforcements arrived at midday the next day from nearby Alcalá de los Gazules and telephone connection was re-established. The reaction started as the anarchists fled to the hills or hid in village houses. A family of anarchists who sheltered in a hut on the edge of the village, expecting that the spark of their revolt would spread across the country, decided to resist. The hut was surrounded and burnt by the Civil Guards. Only two of those inside survived. Later, 14 other men were randomly arrested around the village, taken to see the incinerated bodies and promptly executed. The measure of the repression was disproportionate.

The incident had one major outcome. A storm raged in Parliament and the right-wing opposition succeeded in overthrowing the government, winning the autumn elections. Captain Manuel Rojas, who was responsible for the massacre, was given a 21-year prison sentence but was liberated at the start of the Spanish Civil War three years later. He was among the conspirators in the murder of the poet Federico García Lorca in Granada during the war. Twenty-six peasants were tried in 1934. Ten were absolved and the rest served prison sentences of between one and six years.

The loss of La Janda therefore must be seen in this wider historical context: the extension into the 20th century of a medieval system of land mismanagement in force since the days of the Christian conquest. Wetland drainage was just one way in which new agricultural land could be created and employment generated. With such a powerful history behind it, any attempt to regenerate La Janda as a wetland will always be met with resistance.

The lake's drainage spelt the loss of many aquatic species of birds, in some important cases not just in the local area. The disappearance of the Spanish breeding population of cranes is one example. To highlight a few other more striking cases I rely on the

White Storks gather in large flocks in La Janda in summer before crossing the Strait into Africa

accurate accounts provided for the pre-drainage 19th-century La Janda by Irby.
The African marsh owl nests today in North Africa right up to the Tangier area but is unknown in Europe. It was regularly seen in La Janda, in the marshes near Casas Viejas during the 19th century in what was their only known European outpost. They are gone.
According to Irby: "In Andalusia, as in Morocco, over all low wet ground, the Marsh Harrier is to be seen in vast numbers, particularly in winter. Great quantities remain to breed, sometimes as many as twenty nests being within three hundred yards of one another." No more than 850 pairs of marsh harriers remain in the whole of Spain. A species decimated by loss of wetlands, it is now confined to protected islands. There are always a few marsh harriers around La Janda, and some may breed in isolated reed beds along the drainage canals, but the numbers are insignificant in comparison to days of old.
According to Irby, purple herons were "extremely abundant" in southern Spain. They nested in La Janda and even in small reed beds around Los Barrios. Their main nesting population is now in the marshes and they are only sometimes seen in La Janda on passage. Only 2,000 pairs are left in Spain. Irby tells us: "On the north side of the Straits

they (bitterns) used to breed at Casas Viejas, at the Laguna de La Janda, and in the Soto Torero near Vejer, and still do so in the marshes of Rocina, near the Coto Doñana."
The birds no longer breed in these haunts, having disappeared even from the marismas. The entire Spanish population is reduced to no more than 25 pairs, most of these in the middle stretch of the Ebro river.
The spoonbill nested in the marismas, the Soto Torero near Vejer and in the Soto Malabrigo near Casas Viejas. They still breed in the marismas but are only seen sporadically on passage in La Janda where they no longer breed. The glossy ibis has made a small recovery in recent decades, now breeding in the marshes in small numbers, but was once very abundant. According to Irby, "We saw great flocks of the Glossy Ibis at the lakes of Ras el Doura (northern Morocco)..." and "...in wet seasons they breed in the Soto Torero, near Vejer, and also in the marismas del Guadalquivir". The glossy ibis is only a sporadic visitor to La Janda while on passage.
The skulking aquatic Baillon's crake bred in La Janda and was "...very common...at Casas Viejas from October to February". The Spanish breeding population is at best 52 pairs and it no longer breeds in La Janda. Although the water rail is not as scarce as the Baillon's crake, its numbers must have also suffered greatly from habitat degradation. Finally, Verner visited a breeding colony of whiskered terns in La Janda and found several hundred nests floating on the water. This bird is now only sporadically seen on passage and no longer breeds in La Janda.
The lakes and wetlands of al-Andalus, landlocked islands of natural diversity, have borne the brunt of Man's impact on the environment of these lands. La Janda, having been the largest of them, deserves special mention but myriad smaller lakes have gone or are still under huge pressure from all kinds of human action. One story gives us hope for the future. It is the story of a strange duck that almost went extinct in the 1970s but has staged a remarkable recovery.
The white-headed duck, which is non-migratory, has never been a common species here, but so rare is this bird that, despite its low numbers, Spain has been its traditional western European stronghold. A series of factors, from hunting, disturbance of breeding sites, drainage of wetlands to pollution of lake waters, had reduced the population to a mere 22 birds in 1977. All those remaining were sheltering in their last refuge, the Laguna de Zoñar in Córdoba province. The duck was about to go extinct.
A group of concerned naturalists, led by my good friend Dr José Antonio Torres Esquivias, decided to take matters into their own hands and save this bird. Tired of lack of response and ineffective action from the administration, Torres and his group started a national campaign and formed the Association of Friends of the White-headed Duck. They raised its profile and sufficient funds to allow the purchase of a lake close to Zoñar, the Laguna del Rincón. The protection that followed allowed some birds from Zoñar to move to Rincón and start breeding there. It was the start of the long road to recovery. The action taken by private citizens eventually started the autonomous government

CHAPTER NINE *Janda*

The colourful Stonechat is a common nesting bird in La Janda

The White wagtail is a common winter visitor to the flooded fields of La Janda

machinery moving, saving other sites and creating a network of protected lakes. The recovery was dramatic. I remember going to the Laguna de Medina in Cádiz, once a traditional site of this duck from which it had long disappeared, in the late 1980s and counting more than 600 white-headed ducks in a single flock. This was just 10 years after the birds had reached their all-time low of 22.

The white-headed ducks, using the Córdoba lakes as core area, started to colonise lakes in adjacent provinces and then beyond. By the year 2000 there were white-headed ducks in most Spanish provinces, as far north as the coast of Cantabria. A national census that year revealed close to 4,500 birds.

This story shows that it is possible to recover species through the protection of their natural habitats. It is a far more successful and less wasteful method than the utopian disease of species reintroduction that seems to have plagued modern-day conservationism (but see a refreshing contrast in the case of the bearded vulture in Chapter 17). If it can be done for the white-headed duck, it should be possible for other birds too and – why not? – for the big ecosystems like La Janda. The white-headed ducks spread because a network of protected sites suitable to their needs was established. If things went bad one year in one site, they had other options to fall back on.

On a much grander scale this is what La Janda represented. It was a key wetland on a large scale, comparable to Doñana. They formed, together with the large Moroccan wetlands and those of central and northern Spain (Villafáfila, Gallocanta, Daimiel) a survival network for many species of aquatic birds. The degradation of this network meant the extinction of species or their reduction to very low levels. The white-headed duck is an example of one bird that made it back, but there are sadly many more examples of collapse than there are of success. Many more species that have gone, or are about to go, because we have failed to protect or recover the large-scale sites of this giant wetland network. To the birds that I have already listed we must add the ruddy shelduck, marbled duck, ferruginous duck and the crested coot, and these are just the wetland species. In the balance of things we have lost much more than we have been able to recover.

THE EAGLE
AND THE FOX

CHAPTER TEN

The eagle and the fox

AL-ANDALUS

A number of Victorian naturalists explored the countryside of al-Andalus during the second half of the 19th century. Abel Chapman, whom we met in Chapter 6, was one of a number using the British contacts in Jerez as pivot for his explorations. The other focal point for the exploration in this region was Gibraltar. William Willoughby Cole Verner embodies everything that was the exploration of 19th-century al-Andalus. More so, his name will be forever connected with the name La Janda. This was his natural home. It was where he was at peace.

The following words from his 1909 book, My Life among the Wild Birds in Spain, sum up his character: "When, in a sudden access of hysteric caution following years of 'go as you please', all the upper portion of the Rock was enclosed by a high spiked iron paling, some unimaginative official had the fatuity to style it officially The Unclimbable Fence, and numerous Orders were drafted with respect to it in which it was thus described. It is hard to imagine a more direct challenge to a man addicted to climbing. At this psychological moment I chanced to land at Gibraltar on leave from England. I climbed that fence, not for pleasure or for vanity, but as a matter of duty to the confraternity of birds-nesters. My 'crime' was never taken judicial notice of, and here I was happier than the luckless private soldier, who not long since committed the same offence and according to report was charged with 'Neglecting to obey Fortress Orders, in that he, at Gibraltar, on April 1 – contrary to the Fortress Order directing all persons to abstain from doing so – climbed The Unclimbable Fence!"

I remember as a schoolboy in the 1960s reading avidly the accounts of the old Victorian naturalists who opened up the southern Iberian landscapes and their wildlife for all of us. Names like Abel Chapman, Walter Buck or Howard Irby and their publications were very much a part of those early days, especially as so little had been written about the area since then. One name, for me, stood above the rest. Verner's writings transmitted more than a catalogue of facts and observations; they painted vivid images of another age, of expeditions on horseback into the wilds of Spain, of life on the Rock of Gibraltar from a very singular perspective, of cliff-climbing in those early days of nature photography. I developed a growing interest in this unique character, realising that there was much more to Willoughby Verner than his love for natural history. In the words of Harold Hodge, who wrote his obituary: "To give a just impression of so many-sided and kaleidoscopic a man is difficult, perhaps impossible. Certainly no one who tries to do it will satisfy himself..."

Verner was born in the year 1852. He was the son of Colonel W.J. Verner of the 53rd Regiment and great nephew of Sir William Verner, one of the founders of the Orange Institution. He joined the Rifle Brigade (now the Green Jackets) in 1874 and his whole life was intimately connected with that of his regiment. That same year he went to Gibraltar with his regiment and remained there until 1880; his passion for this land continued until the day of his death and he visited the area for two weeks to six months at a time for the rest of his life. Verner, writing on the need for time to undertake

The Blue Rock Thrush is a typical nesting bird of cliffs in Mediterranean Iberia. It is a bird that gave Verner headaches trying to find its nest.

research, gives us this view of life in Gibraltar at this time:
"At no period was this more clearly brought home to me than during my six years at Gibraltar, between 1874 and 1880. That was in the days when no railways or other facilities for travel existed in the vicinity (for even the road from Algeciras to Tarifa was not then constructed), hence every expedition from the Rock was limited to riding out between the hours of morning and evening gunfire, when the gates of the fortress were opened and closed. And closed they indeed were and the keys were taken to the Convent, the Governor's residence, and kept there."

During this first time in Gibraltar, Verner met another great naturalist, Colonel Howard Irby (in 1876) and until Irby's death in 1905 they were constant companions in innumerable birding expeditions. A highlight in his early days as subaltern came in 1879 when Crown Prince Rudolf of Austria, a keen ornithologist, visited Gibraltar. Verner received an invitation from the Governor, Lord Napier of Magdala, to meet him at dinner. Verner tells us: "Our meeting resulted in the Prince requesting me to take him for a ride into Spain the following day, the upshot of which was that when the Miramar sailed for Tangier I was bidden to accompany him. We subsequently went for a cruise up the Guadalquivir when, thanks to the kindness of the late Henry Davies of Jerez and his comrades, we were permitted to explore that most fascinating region the Coto de

Doñana."

In 1881 he passed through Staff College (passing both in and out with first place – evidence of his academic distinction), was promoted to Captain and was awarded the Royal Humane Society's Medal for life saving. That year he married the Hon. Elizabeth Mary Emily Parnell who was daughter of the third Baron Congleton. He had a son and a daughter: his son, Commander Rudolf Verner was killed in action in the Dardanelles when a shell fell on H.M.S. Inflexible.

In 1884 he was sent to Egypt where he saw action in the Nile Expedition of 1884-85. This early part of his career promised much for the future and those who knew him expected rapid promotion for him. He and Kitchener were captains at the same time and worked closely in operations in Africa. In 1891 he was promoted to major and in 1896 to lieutenant-colonel. That same year he became Professor of Military Topography at Sandhurst. On the outbreak of the Boer War in 1899, Verner was appointed to serve as Chief Staff Officer to Lord Methuen in South Africa. He was present at the actions of Belmont and Graspan. At Graspan he sustained severe injuries which were to severely limit his career in the army and affect him for the rest of his life. He received the Queen's South African Medal with Clasp inscribed "Belmont" and in 1904 was promoted to brevet-colonel and retired later that same year.

Verner's qualities as an officer were outstanding. He was famous throughout the army as a cartographer and a draughtsman and his interest in military matters extended to every branch of military science. The accident at Graspan was unfortunate. Verner was galloping on a strange horse, taking despatches from Lord Methuen, when the horse crossed its feet and fell. Verner fell on a boulder and the horse on him. His injuries were severe and few thought he would survive. Though his energy pulled him through, he never recovered fully. His heart was badly displaced and he had serious internal injuries, but he lived for another 20 years during which time he did much valuable work even though his military service was over. It is said that the great grief of Verner's life was that he was unable to take part in the Great War.

Verner retired to the Gibraltar area and built himself a house, El Aguila (The Eagle), in Algeciras, with a full view of the Rock. He died there on January 25, 1922 at the age of 70. He was buried at the North Front Cemetery in Gibraltar with the 4th Battalion, under Lieutenant-Colonel Seymour representing the Duke of Connaught, rendering full military honours.

Verner distinguished himself in many fields, but especially as a writer. He wrote several books about the history of his regiment and in 1890 published the first British Rifle Corps. He started that same year the Regimental Chronicle which he edited, combining his literary ability with his military knowledge. His book, The Military Life of H.R.H. George Duke of Cambridge, written at the duke's command, was published in 1905. He was a keen naturalist from his early boyhood and wrote extensively about birds; his main work was My Life among the Wild Birds in Spain which was published in 1909. For

CHAPTER TEN *The eagle and the fox*

many years he contributed important sections to the Gibraltar Gazette. He had other skills, being a distinguished inventor, producing the magnetic and prismatic compasses, the cavalry sketching case and plane tables.

These facts tell us a great deal about Verner but, as Hodge put it, "about many men the facts of their life are not the main thing... What a man is, is more than what he does". Verner spent most of his second period in Gibraltar and southern Spain studying birds, a great credit to him in view of his injuries. He tells us himself: "Owing to my intimate knowledge of many remote spots in this beautiful country, explored during many expeditions made before the war in South Africa, I am able, in spite of the serious handicap due to my injuries, with the aid of horses or mules to re-visit these parts. Once on the spot, I can still render a fair account of most cliffs or do a day's wading in a marsh, sufficient in any case to reach a nest I want to photograph."

So what else can we glean of Verner's character? The episode with the Abbe Henri Breuil, the famous French palaeontologist, reveals his great scientific vision. In 1911, Verner had heard of a cave with paintings in the Ronda area and was responsible for making known the existence of the Cueva de La Pileta and its spectacular Palaeolithic cave art. The eminent prehistorians Professor H. Obermaier and Breuil visited the cave with Verner in 1912. The relationship between Verner and Breuil developed from this contact, not surprisingly as they were both men of great intellect and energy. Breuil, who was professor at the famous Institut de Palaeontologie Humaine de Paris, visited Gibraltar in 1914 at Verner's instigation and, while walking together along the northeastern side of the Rock, commented to Verner that the brecciated talus he had observed should prove fruitful in investigating the existence of prehistoric man at Gibraltar. (A brecciated talus is an old slope formed by a landslide in which the mud has fossilised to bind the loose boulders.)

Breuil encouraged the young Dorothy Garrod at Cambridge University to excavate Devil's Tower between November, 1925, and January, 1927. Breuil's intuition proved astonishing for Garrod found the fragments of the skull of a Neanderthal child. Garrod would become, in due course, the first female professor at Cambridge. Verner, by then, was dead and could not share in the triumph in which he had had such a great part. Verner was indeed a great man. His friend Hodge described him thus: "Unique personality does not necessarily engender love – perhaps as often it provokes antipathy – but it does command attention. You might dislike Verner – all dull men did – but you could not ignore him. You had to notice him even if he might not notice you – a situation which we must admit does not make for general contentment. Naturally this strong personality affected various people variously. Those who like brilliant people were compellingly attracted to Verner, and with them, if opportunity allowed it, admiration deepened into affection. Those who are not attracted by brilliancy he tried sorely. Such a man does not easily admit others into his inner being; he has a wide, very wide, acquaintance, but his friends are not general. Probably very few knew more

people, both in and out of the 'great world', than Verner. In the conventional phrase he 'knew everybody'; but in sober fact he did know nearly everybody who to an intellectual man, interested in everything and keen to pick up knowledge from everybody, was worth knowing. But the number who knew him was very much smaller than the number he knew. It was impossible to know Verner unless you knew him well. His very attractiveness, the easy soldierly bearing, the charm of address, all the external man, while it made superficial acquaintance with him very easy, was really very much a defence against entry (intrusion is perhaps the word) into the arcana of his real self."
Hodge has highlighted Verner's versatility as one of the main features of his character. He was soldier, sailor, inventor, historian, antiquary, writer, artist, naturalist, sportsman, society man, churchwarden, Orangeman, raconteur, conversationalist. Unlike most versatile persons, he lacked shallowness. He was genuinely interested in all that he did. He made an important contribution to knowledge and progress, and was able to give pleasure and help to a large number and variety of people.
For me, Verner's character best comes through in his writing for it is here that we most closely receive the thoughts of a man who committed them to paper those decades ago. It is from his book My Life among the Wild Birds in Spain that the following passages are taken at a time when egg collecting was regarded a legitimate form of doing science:
"I had long cast covetous eyes on the Osprey's nest at the back of the Rock. It was in a bad situation and inaccessible save with a rope. Accordingly one day, in defiance of all Garrison Orders prohibiting the molestation of wild birds on the Rock, and accompanied by a naval officer and another soldier, I proceeded to Catalan Bay. Here we lunched with the Detachment officer and afterwards started on our expedition. After a most fatiguing struggle across the great slopes of shifting sand we reached the first serious obstacle, a low cliff. Skirmishing on ahead, I picked out a practicable line and we set to work to sidle along the narrow terraces, at times not very high up and at others several hundreds of feet above the sea. Arrived above the Osprey's nest, we found a nasty sloping terrace of loose stones which made it dangerous for two men to lower a third, also our rope was totally inadequate for such a purpose. My companions refused to lower me over, and I am not ashamed to say I inwardly rejoiced, for it would have been perfectly foolhardy to attempt it in the circumstances.
"Many years afterwards, I revisited the same spot but with proper appliances and, despite all orders to the contrary, took the eggs! That very night I chanced to be dining at the table of the Admiral and among the guests was the Governor and by ill-luck the conversation turned upon the Osprey's nest on the Rock. Somebody remarked that no man could get at it and I was suddenly appealed across the table as a known climber and expert. To make things worse, some of my guilty accomplices were present and eyed me anxiously. Mercifully the question put to me was whether I thought it was possible for anybody to take the Osprey's eggs? All eyes were turned on me, as with a supreme effort, begot of the perils of my position and with the thought of those two lovely eggs

CHAPTER TEN *The eagle and the fox*

Verner spent most of his life in search of the nests of raptors such as the Egyptian Vulture, a migrant from Africa that is now threatened.

still unblown locked up in my dressing-case, I replied 'No, Sir, I feel sure that anybody who tries to take them will fail."
He was clearly very stubborn and not easily defeated. He took up almost any challenge but was prepared to see the humorous side of any situation as his description of an encounter with blue rock thrushes shows: "I watched him (a male blue rock thrush) fly to Rosia Bay where I spent no less than six days in March watching the movements of a pair in the sea-cliffs. At this time Lord Lilford was at Gibraltar in his yacht the Glow-worm, and with the assistance of his son, Thomas Powys, and some of the crew I was lowered over the cliffs between the New Mole and Camp Bay in all directions. It was now that I learnt by painful experience the deceptive ways of the Blue Rock Thrush. One of their practical jokes was to simulate great interest in some cavern or fissure in a cliff and to disappear into it for a considerable time with the result that I was committed to a perilous descent only to find that I had been grossly imposed upon. At last on 5 April we decided that there must be a nest in a cave below Parson's Lodge Battery. This happened to be quite inaccessible from above so I swam out from Camp Bay and scaled the cliff but found nothing. I realised however that between sharp rocks, barnacles and thorny scrub it was an over-rated amusement to go birds-nesting unclothed."
Perhaps the funniest episode of all is that with the eggs of a Bonelli's eagle. Verner

had placed the egg of a wild goose in the eagle nest when he took an egg, a practice which induced the adult eagle to remain incubating. He found the eagle's egg had been considerably incubated so that there was no chance of the eagle laying a second egg. As he was by then physically unable to climb a second time to the nest to remove the goose's egg, he left it there. But that was not the end of the story.

"A few days after the last visit to the Bonelli's crag, on our return from a long expedition one evening, I was informed that two Englishmen had arrived and had installed themselves in the kitchen of a cottage adjoining my own which I had temporarily hired….On enquiry I found them to be a professional bird photographer and his assistant out on tour in quest of 'copy', who by some curious chance had come to stop at the identical spot where I have lived for so many years and which, it should be mentioned, is many hours from the nearest civilisation. They assured me they were not collectors, in fact they did not take nests 'only photographed them'. During their stay they made various expeditions in the neighbourhood and then disappeared as suddenly as they had come, as also by the way did sundry Neophrons' (Egyptian vultures) and other eggs about the same time. This occurred in the month of April. In the following March I was as usual staying in the same place and had forgotten all about the incident when one day I received a copy of Country Life sent me by one of the party who had lowered me to the Bonelli's nest the previous year and had seen me place the goose's egg in it. In this number, to my intense amusement, as well as to that of all who were concerned with the expedition, there was a most graphic account of the identical nest of Bonelli's Eagle, describing how my photographing friend had obtained the egg from it! With the set purpose, apparently, to place on record for all time his ignorance of Eagles and their eggs, the unfortunate writer went into the most minute details as to how the egg he had so gallantly obtained was "white and somewhat pointed at both ends"; in fact an unmistakable tame goose's egg!"

This energy and vitality persisted virtually to the end. Smith-Dorrien, Governor of Gibraltar, thus tells the story of a dangerous expedition to an eagle's nest with Verner shortly before his death. This was indeed this unique man's way. He was an intellectual whose personality comes across to us in his writings even today. His heart was first and foremost in the wild countryside of southern Iberia, most of all in the great wilderness of La Janda. Here was a man who fell in love with Gibraltar and the surrounding countryside. Apart from his military career, he stimulated interest in Gibraltar's caves and prehistory, he explored such caves as St Michael's and Judge's in Gibraltar and La Pileta in Spain, he climbed trees and cliffs, he sought out the track at the back of the Rock which the Spanish goatherd Simon Susarte had used to lead Spanish troops into Gibraltar in 1704, he studied birds and other wildlife; and most of the time with injuries that would have confined most mortals to a sedentary life. In his day his intellect brought him renown. Today, as often happens to individuals of great spiritual and intellectual calibre who devote their lives to inquiry and not to self-glorification,

CHAPTER TEN *The eagle and the fox*

he is largely forgotten or unknown to most. I still remember the first time that I inadvertently came across his grave at North Front, ironically while bird-watching. There he was, where he belonged, in his beloved Gibraltar.

I can only conclude with a passage from Hodge's posthumous "impression": "There amongst the wild birds, the (almost) wild bulls, and the unsophisticated peasantry with his horse, his dog, and his gun, Verner felt a free man. In England you can get no wild life, he used to say, and English shooting parties seemed tame to him after the great spaces and unrestricted movement of La Janda. Altogether it was fitting that he should die in his Spanish home in sight of Gibraltar, in Algeciras near the church where a window had been installed in memory of his beloved son. His wife and daughter were both with him and his own regiment was at Gibraltar. For the first time for many years a battalion of The Rifle Brigade (the 4th) was stationed at Gibraltar, and so the regiment was able to render the full military honours at the funeral. While his body lies in the North Front Cemetery, his monument extends far beyond his grave."

The second character in this essay is a Spaniard, descended from an eighth-century Castilian family from the beech-and-oak mountain forests around Logroño in the medieval Kingdom of Navarra, on the upper reaches of the Ebro river. The 18th-century survivor of the lineage was Pablo Larios y Las Heras, born in 1755, who moved with his family to Andalusia where they set up a large industry based on the exploitation of cork and the manufacture of sugar. Martín, the younger of Pablo's two sons from his second marriage, settled in Málaga and was given the title of Marqués de Larios in 1865.

Pablo Eustaquio, the elder, married a Gibraltarian woman in 1818, Geronima Tashara Celli, who was in all probability of Genoese descent. The family of Pablo Antonio, the eldest of eight children from the marriage, became well established in Gibraltar. The marriage of Pablo Antonio's two youngest sisters to British officers serving in Gibraltar firmly cemented the connection with the British. Like his father, Pablo Antonio married a Gibraltarian woman, Leocardia Sánchez de Pina, and, on his early death in 1879, his will divided his estate equally among his five sons. One was Pablo Gerónimo Larios y Sánchez de Pina, the subject of these lines, whom we shall refer to simply as Pablo Larios.

Pablo and two other brothers studied at Beaumont College, from where he went to Owen's College in Manchester to study chemistry, a subject that would have been of great practical application to the family business. While in Manchester he became a regular participant in the Cheshire fox hunt. After a stay in Brunswick, Germany, Pablo returned home. In Gibraltar he is best remembered for his large mansion, now the City Hall.

Although contemporary texts do not make a direct link, Larios' activities and interests at the end of the 19th century and beginning of the 20th must have brought him in close contact with Willoughby Verner. Unlike Verner, Larios did not write about his exploits so we have to dig from other sources to build up his profile.

He was first and foremost a keen all-round sportsman. He was excellent with the gun and took part in many organised hunts after ibex, red deer, wild boar, lynx and even wolf. He travelled widely and knew every corner of the Iberian peninsula and beyond. Like Abel Chapman, he went to the Picos de Europa after chamois and spent time hunting large game in Africa. At home he was credited with being one of the first to have successfully stalked ibex in Andalusia. Like Chapman and many of the Victorian naturalists, who have often been misunderstood because of their shooting of game, Larios was a keen and practical conservationist. Much of the mountain ground between Gibraltar and Málaga was the property of his family and he personally dedicated it to the protection of the ibex. While Chapman contributed to the conservation of the ibex in the Gredos, Larios made an important contribution that helped save the Andalusian stock.

His time in England converted Larios into a staunch supporter of British sporting traditions. He tried to introduce the pheasant into the Spanish countryside but, meeting with little success, loved instead to shoot red-legged partridges, driving them the English way. He was happy to absorb the best of each of his traditions so, when it came to large game, he resorted to the Spanish system of montería.

Larios was also an excellent rod fisherman. He had learnt to fish salmon and trout in Britain and became an authority on fly fishing in Spain, contributing to the conservation of freshwater fish and even drafting Spanish fishing laws that survived into modern times. Living in Gibraltar surrounded by the rich waters of the Strait of Gibraltar, he was also attracted to the sea. He was credited to have been the first to have caught a tuna with rod and line, Romans permitting that is.

The Duke of Wellington encouraged his officers to hunt foxes on horseback when not fighting the French during the Peninsular War. It was a practice that kept his cavalry well-trained and proficient. Among the first hunts established was the Calpe (after the classical name for Gibraltar) in Wellington's time, in 1813. The fox hunt spread far and wide across the British Empire and Lord Kitchener himself approved of it in 1903.

We cannot begin to imagine the image of British officers on horseback, chasing foxes across the Spanish countryside in time of war. A bizarre incident occurred at Bidasoa in October 1813. The Bidasoa river separated the British and French armies when the British started a hunt. Determined not to lose the fox the hunt entered the enemy lines and scattered a French drum major and his band. Once inside enemy lines they could only get out with a flag of truce, to the amusement of the French.

The Calpe Hunt became a Gibraltar institution, in which officers and civilians actively took part, continuing until the 1930s. In 1891 when a new master of the hunt, a position always previously held by an officer of the garrison, was to be elected there was no suitable or willing candidate. But there was Pablo Larios. He was a keen supporter and the hunt was only possible because he allowed access through his lands in the Spanish

CHAPTER TEN *The eagle and the fox*

The Red-legged Partridge is an Iberian endemic that has been the favourite prey of hunters for centuries.

hinterland (it is said that one could ride along the coast from Los Barrios to Marbella without leaving Larios land – a fine example of the continuing tradition of large estates owned by wealthy families that had started with the capture of Muslim-held lands in the eighth century).

A number of British officers opposed the move to have a civilian, and a Spaniard at that, in the prestigious position of Master of the Hunt. But Larios was well liked and respected both by the members and the Spanish landowners. On the somewhat reluctant advice of the Duke of Cambridge, the hunt's most senior member, Larios was elected. So it was that, at the height of the British Empire, a Castilian became the most senior officer of a prestigious British sporting institution. Larios was to have a say in an even more remarkable turn of events 14 years later.

Early in 1906 it was proposed to make King Edward VII, who had joined the Calpe Hunt in 1859, the hunt patron. When the Governor of Gibraltar wrote to the king's private secretary, he added a novel suggestion, that the Spanish monarch should also be invited to become a patron. The reply from King Edward was positive on both counts. The Governor of Gibraltar was asked to formally put the request to Madrid once the British Ambassador returned there, but Larios could not wait. Breaking with protocol, he had been in touch with the Marqués de Mina, the Spanish king's Master of Horse, who had transmitted the message to the king. When the British Ambassador finally wrote to the Marqués, he received the following reply: "According to what His Majesty told me, you can let the Governor of Gibraltar know that the King has accepted to be a Patron of the Calpe Hunt as I wrote to Mr Pablo Larios and it will be unnecessary to make a formal application."

In this somewhat informal and unorthodox way, the Calpe Hunt achieved the unique distinction of having the kings of both Great Britain and Spain as patrons. In a final twist to the story, General Sir Dighton Pobyn, VC, Comptroller and Treasurer to His Majesty's Household, wrote to the Governor of Gibraltar with the following message: "With our King and with this Spanish King both patrons of the hunt, I think it will certainly deserve the prefix of Royal, and on return of the King to England early next month you may depend on my submitting your request to His Majesty…"

In this way the Calpe became the first British hunt to be honoured with the title of "Royal". When on June 8 it became the Royal Calpe Hunt new buttons arrived with the Crown of England and the Crown of Spain superimposed, side by side, over the traditional CH on the original button. A week earlier King Alfonso XIII had married Princess Victoria Eugenie of Battenberg, a niece of King Edward VII and granddaughter of Queen Victoria.

When the Second Spanish Republic was proclaimed in 1931, King Alfonso XIII abandoned the country without formal abdication. The monarchy would only be restored to Spain more than 40 years later through Alfonso's grandson, King Juan Carlos. Two years after the proclamation of the republic the Spanish countryside was ready to revolt. The poor countryfolk of Casas Viejas may well have seen, or heard of, gentlemen riding across the land chasing foxes while their children died of starvation. Three years later Spain was immersed in civil war.

Larios and Verner, men with totally different trajectories, came together in the south of al-Andalus at about the same time. Their respective characters and their means allowed them to pursue the sport of hunting, in its many versions, and to contribute to the conservation of species that might otherwise have gone extinct. It is the paradox of the 19th-century hunter-naturalist. Larios may have been at home on horseback chasing foxes in the lowlands of al-Andalus, but he was equally at home among the ibexes in the sierras. If the wetlands and plains of La Janda were Verner's passion, the mountains of southern and central Spain and their eagles were not far behind. It is to these mountains that we now turn.

CHAPTER TEN *The eagle and the fox*

Larios was a key figure in the fox hunts around southern Andalucia. The fox remains today a common carnivore.

"Larios and Verner...came together in the south of al-Andalus at about the same time. Their respective characters and their means allowed them to pursue the sport of hunting, in its many versions, and to contribute to the conservation of species that might otherwise have gone extinct."

Meltwater feeds the clear mountain streams of northern and central Iberia, as in Gredos (Photo by Stewart Finlayson)

Europe in Africa

Chapter Eleven

Europe in Africa

AL-ANDALUS

Gallant efforts saved the white-headed duck from extinction, as I noted in Chapter 9. The passage of time has almost rubbed out the memory of another valiant effort, at the beginning of the 20th century, which saved the Spanish ibex. The ibex, a distinct species endemic to the Iberian peninsula, had been separated into mountain refuges. These "islands", not dissimilar in this sense from the "island lakes" of the white-headed ducks, had been isolated long enough to have produced genetic differences so that four races of ibex could be identified, one in the Pyrenees, another in Portugal, a third in southeast Spain and the last one in the Sierra de Gredos in central Spain. Ibexes had been traditionally hunted in these mountains and the Portuguese race went extinct in 1892. It was followed by the Pyrenean population eight years later. The southeastern one managed to survive but, by the late 19th century, the Gredos population was also on the verge of extinction. It would have gone the way of the Portuguese and Pyrenean animals had it not been for the foresight of some amazing characters.

We owe the survival of these animals to Abel Chapman and Walter Buck and to the response of enlightened Spanish landowners of the time. It is ironic that Chapman and Buck are often considered by modern self-styled naturalists to have been hunters who traversed the wilds of Spain killing any animal on sight or removing eggs from the nests of rare birds for their personal satisfaction. I wonder how many of these eco-friendly 21st-century naturalists can claim, from the comfort of their arm-chairs, that they have personally and actively contributed to the salvation of a species from extinction. Chapman and Buck did.

There is no better way for me to describe the brilliant manner in which the ibex was saved than by quoting Chapman himself. In his 1928 Retrospect, he related his recollections from 40 years earlier:

" ...but among those ancient memories few remain so vivid than our surprise and disappointment to discover how perilously near to total extinction the Spanish ibex had already been reduced on several of those great mountain ranges which, during the ages, had formed its ancestral strongholds. Nowhere, in those days, was protection afforded it: everywhere the mountaineers, who alone shared these Alpine solitudes, carried guns and shot the vanishing ibex – regardless of size, sex, season – whenever opportunity offered. By the close of the 19th century the scant remnants of the race in the great Sierra de Gredos had been reduced literally to units; nor is it too much to say that another 10 years would have witnessed the last of this noble game-animal wiped off the face of the earth in its main haunts...

"By supreme good fortune, ere the fatal hour had struck – as it were, at the 11th hour – a deus ex machina intervened. The co-authors of Wild Spain became associated in the Coto Doñana and elsewhere with Spanish friends in whose hands lay the power to save the situation. There thus occurred the opportunity to point out the impending peril to some of those great Spanish land-owners within whose titles were included vast regions

Male Spanish Ibex in Gredos (Photo by Stewart Finlayson)

of the chief ibex-haunted cordilleras; but who, at that time, were only vaguely conscious of the existence of ibex on their remote and ill-accessible domains, while none had then realised that the threatened race belonged to a species endemic to Spain – that it was confined to the peninsula and known nowhere else on earth.

"At first sight the practical difficulties of affording any effective protection to wild animals on such vast areas of mountain solitudes, some extending to, say, 60 to 80 miles in length and rising over 8000 or even 10,000 feet in altitude, might well have been deemed insuperable, not to say appalling. At home we have no such fearsome propositions. These grandees of Spain, nevertheless rose to the occasion in the spirit that overwhelms difficulties – as it overpassed our utmost hopes – the spirit that emphasises the traditional chivalry of their race, and of Spain. All honour to them.

"Spontaneously, they ceded in perpetuity the rights-of-chase to the King of Spain. His Majesty accepted the trust and commissioned the Marqués de Villaviciosa de Asturias to organise the great Sierra de Gredos, as well as the Picos de Europa in the Cantabrian chain, as "royal reserves"; the identical goatherds (our old friends) who had hitherto been the most deadly enemies of the ibex, being now transformed into their royal guardians! No happier selection could have been made: for it is no exaggeration to describe these lithe mountaineers as a specialised human type, bred during generations lightly to traverse regions so terribly rugged and abrupt that even the strongest and most active of normal build can only crawl.

"The happy change occurred in 1905, and the results of royal protection have been equally surprising and gratifying. From the start, the scant remnant ibex increased and multiplied so rapidly that within the first few years of absolute sanctuary, their numbers were approximately estimated to have reached between 200 and 300 head, while shortly thereafter it was even deemed desirable to pick out some of the older and redundant rams. Within less than 10 years the ibex on Gredos were reckoned at 500: and here it will be appropriate briefly to glance back at the tiny nucleus from which those hundreds had emanated.

"Forty years ago, or at the period of our earlier expeditions, there might still remain at the utmost 100 head of ibex, all told. By 1896 that sorry remnant had been reduced by one half – 50 was the estimate we gave in Unexplored Spain, a figure which was confirmed by Dr Angel Cabrera, as cited in his standard work, Fauna Ibérica. So rapid, after that, was the process of extirpation that by 1905, when royal control was established, it was virtually all but an accomplished fact. Certainly at that date no more than a few units remained. Indeed Dr Cabrera gives the census as 'One old ram, seven females, and three or four kids.' That, however, in view of the subsequent increase, may have been an under-estimate and, of course, in so big a terrain, no exact computation was possible. Still it is clear that royal protection came in at the very nick of time – the ibex had had the narrowest possible escape from total extinction.

"To turn to a happier aspect. Since 1914 the cumulative increase has been rapid and continuous, as the following details kindly sent me in January, 1927, by His Excellency the Marqués de Viana, Montero Mayor to H. M. King Alfonso, testify: 'Since the Coto of Gredos was established, the race Capra hispánica has gone on increasing in number in an ever-ascending ratio till, at the present day, they may approximately be reckoned at 1000 to 1200 head.'

"This surely bespeaks a marvellous transformation? Compare this abundance with the melancholy memories of 25 years ago, when a sorry remnant was barely holding out on those majestic altitudes that encompass the snow-clad Plaza de Almanzor! Today, without the slightest danger to their race, where only yesterday the ibex had been reduced to units."

What a lesson to us all. Today, we have the luck to be able to see the ibexes in Gredos, and what a sight they are. I remember my first visit, in the footsteps of Chapman and the first contact with the ibexes. I was high up, well above the tree line, where only low scrub and mosses grow. It was spring. Alpine accentors searched the ground for insects among the rocks while a wheatear stood boldly on some rock that marked the boundary of a territory. As I looked up towards the horizon all I could see was the intense blue

Spanish ibexes in Gredos – my first encounter

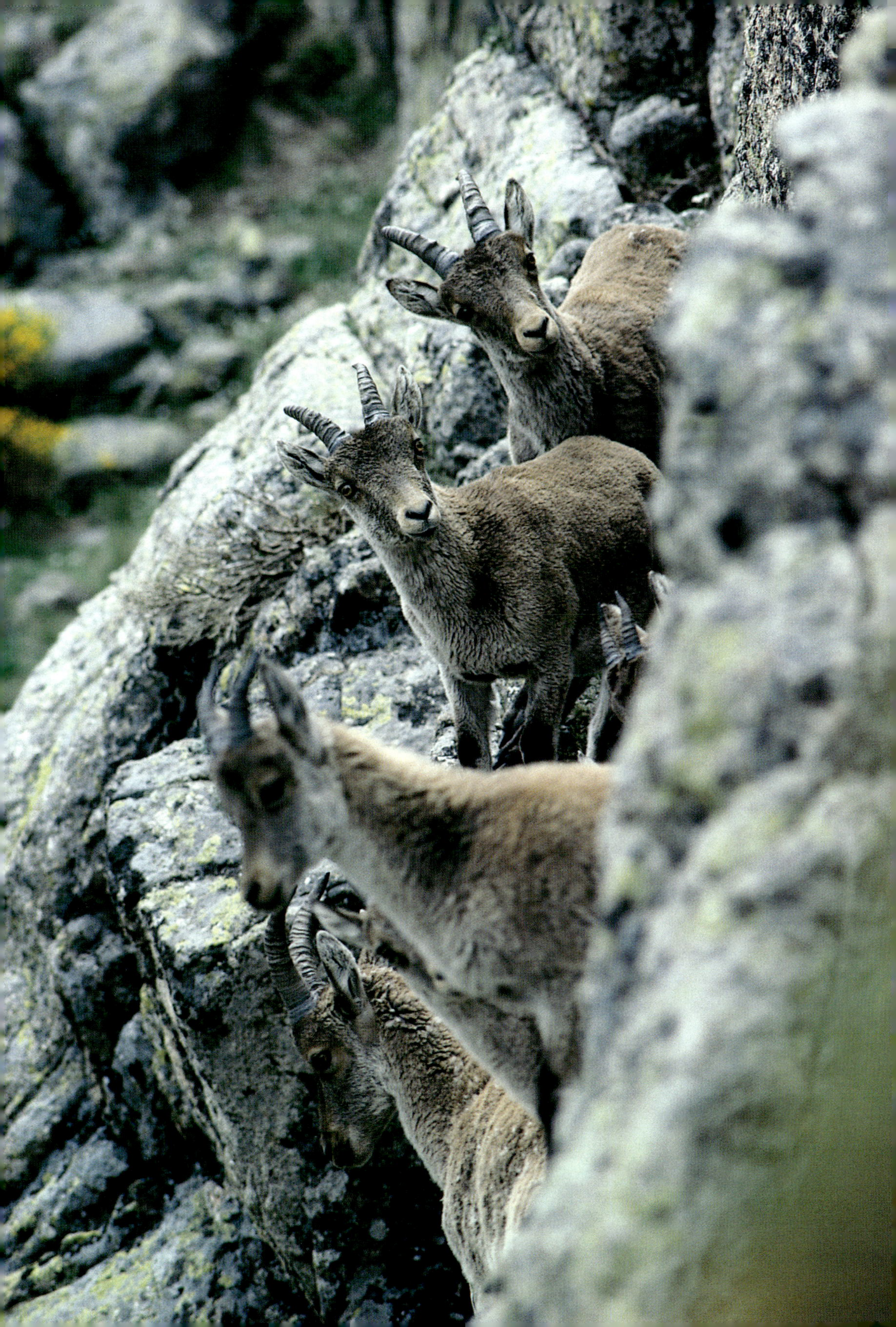

of the sky. A movement caught my eye and through the binoculars I could just see the head and small horns of a young ibex. I decided to make for the ridge. Climbing over rocks above 2,000 metres takes its toll so an apparently short climb of 100 metres or so is actually quite hard work. Usually in these cases as you approach a ridge and think that you have conquered the peak, another one appears, higher and further away. This one was true to form except that there was a clear incentive to keep climbing. A group of five young ibexes were silhouetted against the horizon.

Eventually I caught up with them. They had slowly walked down a gully and I carefully crept up, looked over and there they were, half-way down the gully on a sheer face looking up towards me, no more than 15 metres away. Safe in the knowledge that they were masters of the vertical and I was not, they inquisitively watched me until they had had enough then walked further down the cliff and behind an outcrop. It was my first, and unforgettable, encounter with ibexes in Gredos and I had Abel Chapman to thank for it.

Gredos is the western extremity of the central chain of mountains that run roughly east-west across Spain. The sierra is a series of granite blocks, some reaching heights above 2,000 metres, others as low as 500 metres, thus creating deep and spectacular valleys and ravines. The highest peak, in the west of the sierra, is Almanzor at 2,592 metres above sea level. Gredos, surrounded by plains on all sides, is a biological island. It is also barrier and bridge between two very different floras and faunas, those of the Mediterranean to its south and those of Atlantic Europe to the north. For this reason the diversity of its fauna is spectacular with between 50 and 64 per cent of all the mammals, birds, reptiles and amphibians of the Iberian peninsula being found in this single chain of mountains. The ibex is its emblem but there are some very special birds here too, among them the Alpine accentor and the bluethroat. The accentor is an Alpine species and Gredos is a southerly isolated outpost. The only other population to its south in Iberia is found in the high peaks of the Sierra Nevada. The bluethroat is essentially a northern European bird that finds suitable habitat only in the high mountains, between 1,200 and 2,000 metres of the south. Gredos is its most southerly outpost. Gredos is also an island refuge for other animals. The Iberian rock lizard is confined to northwest Spain with a southern population in the central mountains including Gredos. That is its world distribution.

The mountains were also human refuges, difficulty of access and harshness of climate barring the entry of intruders. When Chapman and Buck visited Gredos in 1896 they remarked how: "Not a yard of that great mountain-land of Gredos has been trodden by British foot (save our own) since the days of Wellington." They were referring to Wellington's campaigns in the Iberian peninsula on the side of the Spanish against the

The foxglove is a typical plant of the humid Atlantic forests

CHAPTER ELEVEN *Europe in Africa*

Small hamlets dot the agricultural landacape of the valleys in the Cantabrian Mountains

French at the beginning of that century. One of the most famous Peninsular War battles was fought at Talavera on the lower slopes of the Gredos in July 1809.

A large high tableland separates the Gredos from the chain of high mountains that run along Spain's northern coast, from Galicia in the west to the Basque country in the east. These mountains, the Cantabrians, stand out above all others as refuges of hardy people. They have always presented a formidable barrier to access and the local inhabitants, intimately acquainted with their mountain refuge, became renowned for their resilience and resistance to invasion. As the Romans gradually conquered Iberia they built an intricate network of roads along the entire coast of the peninsula, connected by others that criss-crossed the interior. The Cantabrian mountains and coast were left out of the network altogether, showing us the degree to which the people of these mountains had managed to remain independent. The climatic and ecological contrasts between the heights of these mountains and the valleys below, the difficulties of access and the intricate network of valleys made this an impossible land to tame. The ecological contrasts from heights to valleys below were neatly described by Chapman and Buck when they visited the Picos de Europa, on the border between Asturias and Cantabria, at the end of the 19th century. As they sat on the lofty snow-clad peaks, they noted:

Imposing landscape at the Picos de Europa in the Cantabrian Mountains

"Far away below, as in another world, lie outspread champaigns; sunlit stubbles, newly stripped of autumnal crops, form chequers of contrasted colour that set off with golden background the dark Asturian woods, while fresh green pastures blend in harmony with the riant foliage of the vine."

One summer, we drove from the Picos de Europa down to the tablelands towards Burgos. The road wove through innumerable mountain valleys and we passed by dense woods of northern trees, amid Atlantic mists that creep in almost daily often bringing heavy rain even in summer. It was hard to believe we were in Spain at all. There was water everywhere, cutting streams through the limestone, creating idyllic waterfalls where the gradient changed abruptly and forming rivers that would flow towards the Bay of Biscay. In these rivers Chapman and Buck spent days fishing trout, a fish which remains abundant. In all, seven species of freshwater fish inhabit the clear waters, among them the Atlantic salmon. There are also otters and dippers and the rare Pyrenean desman, a small (100-135 mm or 4 to 5 inches) mammal that nests in river banks and catches small invertebrates from stream beds. It is exclusive to these mountains and the Pyrenees.

The controversial comment that Africa started south of the Pyrenees is attributed to

AL-ANDALUS

Napoleon. Had he been a bio-geographer instead of a dictator, studying the distribution of plants and animals instead of invading nations, he would not have been far off in his remark. Bio-geographers classify this northern region as Euro-Siberian. It means that its flora and fauna is essentially that of Western Europe and quite distinct from that of the drier and more seasonal Mediterranean regions to the south. In the Cantabrian mountains and the Pyrenees exist incursions of temperate European plants and animals into the Mediterranean realm, and it is altitude that has kept them there.

As we made our way across the deep valleys, we could see the snow still on the almost barren peaks where only Alpine vegetation survived. These rocky peaks, reaching a maximum altitude of 2,648 metres, were home to some very special animals, among them the chamois. This goat-like animal is truly an Alpine inhabitant which, with a population of around 6,500, finds here its southernmost outpost. Then there is the wall creeper, a wonderful little bird that lives on sheer rock faces where it feeds on insects taken from the cracks in the rock. It is a grey bird with broad crimson wings that, in flight, give it the appearance of a gigantic butterfly. Spain's wall creepers are confined to these mountains and the Pyrenees, but they are also found in Europe's big mountain chains, like the Alps. The Spanish population, between 9,000 and 12,000 birds, is Europe's largest. Here in its Iberian stronghold we also find the Alpine accentor, briefly encountered in the Gredos. The accentor and the creeper are both high-altitude specialists, breeding more than 2,500 metres above sea level.

Lower down, below 1,800 metres, the slopes became clothed with copses of beech trees and scattered yew, holly, rowan, birch, hawthorn and sloe, the latter providing the fruit for patxarán, the traditional liqueur of these mountains. Lower still, below 1,400 metres oaks made an appearance, anticipating the lower forests that surrounded us. This was the land of the capercaillie, a large game bird in serious decline with fewer than an estimated 100 territories. The capercaillie is doing well in comparison with the wolf, with fewer than 20 left, and the brown bear which was almost extinct.

These mixed forests recall Europe before agriculture, when huge tracts of virgin forest occupied vast stretches of the land. In the moist and mild temperate climate of the lower hills of Cantabria the forests hold a huge diversity of trees making up the broad-leaved mixed forest: ash, maple, alder, oaks, lime, chestnut, walnut, wild cherry, wild apple, hazel, laurel and elm. The forests are home to a variety of animals, which include roe and red deer, wild boar, wild cat, badger and some very special woodpeckers like the large black woodpecker and the rare middle-spotted woodpecker.

As we descended gradually through the mountain passes towards the southern slopes we started to get indications of Mediterranean vegetation, trees that were familiar to us, holm, Portuguese and even some cork oaks, replacing the Atlantic forest. The real shock came abruptly as we reached the lower ground of the tableland north of Burgos, to be confronted by the dry heat of the Castilian summer and the parched, treeless, landscape of the northern meseta. The mists and drizzle had gone and we were under

CHAPTER ELEVEN *Europe in Africa*

The Jay is a typical crow of the northern broad-leaf forests

The red-backed shrike only breeds in northern Iberia. It is a central European bird that winters south of the Sahara

Autumn in a mixed forest in the Pyrenees

a scorching sun giving us 35 degrees C in the shade. In an hour the step in altitude and orientation had changed the world. Immediately we understood why the Arabs and Berbers who conquered these lands in the eighth century had stopped short on reaching these mountains. Reluctant to leave the dry warmth that they were familiar with at home, they found little to interest them in this thinly populated and poor mountainous region and moved instead along the coastal strip to the east, entering the Mediterranean lands of France instead. It raised questions in our minds: to what degree did the start of the expansion of Christian kingdoms in northern Spain in the eighth century have to do with a genuine quest for retrieving lands lost to the Muslims? Or rather was it related to the slow growth in a land which the Muslims had decided, like Romans and Visigoths before them, was not worth the effort of conquest.

It will be useful to recall at this point the historical events that were pivotal to the eventual expansion of the Christian kingdoms and the withdrawal of the Muslims. Although the term re-conquest has been applied freely to this process, it is a misnomer as the expanding Christian kingdoms had little in common with the Hispano-Roman peoples who had lived under Visigothic rule for around 300 years prior to the Muslim conquest. For that reason, in this book I have tended to refer to the process simply as the

The wet valleys of the Pyrenees make excellent pasture and agricultural land

Christian conquest of al-Andalus.
With the death of the Prophet Muhammad in the year 632 AD, there was a rapid expansion of Muslim armies across the Middle East. These Arab peoples entered Egypt in 642. Following the North African coast, a region with a climate and geography very similar to their Arabian home, they took the Byzantine North African capital of Carthage in 698, conquering and converting people on the way. The only resistance to the rapid Arab expansion came from the North African Berber tribes of the coastal mountains and desert, but these were gradually assimilated into the religion. By 710 the Muslims were on the southern shore of the Strait of Gibraltar, poised to cross into Europe, into the territory that they knew historically as al-Andalish, the land of the Vandals. The Vandals had settled here 300 years before moving across the Strait of Gibraltar into North Africa. It is from al-Andalish that al-Andalus was derived.
The Arab invasion of Spain was allegedly provoked by an incident involving the Visigothic Governor of Ceuta, Count Julian, although its veracity cannot be confirmed. Julian had sent his daughter to Toledo, the Visigothic capital of Spain, to be educated with the king's daughters in the court. Attracted by her beauty, the Visigothic King Roderic is said to have made advances to her. When she rebuffed him, he resorted to

force and raped her. Julian, on hearing of this, brought his daughter back to Ceuta and in anger approached Musa ibn Nusayr, the Arab commander in North Africa, urging him to conquer Spain. Musa paid heed. He ordered a Berber captain under his command, named Tariq ibn Ziyad, to undertake the quest.

In September, 710, Tariq sent an exploratory force under the leadership of Zar'a Tarif ibn Malik al-Mu'afiri, or Tarif for short. Tarif took with him 400 footmen and 100 horsemen and crossed in four ships provided by Count Julian. They landed on the island of Las Palomas close to the mainland where the town of Tarifa would one day be established. Tarif's incursions into the hinterland were virtually unopposed and his return with rich booty convinced Tariq to make his move. In April, 711, Tariq and 12,000 men, mostly Berbers and some sub-Saharan Africans, crossed the Strait of Gibraltar from Ceuta. Using Count Julian's ships, they landed on the northern Pillar of Hercules, the Mons Calpe of the Romans. The historic landing was immortalised in the new name of this hill, the Jebel Tariq – the hill of Tariq – Gibraltar.

On hearing of Tariq's landing King Roderic, who was in northern Spain subduing the Basques, rushed south to meet the invading force. The opposing armies met on July 19, probably by the Guadalete river near present-day El Puerto de Santa María, though some suggest it was in the vicinity of La Janda lake. A Visigothic force put at anything between 40 and 100,000 men, though the figure is likely an exaggeration, faced 12,000 Berbers. The battle lasted for eight days, the Visigoths were defeated and Roderic was killed. Although 3,000 Berbers were killed, the depleted army pressed on. They defeated a second Visigothic army near Ecija in the Guadalquivir valley, took Córdoba and proceeded to Toledo. On reaching the capital, they met little resistance. Tariq then sent reconnaissance parties deep into the north, as far as the Duero river. A small contingent of light troops was despatched south to take Málaga.

Musa, Tariq's Arab general, landed in Algeciras the following year and pushed north. He took Carmona and Sevilla, laid siege to Mérida and sent his son to pacify the upper Guadalquivir valley and take Murcia. Further raids took Tariq to Tarragona and Barcelona while Musa conquered Zaragoza and Lugo. The speed of the conquest was impressive. Between 711 and 718, in a series of uncoordinated expeditions and with very few pitched battles, no more than 25,000 soldiers had conquered all but the most mountainous regions of Cantabria.

The first king of the first Christian kingdom, Asturias, was Pelayo (718-737). This enigmatic man was almost certainly a Visigothic noble who had escaped the Muslim onslaught. He is credited with the victory over the Muslims at Covadonga in the Cantabrian mountains in 718/19, an event that has been repeatedly indicated as the turning point of the Muslim conquest. Actually it was a small territorial victory in a region that was of little interest to the Muslims. Pelayo must have been a good politician. The Visigoths had never fully tamed the mountainous people of the north, but he seems to have found a way of incorporating their tribal society to create an

The Pyrenees (this image) and the Cantabrians trap the rain from the Atlantic weather fronts that reach it

embryonic kingdom.

To consolidate his position among the Cantabrians, Pelayo married his daughter to the son of the "duke" Pedro of Cantabria. The union was strengthened further after the death of Pelayo's successor, his son Fáfila (founder of Villafáfila), when Pedro's son took the throne as Alfonso I of Asturias. Later on, Alfonso's son, King Freula I, married Munia, a Basque woman, strengthening further the tribal bonds. By the reign of Alfonso II of Asturias (791-842) the new kingdom stretched from Galicia in the west to Cantabria and parts of the Basque country in the east.

The territory was also spreading southwards towards the Cantabrian mountains' lower slopes, then into the tablelands north of the Duero river, a movement that had to do with the invaders' weakness. The Muslims who conquered al-Andalus were a mix of Arab, Syrian, Egyptian and mostly Berber. During the eighth century the Arabs settled in the Guadalquivir valley, the Syrians in Granada and the Egyptians in Murcia. The Berbers settled in the poorer lands to the north, the hills of northern Andalusia, Extremadura and the meseta. Dissatisfied with their lot, the Berbers revolted in 740 against Arab domination and there was a large Muslim withdrawal from the marginal northern lands around Galicia and the Duero valley that could not be controlled. A series of famines between 748 and 754 added to the depopulation of these peripheral lands.

AL-ANDALUS

King Alfonso I of Asturias took advantage of the situation to carry out extended incursions from his mountain stronghold into the nearby lowlands. He took León, Astorga and Braga (in present-day Portugal), raiding as far south as Salamanca. In parallel the northern tribes were being converted to Christianity and the growth of the church became connected with the growth of the kingdom, Alfonso I founding the first bishopric of the new kingdom in Lugo. After a period of internal strife the momentum gathered once again under King Alfonso II.

During his reign, around 830, Teodomir, Bishop of Iria Flavia, discovered in a ruined shrine the human remains said to be of the apostle St James. Alfonso subsidised the construction of a church at the site of what would become the city of Santiago de Compostela. The young kingdom had found for itself a mighty patron. Alfonso moved his capital south to Oviedo, which was less hemmed in and with easier access to the south, and created another bishopric there.

So the mountain refuge of the Euro-Siberian region of Spain, that had been a stronghold of wild tribal peoples since prehistory, had become the nucleus for the expansion of a new kingdom of a new people, a combination of indigenous mountain groups with some Visigothic institutional and political direction under the increasingly weighty influence of the church. Geography, climate and ecology had played a central part in their survival and success.

It is safe to say that Pelayo, after the victory at Covadonga, had nothing further from his mind than the expulsion of the Muslims from Iberia. He had no master plan that would take him in a few years to Tarifa. Instead, and setting the norm for centuries of battling to follow, Pelayo was carving a territory for himself and his lineage. For the first 250 years the local monarchs never described themselves in relation to any kingdom of Asturias or León. Re-conquest was not in their minds. That would only slowly percolate the thinking of future kings under the increasing influence of the church and its leadership in Rome. Instead, with a neighbour in disarray, they exploited opportunities that presented themselves and allowed the aggrandisement of their territorial ambitions.

The Avocet is an elegant wading bird of the Iberian wetlands

Among Canes and Mud

CHAPTER TWELVE

Among canes and mud

AL-ANDALUS

In 1902, the Spanish author Vicente Blasco Ibáñez wrote Cañas y Barro (canes and mud), a novel centred around life in the Albufera, a large lagoon on Spain's east coast near Valencia. This chapter is about life in the rivers, deltas and coastal lagoons of Iberia and the influence that the rivers had in its history. We start once again with the Romans. They were, after all, the first people to introduce a measure of order and unity into the Iberian peninsula. Six centuries of Roman rule brought some kind of imperial order and structure to the Iberian lands, as it had done across the entire empire. The basic territorial unit of the empire, the province, was introduced. Any semblance to the modern political configuration of the peninsula would have to await the gradual expansion and development of the Christian kingdoms between the ninth and the 15th centuries. Until such time, and arguably even afterwards, the geography of the Iberian peninsula was to closely dictate the distribution of people who lived there.

The major problem with settling in Iberia was the nature of its climate. The peninsula is large but mostly dry as much of the Atlantic rains are trapped by the mountains of Cantabria, Galicia and the Portuguese highlands. Rains and snow also fall intensely between autumn and spring on the high ground elsewhere. Grazalema, a small town 823 metres up in the Cádiz mountains facing the Atlantic, boasts the highest rainfall in Spain with an average of more than 2,200 millimetres per year. The rain trapped by the mountains largely flows, in the case of most of the major rivers, towards the Atlantic. They have historically created belts of greenery in an otherwise parched land and it is around the main rivers that the agricultural civilisations of antiquity developed.

Five major rivers dissect the Iberian landscapes. Four drain westwards into the Atlantic and the fifth eastwards into the Mediterranean. In Roman times they were largely responsible for the basic shape of the provinces. The longest of these rivers is the Tagus (Tagus in Latin, Tajo in Spanish, Tejo in Portuguese) which drains a watershed of more than 80,000 square kilometres. From its source in the Albarracín mountains of central Spain it flows due west. Roughly three quarters of its length of 1,038 kilometres flows through Spain and the rest through Portugal, where it reaches the Atlantic at Lisbon. The valley was particularly useful for agriculture and livestock as it traversed the dry plains of the lower meseta, south of Madrid and the central mountains including Gredos. Its sharp drop from the meseta to the Portuguese coastal plain limited its use for transportation as ships could not go beyond Santarém, approximately 75 kilometres northeast of Lisbon. Much of the basin of the Tagus was, together with the Guadiana to its south, the Roman province of Lusitania.

The Ebro (Iberus in Latin, Ebre in Catalan) is the second river by length, 910 kilometres, and the only one to drain into the Mediterranean. It too has a watershed of more than 80,000 square kilometres. It originates in the Cantabrian mountains and flows southeastwards across the Rioja towards the plains and semi-desert of Aragón, passing the capital Zaragoza on the way. It reaches the sea south of Tarragona where it forms a large delta. In this respect it differs from the other major rivers. The low tidal range

CHAPTER TWELVE *Among canes and mud*

of the Mediterranean allows the silt carried by the river to settle close to its mouth, forming the delta. The large tidal regimes of the Atlantic remove the silt brought by the other rivers, so these open into the sea in the form of estuaries.

This peculiarity has made the Ebro delta one of Spain's most important natural reserves. Within its 320 square kilometres 50,000 people live off the richness of its alluvial soils. Unfortunately, crops and nature do not often come together as we saw in La Janda and the delta has progressively lost animals and plants at the expense of the expansion of the area dedicated to agriculture in the last century and a half. The landscape of the delta has been significantly transformed in many parts, in particular through the massive use of flooded areas as paddy-fields. Despite the losses there are important areas of natural coastal vegetation within the park, among the last refuges on the Spanish Mediterranean coast.

Amid the surviving salt marsh and dune and within the deep reed beds of the coastal lagoons animals are still able to live in relative peace. Thirty-seven different species of fish live in the waters of the delta, where freshwater meets salt. They make up a peculiar gathering of marine and freshwater species, from bass and bream to eel and barb. Ten species of amphibians and 19 different kinds of reptiles are also able to survive close to the life-giving water, in large numbers too, most unusual in the 21st century.

The stars of the delta are its birds. Among them the water birds shine brightest. The delta is the only breeding site of 23 species in the whole of the Catalan region and it shelters a rare species that only just makes it to Europe. This is the lesser-crested tern, a seabird at home between the tropics of Capricorn and Cancer, from eastern Australia to the east cost of Africa. A small population escaped its tropical shackles and entered the Mediterranean via the Red Sea, establishing itself on the Libyan coast. A few have since managed to settle on the rich waters of the Ebro. Terns and gulls are a major feature of the delta. The wintering population of Mediterranean gulls, at 30,000, is the largest known. There are more than 400 nesting pairs of the slender-billed gull, making this Europe's second largest colony, but the king is the rare Audouin's gull.

For a long time the Audouin's gull was a Red Data Book species, a bird in danger of extinction. For reasons that are not clear, the species' numbers increased dramatically in the late 1970s and early 1980s. At the time its main stronghold was the Chafarinas Islands off Melilla in North Africa. In 1981 36 pairs nested for the first time in the Ebro delta. By 1989 there were 4,200 breeding pairs in the delta, one of the most dramatic increases for a species on record. I was privileged to experience the amazing increase first-hand. During the 1970s and 1980s I spent many hours monitoring the migration of seabirds past Europa Point in the Strait of Gibraltar. When I started, the Audouin's gull was a rare bird; when I finished, it was a regular migrant. Today, flocks of Audouin's gulls pass the point in July and August en route to the Atlantic and it is not unusual to find them along the coast throughout the year. My records show that the average number I saw passing the point in summer had been 1.5 birds every hour in 1982. By

1989 it had risen to more than 18 per hour. Because its colonies are few and far between, the Audouin's gull remains vulnerable. The world population is estimated at just over 17,000 breeding pairs, 65 per cent of which nest in the largest breeding colony in the world – the Ebro delta, colonised for the first time in 1981.
The colonies of water birds are spectacular: night heron (50 pairs), purple heron (300 pairs), little bittern (a few hundred pairs), cattle egret (2,000 pairs), little egret (500-600 pairs), red-crested pochard (900-1,700 pairs), mallard (5,000 pairs), avocet (400 pairs), black-winged stilt (700-1,500 pairs), Kentish plover (more than 1,000 pairs), collared pratincole (30-40 pairs). One bird, above all, characterises the lagoons and deltas of the Mediterranean. It is a species that nested in the delta until the 16th century and, because of protection of suitable habitat, returned as a nesting species in 1993. I am referring to the greater flamingo. The colony on the Ebro delta was described as far back as 1557 by Cristófor Despuig in his "Col·loquis sobre la Insigne Ciutat de Tortosa": "...they found a place where a genus of these birds known as flamingoes nested, smaller than cranes, and the number of eggs that they found there was so great that the boat that usually took fish to Tortosa could be filled and the boat could take up to 150 quintales (approximately 7,000 thousand kilos),...in this way the fishermen took eight or 10 full bread baskets as they did not want any more and they left the remainder there..."
One of my favourite descriptions of this colourful bird is that of the British naturalist G. K. Yeates, reporting first impression of this bird in the 1940s, in Doñana: "In a host of bird memories I can think of nothing so inspiring, so exciting, so beautiful as the experience we have had today... We first saw the birds as a long thin pink line through the mirage. As we came closer, they assumed more definite shape. When wading through the shallows, the flamingoes' general colour scheme is a very soft pink. The body appears like a round ball precariously balanced on two long pink stilts. The long thin serpentine neck with the curious heavy downward-tilted bill completes a strange picture... The soft reflections of the long thin pale-pink line in water that took its colour from the blue of the sky defeat my poor pen for description.
"Yet if the mere bird at rest leaves me without words, what am I to say of it in flight? Lovely as the flamingo is as it wades, it is a flash of glory when on the wing, for then instead of the soft pinks which predominate on the ground the bird exposes the brilliant scarlet of the covert feathers, scarlet that ends in the quill feathers of the primaries and secondaries in a marginal line of black."
With the flamingoes I leave the Ebro and continue my virtual journey of the Iberian rivers, but not without first returning to the Romans. The area around the Ebro delta was the first to be colonised by the conquering armies. Saguntum, the town that had sparked the flame between Hannibal and Rome was just 150 kilometres southeast of the Ebro delta and Tarraco (now Tarragona), the Imperial Roman capital just 60 kilometres to the northwest. Among the rivers of Iberia, the Ebro had the second greatest volume of water. The flow was evenly spread through the year thanks to the constant rainfall

CHAPTER TWELVE *Among canes and mud*

An adult Audouin's Gull on migration past Europa Point, Gibraltar

Stunning display of red as flamingoes take to the wing

The dainty Black-winged Stilt is a typical bird of Iberian wetlands

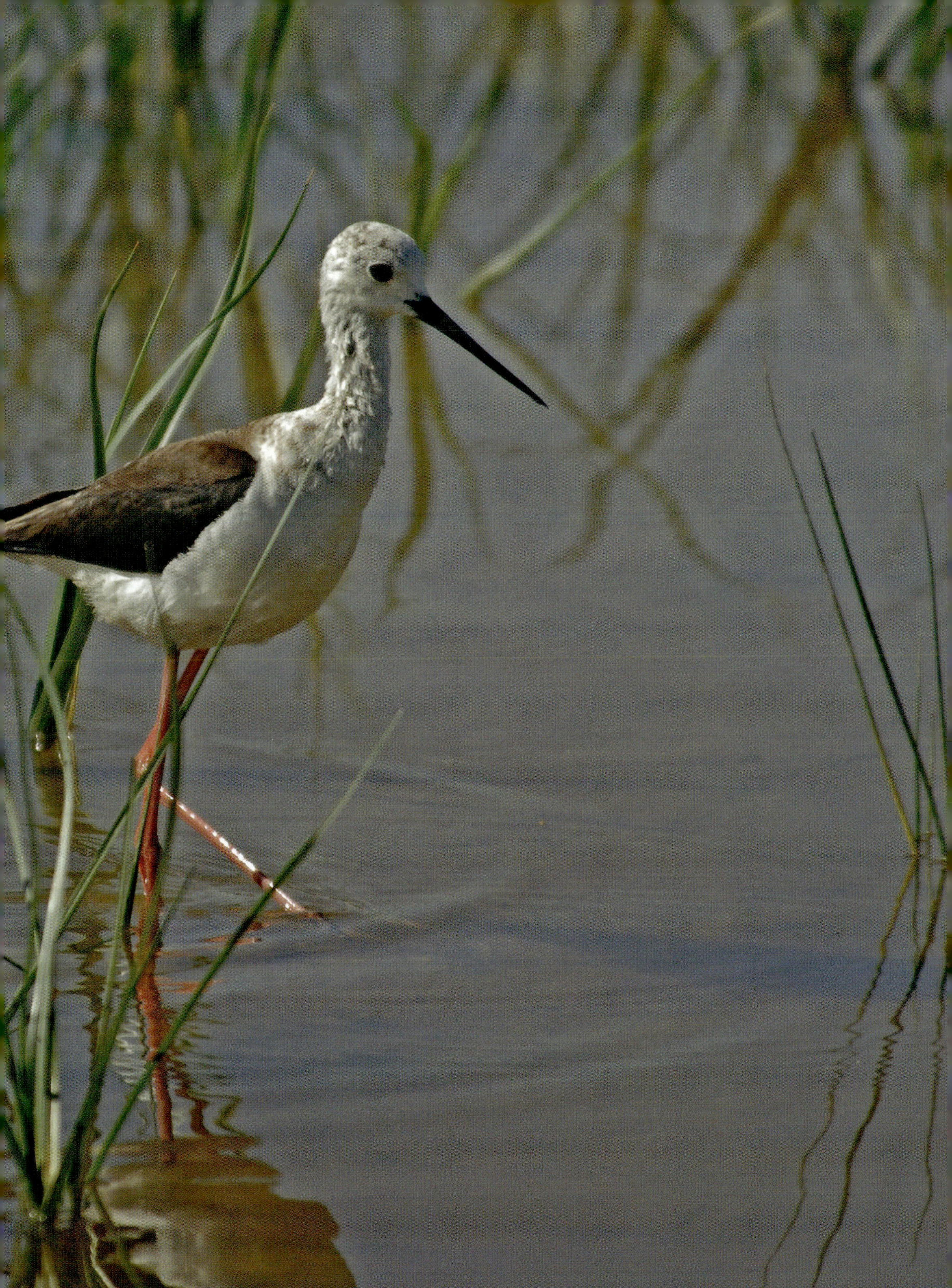

Greater Flamingoes are a colourful addition to the salt marshes of Iberia

regime of the Cantabrians that fed it, supplemented by summer snow melt. The river allowed navigation well inland and was the lifeline and binding force of this first Roman province, Tarraconensis.

The third in the hierarchy of rivers is the Duero (Durius in Latin, Douro in Portuguese). It has a length of 897 kilometres and runs east to west from its source in the central mountains of Soria, across the northern meseta towards the Portuguese Atlantic coast at Oporto. Its watershed, at 98,000 square kilometres, is greater than those of the preceding rivers. The Duero marked the northwestern boundary of the large Roman province of Carthaginensis which stretched from the southeastern Spanish coast, where its capital Cartago (modern Cartagena) was located, right across the meseta. The province was kept together by administrative, rather than natural, means. From the meseta, the Duero plummeted down to become the Portuguese Douro along its final short lap, which made it un-navigable except for a very short distance towards the Portuguese coast. The Duero marked the early boundary between Christian and Muslim. The next on the list is the 778-kilometre long Guadiana (from the Arab wadi – river, and the Latin anas – duck), with a catchment of more than 67,000 square kilometres, that flows from the region of Albacete in the southeast of La Mancha to the complex of 15

La Mancha is the land of Don Quixote and his windmills

inland lakes known as the Lagunas de Ruidera, an oasis in otherwise barren lands. From there it flows westwards across La Mancha, the land of Don Quixote, immortalised by the poet and playwright Miguel de Cervantes, towards the Portuguese border where it turns south to reach the Atlantic in the Gulf of Cádiz. For much of the lower course the Guadiana is the frontier between Spain and Portugal and in Roman times marked the boundary between the provinces of Lusitania and Baetica. The centre of the former was Emerita Augusta (present-day Mérida), up to which point the river was navigable. Chapman and Buck visited La Mancha too, leaving no doubt about their impressions in Unexplored Spain, written in 1910:

"Immediately to the north of our 'Home Province' of Andalusia, but separated therefrom by the Sierra Morena, stretch away the uplands of La Mancha – the country of Don Quixote. The north-bound traveller, ascending through the rock-gorges of Despeñaperros, thereat quits the mountains and enters on the Manchegan plateau. A more dreary waste, ugly and desolate, can scarce be imagined. Were testimony wanting to the compelling genius of Cervantes, in very truth La Mancha itself would yield it.

"Yet it is wrong to describe La Mancha as barren. Rather its central highlands present a monotony of endless uninteresting cultivation. League-long furrows traverse the landscape, running in parallel lines to utmost horizon, or weary the eye by radiating from the focal point as spokes in a wheel. But never a break or a bush relieves one's sight, never a hedge or hill, not a pool, stream, or tree in a long day's journey. Oh, it is distressing, wherever seen – in Old World and New – that everlasting cultivation of the flat."

The Ruidera lakes are mentioned by Cervantes (Don Quixote slept for one night in the Cave of Montesinos in the vicinity). Apart from the lakes the Guadiana is also responsible for the inland wetland complex known as the Tablas de Daimiel. Tablas, or tables, refers to the large shallow lakes produced when the Guadiana and its tributaries burst their banks. In 1325 the Book of Hunting of the Infante Don Juan Manuel describes this place, the property of the Order of Calatrava, as very appropriate for hunting. King Felipe II visited the wetland in 1575 and was so impressed by it that he ordered that it should be well maintained.

Chapman and Buck were more generous towards Daimiel than the rest of La Mancha: "Yet there is no rule but has its exception, and it is, in fact, to the existence of a series of most singular Manchegan lagoons, abounding in bird-life, that this venturesome literary excursion owes its genesis.

"In the midst of tawny table-lands, well nigh 200 miles from the sea and upwards of 2,000 feet above its level, nestle the sequestered Lagunas de Daimiel extending to many miles of mere and marsh-land. These lakes are, in fact, the birthplace of the great river Guadiana (in actual fact they are the meeting point of two tributaries), the head-waters being formed by the junction of its nascent streams with its lesser tributary the Ciguela.

"In the confluence of the two rivers mentioned it is the Guadiana that chiefly lends its serpentine course to the formation of a vast series of lagoons, with islands and islets, cane-brakes and shallows overgrown by reeds, sedge, and marsh-plants, all traversed in every direction by open channels (called trochas), the whole constituting a complication so extensive that none save experienced boatmen can thread a way through its labyrinths.

"Isolated thus, a mere speck of water in the midst of the arid table-lands of central Spain, yet these lagoons of Daimiel constitute not only one of the chief wildfowl resorts of Spain, but possibly of all Europe. Upon these waters occur from time to time every species of aquatic game that is known in this peninsula, while in autumn the duck-tribe in countless hosts congregate in nearly all their European varieties."

What we see in Daimiel today is a pitiful token of what once was this large and ecologically important inland network of wetlands that provided a link between those of Andalusia and Morocco and those of Aragón and Castile. Hope came in 1959 when a ministerial order prohibited hunting, a dictum that was exceptionally broken on October

Medieval Muslim water wheel on the Guadalquivir by Córdoba

CHAPTER TWELVE *Among canes and mud*

17, 1965, so that General Franco could hunt there.

Disaster struck in the 1960s. As was the case in La Janda, extensive channelling of the rivers of La Mancha started to alter water tables. The drying of the wetlands commenced with the drainage and channelling of the Guadiana and its tributaries. At the same time the underground water table began to be tapped. All this was done to favour the large-scale development of irrigation schemes. In a few years the Guadiana had dried up almost completely and an ecological disaster of unprecedented proportions followed. The peat bog forming the lakes' bottom dried up for the first time in hundreds of years. Spontaneous combustion soon followed and the plant remains that had been waterlogged for centuries caught fire. The bogs burned without flames, internally, with an excess of gases that escaped through cracks in the ground.

Some hope returned in 1996 and 1997 as a result of heavy rains, but subsequent dry years have made matters worse. When I visited Daimiel, full of anticipation, in 2004 I could not believe that I was in a National Park, on the very river that the Romans had christened 'of the ducks'. I cut short my stay. The pain was too great to bear.

A report in the Spanish media dated July 16, 2007, stated that the capture of waters from the Segura river to the Guadiana had meant that 360 hectares of a possible 1,750 had been flooded in Daimiel. The flooded area had been reduced to a mere 17 hectares, less than one per cent of its total capacity (in modern times). Having sucked the Guadiana dry and brought it to its knees, we now resort to extreme measures by taking water from another source to allow this agonising jewel a last gasp.

The Guadiana became the southern frontier of Christianity once Trujillo and the other Extremaduran towns had been taken. From there the assault on the core of al-Andalus, the valley of the Guadalquivir, commenced. The Guadalquivir (from the Arabic al-wadi al-kabir, the great river), formerly the Baetis of the Romans, is the fifth of our large rivers. It is 657 kilometres long, originating in the high mountains of the Sierra de Cazorla in southeastern Spain. From there it flows steadily west past the great cities of Córdoba and Sevilla, draining 58,000 square kilometres of land, to reach the sea at Doñana. As with the other rivers that open into the tidal Atlantic, the Guadalquivir does not form a delta. The formation of a bar and sand spit near its mouth contributed over hundreds of years to the accumulation of the sediment carried downstream which was not lost to the sea. The great marshes of Doñana were created as a result.

The Phoenicians, and the Carthaginians and Romans after them, learned to approach the great river from the sea. Rather than land on the rugged coast of southeast Spain, these Mediterranean mariners would continue their sea journey west past the Pillars of Hercules and land in Cádiz from where they controlled the river's entrance that was a short distance to the north. The great advantage of this river was that it was permanently navigable to Sevilla and intermittently right up to Córdoba. Thus the basin of the Baetis river, along with the mountains and coast to the south, became the Roman province of Baetica and its capital became Hispalis (present-day Sevilla).

CHAPTER TWELVE *Among canes and mud*

The significance of this major route did not escape the Arabs centuries later and it was upstream, in Córdoba, that Islam reached its finest hour in al-Andalus. The remarkable story of the rise of al-Andalus started with a lucky refugee. When the Umayyad Dynasty that had ruled the Islamic world from Damascus was overthrown by the Abbasid dynasty in 750, Abd al-Rahman I managed to escape west to al-Andalus. Here he became the first emir of the surviving Umayyad dynasty. He ruled from 756 to 788 and started a line that would survive until 1031. From his base in Córdoba, Rahman started to organise the government of al-Andalus, which had been in tatters since the Berber revolt of 740. He created an administration that was less centralised than it had been under Roman or Visigoth and created a number of small provinces or guras: Málaga, Medina-Sidonia, Morón, Jaén, Elvira, Talavera, Tarragona and Barcelona. The governors of Badajoz, Toledo and Zaragoza had even greater independence. The provinces mirrored the central government of Córdoba, which appointed the provincial governors from local families.

Rahman issued a stable coin, the silver dirham, and maintained a standing army of mercenaries made up of Berbers and slaves of Christian origin (the mamelukes). The nature of the army meant that, if necessary, it could be used against the Arab aristocracy. Rebellions were short-lived and stability was the norm in the Umayyad period. Córdoba became a cosmopolitan city under Rahman. A thriving, literate Jewish community was very useful in the urban environment. They were permitted to practise their religion, a giant step from the earlier Visigothic repression, and the Umayyad period became the golden age of Iberian Jewry. Most of the population consisted of the other subject peoples, the Christians or Mozarabs. They adopted Muslim dress, some of the diet and a measure of bilingualism but retained their religion and the use of vulgar Latin, that would evolve in the direction of Romance.

The Muslims carried the development of Iberia much further than the Romans had. By the year 1000 Córdoba was the main city, with 90,000 inhabitants. Sevilla had grown to 52,000 and Toledo to 28,000. The economic basis for this growth was a new kind of agriculture. New crops arrived from the east. Banana and cotton came in the ninth century; hard wheat, rice, sugar cane, egg plant and water melon in the 10th; sorghum and spinach in the 11th. These products naturally increased the dietary diversity of the population and so its health. Some of these crops (sugar cane and rice) gave a higher yield than existing crops. Others (sorghum, hard wheat and cotton) were more resistant to aridity than existing plants so new lands could be cultivated. For the first time the dry summer became a new growing season. Land dedicated to olive and grape was significantly extended. With new agricultural techniques, including the spread of the water wheel and a greater use of underground water, the available agricultural land tripled.

The richness and climate of the Guadalquivir valley proved to be the catalyst. It allowed Rahman to import trees from all across the Mediterranean to grace the gardens of his

The Córdoba Mosque is a forest of arches

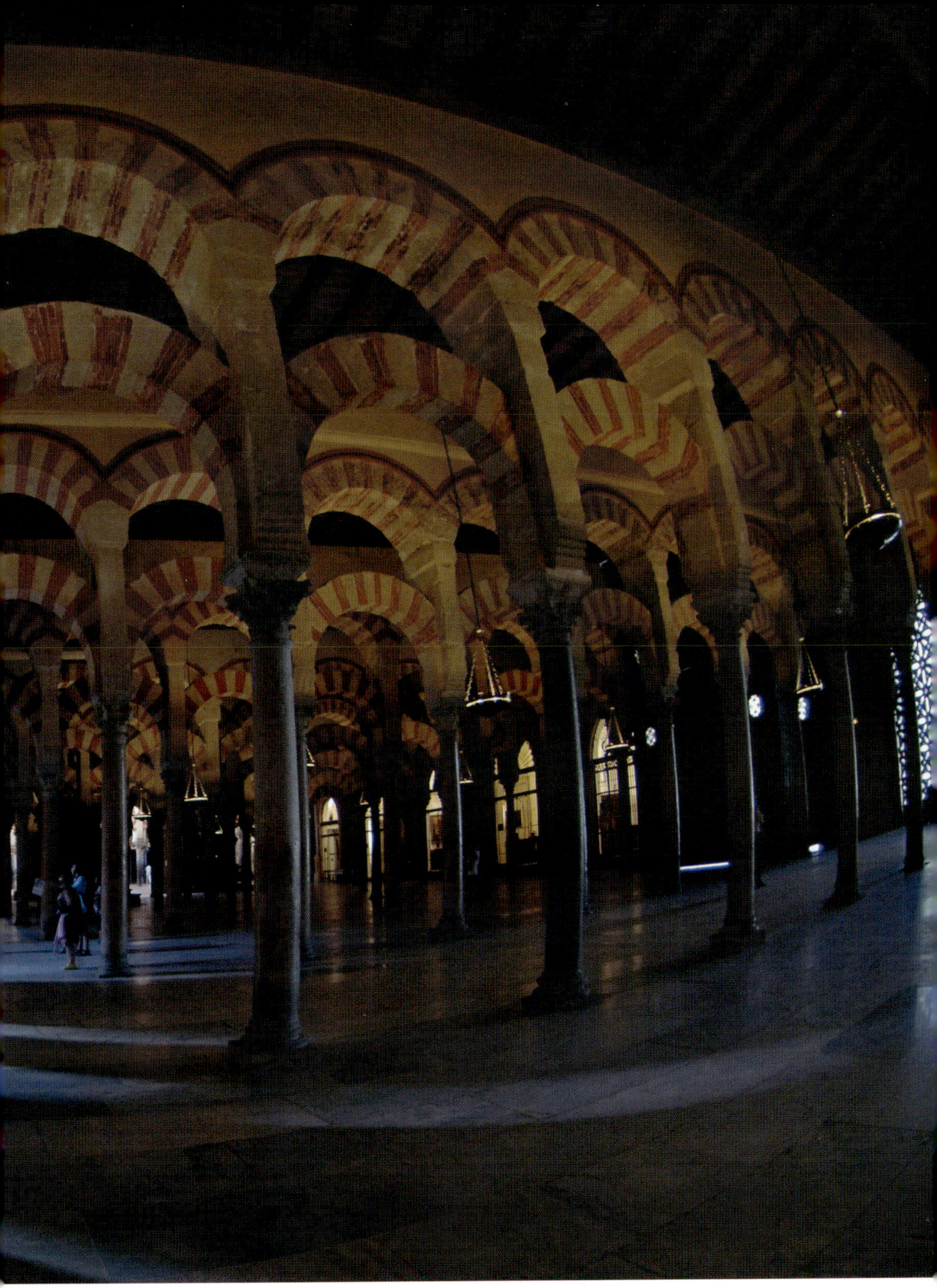

AL-ANDALUS

palace. He introduced a variety of the pomegranate and the date palm. Others were introduced by Abd al-Rahman II (822-852), including an improved variety of fig as well as lemon, lime and sour orange. The activity generated by the new rulers, in the context of a fertile valley, placed al-Andalus within the sphere of a revitalised Mediterranean trade.

The heyday arrived when Abd al-Rahman III (912-961) declared himself Caliph and thus completely independent from Baghdad. The richness of the Caliphate was enhanced by trade with the Near East and North Africa, even from south of the Sahara Desert. Shipyards were built on the Mediterranean coast and in the Atlantic southwest using the plentiful sources of wood in the mountains around the Guadalquivir. Mining and manufacture also took off. Toledo steel and Córdoba leather acquired international fame. The former Christian church of Córdoba was razed and the Great Mosque, the symbol of the new-found wealth, erected in its place.

Rahman III built his palace at Madinat al-Zahra, outside Córdoba itself where he entertained the embassies of Byzantium, the Franks, the Norse and the German Saxons. Amazingly, given the existing conflict with the Christian north, his palace guard was made up of Leonese and Frankish mercenaries as well as east European Slavs. His main army was Berber. Neither race nor religion was important in the caliph's choice of high ranking military and civil officials and Rahman maintained the policy of cordial relations with Christian and Jew. In the Guadalquivir valley flourished a culture and civilisation like never before or after.

Rahman III was, above all else, the king of spin. He excelled at projecting his own image. We see this in the titles he awarded himself. In 929 he declared himself khalifa, the caliph. He was the first Muslim ruler of al-Andalus to do so and was signalling his independence from Baghdad. As caliph he signalled that he was the successor to the Prophet, which was somewhat ironic as in his close ancestry he was of three-quarters Christian descent. His paternal grandparents were the Emir Abd Allah and the Christian princess Onneca. Rahman himself was born of the union of his father, Muhamman, with a Christian slave concubine. He had blue eyes, pale skin and reddish hair, which he tinted black to appear more like an Arab.

As part of his campaign of spin, Rahman awarded himself a number of titles: "He who fights victoriously for the faith of Allah" and "Prince of the Believers", as well as "Caliph". He established an elaborate protocol in the palace and processions and other ceremonies became a regular feature of life. When he wanted to impress visitors he made them approach Madinat al-Zahra from Córdoba itself, along streets lined with soldiers and cavalry. Córdoba under Rahman III was a splendid city that rivalled all others in Europe. In creating it, this master of propaganda ensured his own immortality…

The sun was low on the horizon as our ship left the port of Valencia bound for Gibraltar.

CHAPTER TWELVE *Among canes and mud*

Amid gigantic gantries and floating juggernauts loaded with containers, sandwich, common and little terns from the nearby Albufera busily hovered and dived into the oily waters of the port to catch an evening meal for their hungry young waiting on some sandy island in the distance. As we left the port, towers of apartments and hotels within the Albufera overwhelmed the horizon. There were no canes and there was no mud. We set course south as the sun began to set against distant hills. It was a millennial view, one that the Phoenicians had contemplated almost 3,000 years earlier for the first time. It was not the same view nonetheless. A continuous, never-ending, line of concrete marked the interface between land and sea. Once again, as in earlier times, the late 20th century had been scarred by the ruthless rape of the land. Darkness fell but neon would not allow us to forget the nightmare. At dawn we passed the Cabo de Gata, a brief respite of natural coast, an illusion that was soon shattered as we turned west into the Sea of Alborán and the Costa del Sol...

Rosia Bay, Gibraltar, is where Nelson's body was brought after Trafalgar

GIBRALTAR AND CADIZ

CHAPTER THIRTEEN

Gibraltar and Cádiz

AL–ANDALUS

In this chapter Cádiz and Gibraltar serve as backdrop to the fatal encounter of two men in October, 1805, on the day of the battle of Trafalgar, and we will see how war, blockade (as a direct consequence of the riches that came from the Americas), siege and disease had an impact on the life of al-Andalus. These two cities, with their well- conserved archives, offer a unique window into 18th and early 19th-century al-Andalus.

This chapter shows how chance events have shaped the history of al-Andalus, an underlying theme of this book. Until now, the story has revolved around Arab, North African and Iberian with a dose of Phoenician and Roman. Here I introduce a new influence from outside, one that would have a major impact on future events, that of England and other Atlantic powers, such as Holland, which began at the end of the 16th century.

During the Great Siege of Gibraltar, on the morning of September 13, 1782, mysterious shapes appeared in the bay opposite the Rock. These were the "floating batteries" designed by the French military engineer, Jean-Claude-Eleonore Le Michaud D'Arcon. Gibraltar's coastal defences had been resisting a land attack since 1779. The massive batteries had been prepared so that, when towed close enough, they could penetrate the defences through the incessant pounding of their guns. D'Arcon had taken every eventuality into account. The British had been heating cannon balls in furnaces and firing them red-hot, a novelty which posed a clear risk to any wooden ship. Within the wooden hulks d'Arcon had introduced a system of channels to wet the floating batteries in the event of the so-called red-hot potatoes of the British penetrating the first layer. Also wet sand had been sandwiched between the wooden layers. Fire would thus be prevented from spreading across the batteries. It was generally believed that this was to be the moment when the fortress of Gibraltar would finally fall. The Duke of Bourbon, the Comte d'Artois (later Charles X) and many Spanish personalities gathered on the Spanish side of the Bay of Gibraltar to see the formidable machines at work.

Ten floating batteries had been prepared and they were towed into position in two columns. In the first column a young Sicilian sailor stood proudly in command of one of these formidable machines. We can only imagine the feeling of expectation and tension in the mind of Don Federico Gravina aboard the San Cristóbal as this technological wonder of the time slowly approached the limestone mass of the Rock of Gibraltar. With him in the columns were 138 guns and 5,190 men. Undoubtedly, as Gravina and the San Cristóbal approached the formidable King's Bastion, he would have seen the British troops aligned along the defences, he would have heard their cries getting closer and closer...

Then, at 10.25 in the morning, the earth shook as floating batteries, support ships and the land batteries opened fire. The battle raged all day. Red-hot potatoes fell on the floating batteries without at first causing much damage. In turn the fire from the floating batteries barely reached the coastal defences. By afternoon fire began to spread across

CHAPTER THIRTEEN *Gibraltar and Cádiz*

some of the floating batteries as their system of irrigation failed against the red-hot shot. Between five in the afternoon and nine at night the floating batteries' fire was becoming increasingly ineffective. Then a floating battery caught fire and, at midnight, blew up. Two others followed, the explosions shaking friends and enemies alike – imagine the noise and panic. Thus ended d'Arcon's project...

The history of naval encounters between the English and the Spanish in this part of the world arguably has its roots in the 16th century. In 1587 Queen Elizabeth, conscious of Felipe II's plans to send the Invincible Armada into English waters, despatched Sir Francis Drake to sack the coasts of Spain and reduce the immediacy of the threat. Drake succeeded in entering the Bay of Cádiz, causing significant damage to the Spanish galleons and putting back the departure of the Armada by a year. Nine years later, a heavily armed fleet under the command of Admiral Lord Effingham set sail from Plymouth. The Count of Essex was in charge of the land army. This expedition succeeded in landing, taking and sacking Cádiz, which was poorly defended.

Further Anglo-Dutch attacks on Cádiz took place in 1625 and 1702, the latter during the War of Spanish Succession. In 1797 Admiral Jervis initiated a protracted blockade of Cádiz that ended with the signing of peace in 1802 only to resume early in 1805. These latter blockades had the desired effect of preventing shipments from the Indies arriving at Cádiz, causing substantial ruin to a city that had prospered for much of the century, especially after it became virtually the sole port for commerce with the Indies in 1717, to the detriment of Sevilla, and particularly in the last third of the century. Between 1717 and 1765, 1,083 ships left Cádiz for the Americas, 87.69 per cent of the entire traffic for all Spanish ports. In the same period, 869 returned, constituting 81.67 per cent of the entire traffic. Just under 400,000 tons of goods left Cádiz and more than 350,000 arrived between 1717 and 1778. The range of goods exported to America was great. The major exports were textiles, wine, vinegar, anisette, paper, oil, iron, wax and spices and the main imports included cocoa, sugar, tobacco and copper. Such movement generated huge commercial activity. One estimate put the number of merchant houses in Cádiz at 720. Interestingly, in 1773, 30 of these were English.

Commercial activity in Cádiz increased notably between 1740 and 1760 and peaked in the 1760s and 1770s. Descriptions of the city by visitors attest to the opulence of life. Major Dalrymple in 1774 found it: "grand and well-populated" with "large and beautiful houses, because the number of people who make their fortunes there from commerce is very considerable".

By the end of the 18th century Cádiz, with more than 70,000 inhabitants, was one of the six largest cities in Spain. Cádiz society was cosmopolitan. Thus, a census in 1791, recorded 8,734 foreigners. The dominant components were Italian (57 per cent), followed by French (31 per cent). The city was well planned and in constant progress, needing eight architects to keep apace with development. All roads to Cádiz, except one, came from the sea. Everything entered and left by the port and life revolved around it...

Attack of the floating batteries (Gibraltar Museum)

Thus the British fleet's blockades at the end of the 18th and beginning of the 19th century had a huge impact on the traffic to and from America and the once-prosperous city was ruined. The British captured 186 merchant ships, with cargoes destined for Cádiz and 54 insurance companies established in Cádiz were ruined. To add to the desolation yellow fever hit the city for the second time in four years. In 1800, it affected more than 48,000 people, of whom 7,387 died. In 1804, more than 9,500 fell sick in four months and 2,273 died. Thus, on the eve of Trafalgar, the city of Cádiz, once a rich and prosperous cosmopolitan port, was barely recovering from the effects of blockade and disease.

The story of Gibraltar during the 18th century is very different from that of Cádiz. A civilian population of between 4,000 and 5,000 Spaniards lived there in 1704 when a combined Anglo-Dutch force under Admiral Sir George Rooke and Prince George of Hesse-Darmstadt attacked on August 4. Most left as the place capitulated. The period between 1704 and 1727 was not conducive to settlement by civilians as there was a continuous risk of the Rock being retaken by the Spanish. Genoese and Sephardic Jews, some of whom may have been in Gibraltar in 1704 and stayed on, were to play a prominent role in its resettlement during the 18th and 19th centuries.

Many Jews came to Gibraltar from North Africa during the early 18th century when there was trade between Gibraltar and Barbary. This trade filled an obvious necessity as

CHAPTER THIRTEEN *Gibraltar and Cádiz*

Gibraltar at the end of the Great Siege (Gibraltar Museum)

fresh supplies from Spain were impossible given the political situation.
The Sultan of Morocco signed a treaty with Great Britain in 1729, the first clause of which stated: "That all Moors and Jews subject to the Emperor of Morocco shall be allowed free traffic to buy and sell for 30 days in the City of Gibraltar, or Island of Minorca, but not to reside in either place, but to depart with their effects, without let or molestation, to any other part of the Emperor's dominions."
Jews stayed beyond these limits, as is obvious from census records and, after 1728 (there had been a six-month siege of Gibraltar in 1727), started to build houses.
The Great Siege, a four-year assault by the Spanish and the French culminated with the attack of the floating batteries, started in 1789. It caused the exodus of a large part of the civilian population and left Gibraltar in ruins. The slight growth experienced in the mid-18th century was disrupted in a way that only men can achieve. Cádiz, with its own history of attacks and assaults, never witnessed such a panorama of desolation as this... With the end of hostilities came recovery and people were quick to return in search of opportunity. The first ship arriving from Genoa carried Genoese and Jews who had left during the siege. The next day Jews started to return from Tangier. The wars with France at the end of the 18th century and early 19th, which continued almost without interruption, prevented the commercial development of Gibraltar to its full potential. Following the Great Siege, conditions were far from ideal and, by 1791, the population

Rock of Gibraltar

had actually declined to 2,890 inhabitants. Conditions were no different at the turn of the century, but the population doubled to 5,339 by 1801. The reason was a mass immigration of young Genoese who were evading conscription in Napoleon's armies or simply having to live under the French regime.

The isolation that Gibraltar was subjected to in 1800 meant that it escaped the yellow fever epidemic that hit Cádiz and many other Spanish towns. But 1804 was very different. A total of 5,733 people died, of whom – some authors estimate – as many as 4,864 were civilians, that is nearly 85 per cent of all deaths. Consider that the civilian population of Gibraltar in 1804 was just over 6,000 and the scale of the impact becomes evident. The epidemic became most severe in the summer months and Gibraltar must have been an awful place in the heat and drought with yellow fever rampant.

The following account gives a clear picture of the situation: "The pestilence was awfully aggravated by drought and famine. The people fainted and expired under the intensity of unmitigated heat. Expedients suggested by superstition or despair, seemed more like preparations for death, than preservation of life. Excess of wretchedness steeled the hearts of the lower classes, and changed them into savages; hiring themselves, at exorbitant rates, to perform for the sick those offices which humanity should have

Sunset over the Strait looking towards Trafalgar and the Atlantic

rendered spontaneously, or they supplied their surviving companions in misery with insufficient morsels and scanty droughts, at arbitrary and daily-increasing prices. Coffins could no longer be furnished for the dead, nor funeral rites performed. Half-infected soldiers were seen reluctantly patrolling the panic-struck natives to carry out the corpses of the poor, whether relatives or strangers, and drop them promiscuously into trenches, opened day by day to receive the multitudes of dead."

Although Nelson knew and visited Gibraltar during his time in the Mediterranean, we have little that can give us his view of the place. Writing in April of 1805, when it was not faring much better than Cádiz, Nelson commented: "Broken-hearted as I am at the escape of the Toulon Fleet, yet it cannot prevent my thinking of all the points entrusted to my care, amongst which Gibraltar stands prominent: I wish you to consider me particularly desirous to give every comfort to the good old Rock."

So it was that Gravina and Nelson came together at Trafalgar. The backdrop was provided by the cities of Cádiz and Gibraltar. Nelson had lived in Gibraltar and had attacked Cádiz. Gravina lived in Cádiz and had attacked Gibraltar. Cádiz and Gibraltar had very different trajectories leading up to Trafalgar but they had one thing in common: war and disease had left them in desolation. Trafalgar lay between the two…

On July 7, 1808, not three years after Trafalgar, the French fleet was defeated by the Spanish at Cádiz. The British were promising support to the Spanish general Don Tomás de Morla; the Gibraltar Governor, Sir Hugh Dalrymple, had offered a division of 5,000 men due to arrive from Sicily. Admiral Collingwood and the British fleet were also offering help. That day Morla wrote: "Let our fleets, the Spanish and the surrendered French, then be armed. Let the dockyard at Gibraltar provide the necessary supplies and bring them to ours in Cádiz…"

Gravina, Nelson and thousands of others were long dead. Enemies now fought alongside against old allies, recalling medieval pacts. Cities once at war now helped each other. Such is the futility of the pain that men inflict upon each other…

Maritime trade has been a characteristic of the ports of Cádiz and Gibraltar for centuries

CHAPTER THIRTEEN *Gibraltar and Cádiz*

Part of the complex network of secret World War II tunnels on the Rock of Gibraltar

Civilising al-Andalus

CHAPTER FOURTEEN

Civilising al-Andalus

When Verner took Henry Breuil to see the painted cave of La Pileta in the mountains of Ronda, what their lamps revealed on the walls, among the stalactites, stalagmites and flowstones, were images that reflected a rich landscape occupied by hunter-gatherers since the last Ice Age. These were people from whom we can claim direct ancestry. Their remote origins were to be found in Africa but they were settled in this environment of southern Iberia. They were the same people who visited Gorham's Cave some time after the last of the Neanderthals, around 18,500 years ago. Other hunter-gatherers kept visiting La Pileta for 11,000 years or so until something started to change. Whether new people were penetrating these lands from the east or whether their ideas and technology changed is still open to debate. Either way, by around 5,500 BC we pick up the traces of people who are switching behaviour. An eastern Mediterranean novelty was replacing the hunting and gathering economy that had persisted here since the first ancestors had arrived more than a million years earlier. People started to change the nomadic lifestyle and began to live in semi-permanent settlements. They replaced hunting by herding domesticated goats, sheep and cattle and they replaced gathering with agriculture. It was an irreversible change that would have profound effects on the landscape.

La Pileta gives us a picture of the life of the early hunter-gatherers. They painted the animals that we presume were their favourite prey or perhaps those that they revered most. At La Pileta mostly the horse, the red deer, the ibex (wild goat) and the aurochs (wild cattle) are represented. These animals fit well with a mountain and inland valley fauna that occupied a mosaic of forest, pasture and cliff. It was not very different from that which the Neanderthals had lived in before them.

Even more exciting for me than La Pileta is the cave at Ardales, in the mountains north of Málaga. There are hundreds of paintings and engravings on the walls, fallen rocks and floor of this cave, contemporary with the hunter-gatherers of La Pileta. The sites are not very far from each other, across mountain valleys, so it is possible that we are observing part of the same painting tradition expressed by different tribes, rivals or friends. For me the exciting thing about Ardales was the distribution of the animals represented within the large cave. The subjects were similar to those in Pileta but here they seem to have been ordered in a strange way. Most of the ibexes were on the cave walls but the horses were low down in the cave, usually on fallen boulders. At the base of the cave there were also a fish and a snake. Near the floor, on a low wall, a flamingo had been sketched. Aurochs and deer occupied intermediate positions. Were these people using the cave as a three-dimensional representation of the environment outside? My idea would fit with the distribution of the images: ibexes on the cliffs, horses on the plains below, fish and snakes by the river and cattle and deer on the forested slopes. Maybe research in the future will confirm these ideas, but certainly Ardales is a cave well worth a visit.

What happened when the new technologies, that allowed a production economy for

CHAPTER FOURTEEN *Civilising al-Andalus*

the first time, arrived on the scene? Were the changes as dramatic as we have been led to believe? I think not. My impression is of a gradual transformation in which many groups continued to hunt while others settled and grew crops. The pattern would have varied from place to place. In Gibraltar, by the rich coast of the Strait of Gibraltar the evidence we find is that people were still living in caves around 5,400 BC. They were not farming either. Instead, the bulk of the fossil material shows they were living from the sea and seemed to be particularly fond of tuna. The early Neolithic people of the Strait were fishermen. The change did come in time as the farmers, able to produce a food surplus, reproduced at a faster rate than the hunters and fishermen. With the spread of farming and agriculture came an active transformation of the environment. Forests were cut back for grazing land and for growing crops. The world had started to change at the hands of farmers.

The change involved, for the first time, the creative use of rocks. Previously such creativity had been confined to painting inside natural cavities. Now, for the first time, humans were making cavities using rocks. On the road from Granada to Orce there is a deep valley in a semi-desert landscape reminiscent of Arizona. Within it is the small village of Gorafe, the site of a large megalithic park. Beginning in the fourth millennium, people in southeast Iberia began to build large monuments from carefully prepared stone slabs. They were used to bury people while others were for worship. This area was one of several across Europe where the practice of the large stone monuments started. By the second millennium it had spread across much of western Europe. Here in Gorafe there appears to have lived a large agricultural population during the third millennium. Megaliths were an important part of the society of these rural people so much so that in an eight-kilometre stretch of river there are 240 of these dolmens, one of the largest megalithic concentrations anywhere in Iberia. People were well on their way towards taming the countryside and civilising the future al-Andalus.

Travelling east from Gorafe towards the Mediterranean coast, we pass the town of Baza on the right and, shortly after, an imposing mountain chain carrying its name. I was lucky recently to have the opportunity to work with my botanical colleague and friend Pepe Carrión, of the University of Murcia, in a project to examine in some detail how humans had actually transformed the environment after the advent of agriculture. Our source of information was a pollen core taken from the waterlogged soils at the head of the Cañada del Gitano Basin, precisely in the Sierra de Baza. To the information from the core we added data from other pollen sites in the area and from archaeological work, as well as documentary evidence from historical accounts. We were able to put together a history of the sierra in the context of the exploitation of the natural environment by people and their impact on it. This is what we found.

Between 6,390 and 4,320 BC, prior to and during the transition to agriculture the sierra was dominated by forests of black and Scots pines. There was also some broad-leafed and mixed woodland with evergreen oaks, hazel, maple, birch, chestnut, alder, ash

Typical rock shelter of south-eastern Iberia with rock art (top right) at Velez Rubio, Almería

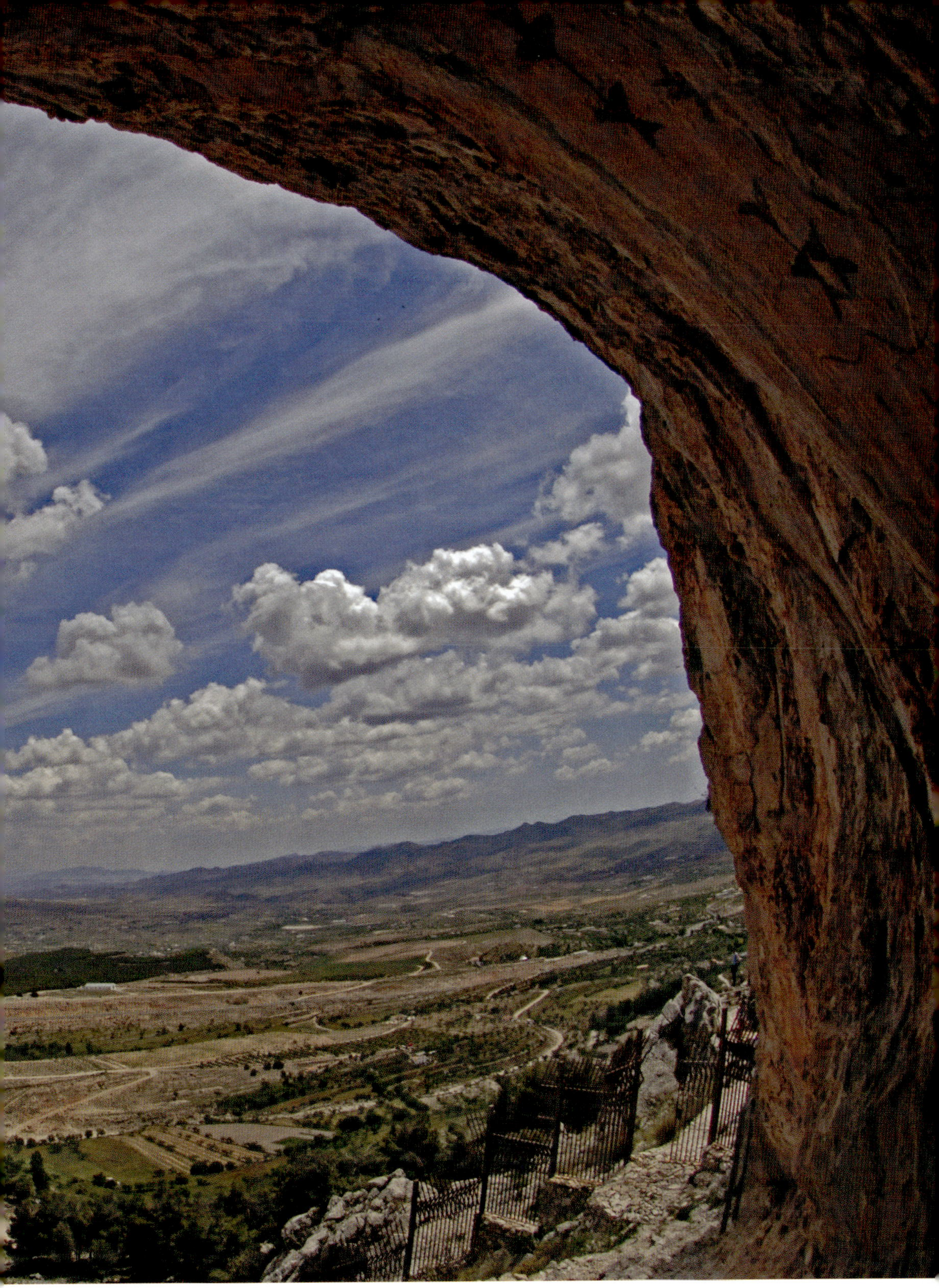

Rows of birds, probably cranes, depicted on the walls of the Tajo de las Figuras near La Janda

Aleppo and maritime pine. There was also some Mediterranean vegetation consisting of wild olive, lentisc, rock roses, heathers, buckthorn and Phyllirea. Mountain prairies and steppes punctuated the forested landscape. This was a typical Mediterranean mountain forest with a zonation of vegetation with altitude, from Mediterranean vegetation low down to pines near the timber line. From the aquatic vegetation we could tell that there had also been a semi-permanent body of shallow water in the vicinity.

There is no evidence of a human presence in the sierra during the early part of this period. The first people appear to be the farmers of the Neolithic (the new Stone Age), between 5,400 and 3,700 BC. The interesting picture that emerged was of people coming into the sierra in search of high mountain pastures, but they also hunted and fished, showing that the change in the economy was gradual. They seem to have practised a seasonal strategy, going up into the mountains in the summer and growing crops lower down in spring and autumn. There is no clear evidence of agriculture in the pollen sequence for this period although the presence of plantain, buckwheat, cabbage, mustard, nettles and beans, which become commoner later on, suggests that the mountain landscape was already being transformed at this early stage.

The presence of these early farmers straddles the period into the next part of the core

Dolmen in the impressive landscape of Gorafe, Granada

that starts at 4,320 BC and finishes around 1,800 BC. It involves the intensification of agriculture followed by the start of mining. Pine forests continued to dominate the high ground but they covered a reduced area as deciduous oaks, other broad-leaved trees and even Mediterranean shrubs expanded their range in response to climate warming. The most humid period was reached between 3,800 and 3,600 BC, after which conditions became more arid and Mediterranean dry-loving shrubs expanded. Later on, after 2,100 BC we pick up an increase in microscopic fragments of charcoal coincident with the drier climate.

The changes in vegetation were clearly influenced by climate change, but human activity begins to intrude into these natural changes. The reduction in high mountain cover is not only affected by the spread of broad-leaved trees in response to climate warming but by an increase in tree-felling to create mountain pastures. It is the start of a one-way trend that spans the entire sequence into historical times, a trend towards a progressive reduction in forest cover.

The increasing aridity between 3,300 and 2,700 BC does not appear to have been solely the product of climate change. Much of it had to do with the replacement of the forests by Mediterranean shrubs as more and more trees were cut down. The microclimate of

The Almond was widely planted by the Muslims in al-Andalus

the mountain was being altered by human action. On the coast this large-scale man-made transformation seems to have begun much earlier, some time between 5,000 and 4,000 BC, but it did not reach the mountains until around 3,800 BC. The archaeology tells us that the main domesticated animals taken into the mountains were goats and sheep, but we also find remains of red deer, roe deer, wild boar and ibex, which suggests that people still hunted wild animals at this stage. We also find cereal pollen which indicates the expansion of cultivation.

The southeast of the Iberian peninsula is one of the areas of western Europe where metallurgy was first practised. As with the change from hunting to agriculture, the transition to a metal-based society was not abrupt. Localised extraction of copper (the period is known by archaeologists as the Chalcolithic) starts around 3,700 BC and we find more and more mining settlements between then and 2,200 BC. The famous archaeological site of Los Millares, north of Almería, is a large, fortified settlement, typical of the settlements of the time – set on hills above rivers and dry river valleys and made up of clusters of circular huts with stone walls, covered with mud and branches.

The culture was extended across southeastern Iberia, in Almería, Granada, Málaga

Monocultures have become a feature of modern al-Andalus

and Murcia. These people showed signs of permanent settlement, with well-defined territorial boundaries, and the archaeological evidence indicates that the population was growing. Their agricultural economy was based on wheat and barley, with beans and lentils, which indicates that the rotation of crops was important. The farming economy was also changing, with fewer sheep and goats and more cattle and horse. The latter were sacrificed at an old age which indicates that they were being used as draft animals. Red deer, wild boar, aurochs, ibex, rabbit and birds were still hunted.

Overall, there is little evidence of large-scale human impact on the environment during this period, but there is a hint that climate may have had an effect. Climate changed rapidly in the period between 4,000 and 3,000 BC. Icebergs drifted well south, Alpine glaciers advanced and there was an increased flow of westerly winds over the North Atlantic and Siberia. At lower latitudes these changes are reflected by increased aridity. In the mountains of Baza we detect an increase in pollen from arid Mediterranean shrubs, which we have linked with this global climate change.

Man's impact on the environment increased after 3,000 BC with the intensification of copper-mining and smelting. In the southwest of Iberia it developed on an unprecedented scale, with systematic deforestation, increased erosion and the start of heavy metal pollution of the Odiel and Tinto rivers. In the southeast, including Baza, the Millares culture is replaced by the Argaric culture after 2,200 BC until 1,500 BC. The new settlements followed the river networks and they reveal a crude urban planning, with streets and passages between houses which are no longer circular but instead rectangular or irregular in shape. Grazing and intensified mining activity transformed the land.

We pick up a major environmental change with this cultural change. Tree cover was substantially reduced at the expense of grasses and arid shrubs. It seems related, judging from the observed increase in microscopic charcoal after 2,100 BC that I have referred to, to a surge of forest fires. Were these fires the result of a drier climate or were they, instead, intentionally started? I cannot answer this and the answer may be a combination of the two. In any case the changes to the landscape were severe, so much so that they almost certainly caused the collapse of the Argaric culture around 1,500 BC. These mountains were abandoned until the arrival of the Romans 1,600 years later.

Even though the sierra itself was abandoned, the surrounding lowlands were occupied by people of the Iberian culture between 1,200 and 220 BC. Very close to the present-day city of Baza, on the foothills of the sierra, was the ancient Ibero-Roman city of Basti. One of the most important fortified cities in the country, it gave its name to the huge southeastern region of Spain, Batestania. The city was founded in the eighth century BC and reached the height of splendour between the fifth and first centuries BC. After the Romans, Basti was occupied by Visigoths and Byzantines and was abandoned in the medieval period. The beautiful statuette known as the Dama de Baza came from a necropolis close to Basti. The territorial organisation of Batestania followed a system of strategically situated cities (with populations of 2,000 to 5,000 inhabitants), close to fertile fields and at the junction of commercial routes, and scattered villages.

The Iberian period saw huge advances in agriculture that included irrigation and the widespread cultivation of the vine, fig and almond. Coinage came into use and richness was converted to currency that separated social classes. For the Iberians the forest was a critical resource. They practised the rotation of cultures, bee-keeping and hunting. They collected wood for fuel for their homes, for ceramic and smelting ovens, for charcoal, for construction, agricultural tools, weapons and ritual objects.

Even though the sierra was depopulated during this period, the people of nearby cities and villages exploited its forests. They had a major impact on the environment as a result. Our pollen core reveals how the forest receded even further and many humid tree species, such as hazel, disappeared altogether. There is a parallel increase in cultivated plants such as the vine and those associated with pastures. Thorny scrub takes off where forest has been cleared and lakes and bogs became clogged up with sediment as a result of the increased erosion. There is increasing evidence of regular forest fires. By this time humans were having a major impact on the environment.

The arrival of the Romans saw the renewed occupation and exploitation of the

Sheep farming was a feature of the new agricultural revolution brought by the Neolithic people

sierra. The driving force was mining for copper, silver, iron and lead. With it came the renewed expansion of agriculture. Mining continued during the medieval period. The exploitation of domestic animals continued for centuries. There are numerous tracks and trails in the sierra as well as archaeological cave sites and shelters that were used to keep animals. The sierra was used for summer pastures for sheep and goats between the 16th and the 18th centuries. Numerous ruins of farms, stables and sheepfolds that once kept animals in the summer remain, but today the mountains are uninhabited once more. There are records of the exploitation of wood from the 15th century. It was used for firewood, charcoal, to build houses, churches, convents and public buildings. Wood was used to build the fortifications of Oran in Algeria and to construct the ships of the Invincible Armada. The forests were protected by law until the latter half of the 20th century when there was massive logging because of the severe shortages following the Spanish Civil War.

Despite the severe deforestation since Roman times, there is evidence of substantial oak, pine and mixed forests at the end of the medieval period. Bears and wolves still roamed these mountains. For all the savage assaults on its forests the Sierra de Baza is today a natural park with substantial areas of forest. We may be tempted to see it as natural, not realising that it is a forest that has been transformed by Man over a period of close to 8,000 years.

If industrial mining was in large measure responsible for the changes in Baza, a different kind of mining, this time for military purposes, transformed the small coastal limestone peninsula of the Rock of Gibraltar between the 18th and 20th centuries. It all started during the Great Siege of 1779-83. The British garrison in Gibraltar was under land attack from joint Spanish and French forces. As the Spanish advanced their lines, the British were unable to aim their cannon at them from the heights of the Rock. To resolve the problem, a Sergeant Major Ince of the Military Artificers took up the challenge of making a tunnel that would reach a promontory on the north cliff known as the Notch. The idea was that a gun placed on the Notch would be able to take aim at the inaccessible enemy below.

During the slow process of excavation work came to a halt as the dust from the mining made breathing impossible. Ince decided to make a tunnel that ran at right angles from the main tunnel towards the cliff. The idea was that this opening to the exterior would create a draught and ventilate the tunnel. Once the secondary tunnel was complete, Ince realised the potential of the newly created opening on the cliff face. A gun could be placed there to fire down at the enemy. In this accidental way the galleries of Gibraltar were started.

The initial tunnelling, using sledgehammers and massive chisels, with powder charges being exploded in cracks made in the rock itself, was painfully slow. Five weeks after starting on May 25, 1782, 13 men had managed to excavate a narrow tunnel (with dimensions of around eight square foot or three-quarters of a square metre) that extended only 25 metres. Aided by the new ventilation, the tunnellers carved out 276 metres by the end of 1783.

The galleries were developed into a three-layered system of tunnels with many openings (embrasures) to the exterior, each with its own gun. By 1790, 1,200 metres of tunnel had been excavated and 14,000 cubic metres of rock removed. The work was undertaken by the Company of Soldier Artificers, created in Gibraltar under Royal Warrant in 1772. The company was the precursor of the Royal Sappers and Miners and became the Corps of Royal Engineers of the British Army in 1856.

Tunnelling resumed 150 years later during the Second World War. The aim of the exercise was to create a city within the Rock, a place where a garrison of 16,000 men could live under siege for a year. The tunnels were to cater for hospitals, power generation, water supplies, sleeping accommodation, in short every basic facility that any city on the outside would need. With the help of Canadian engineers who were skilled at mining using diamond-drill blasting, a total length of 54 kilometres of tunnel were excavated in the five-kilometre-long peninsula. Even today the Rock has more road in its interior than outside.

These tunnels included major roads capable of taking the largest military vehicles from

CHAPTER FOURTEEN *Civilising al-Andalus*

There are over thirty miles of tunnel inside Gibraltar. Many carried familiar English names, like Harley Street, and took the largest military vehicles

one end of the Rock to the other. They were excavated at different levels, each connected with the one above or below by narrow flights of steep steps. One ran to the roof of a cave close to Gorham's Cave, a cave into which the sea reached. A trap door was placed on the roof of the cave, known as Boat Hoist Cave. Should the Nazis have invaded Gibraltar, its governor would have escaped along one of the many tunnels to reach a boat waiting in the cave to take him out to a submarine and safety.

The spoil from the tunnels was used mainly to build the airfield which is now used by commercial airlines. General Eisenhower set up base in the tunnels inside the Rock to direct operations for the North African landings and the airport was to be used to carry men and equipment across. In the end the theatre of operations shifted to the central Mediterranean, from where the invasion took place.

The degree of planning for a possible invasion of Gibraltar was meticulous. In 1997 local cavers reported to me that they had discovered a series of hitherto unknown tunnels. I still remember my first impressions on visiting the place for the first time. We entered one of the many known tunnels near the top of the Rock. This one was lined with corrugated metal sheets for added protection. It was not unusual as many other tunnels had such a covering. We walked by torchlight for about 100 metres when the tunnel turned sharp left, then right and continued in a northerly direction. After another 20 metres or so there was an opening to the right in the rock face, which had been hidden by the sheets of metal. It had been bricked up.

We entered through a small gap that the cavers had made and a new tunnel opened up in front of us, one that had been sealed off behind the bricks and metal sheets. At the end of it an old wooden door had collapsed to the floor. Beyond we entered a large room. Immediately my attention was drawn to a perfectly laid floor of cork tiles. On the right there was a large open pit with a tap over it. I realised that the tap led from a carefully concealed large metal water tank that we could not have seen from the outside. I suspected that the tank drew water from the winter rains. The tap was stiff, not surprisingly after 50 years of disuse. I kicked it gently, then more forcefully, and freshwater rushed out. It was crystal clear and perfect to drink.

We moved to the other side of the room where there was another door. Through the door were two small rooms. On the right was a radio room and on the left there were toilets. By the radio room there was a fixed bicycle, a leather strap replacing the chain. From it a long, thick copper wire, in a protective sheath, and a long, hollow square duct led up some steps towards daylight.

At the top of the steps we could squeeze through a narrow opening that led to a narrow ledge, three-quarters of the way up the sheer eastern cliff of Gibraltar. I understood. We were in the secret "Stay Behind" tunnels rumoured to exist inside the Rock. Operation Tracer was a British military plan to be put into operation should the Nazis capture Gibraltar. In that event, six men would seal themselves in a secret tunnel inside the main tunnels and spy on the Germans from there. Silence would have been essential which explained the cork floor and the leather bicycle chain. From our ledge we could see the Mediterranean below so from their hideout the British could have observed, brought out the copper aerial at night and transmitted intelligence back to London. Electricity was generated by one of the men pedalling and the hollow square tube provided ventilation.

Were these intrepid men able to observe the strategically important bay and harbour to the west? We found a second tunnel leading from the steps. It turned on itself and back westwards. At the end a concrete wedge was fixed on the wall. I removed it and a ray of light came in through a narrow slit. Looking through it, below me I could see the Gibraltar dockyard and harbour. I replaced the wedge and later, looking for the slit on the outside, could not see it. Nobody would have known it was there.

A pile of bricks had caught my eye as I had entered the first tunnel. I realised that, should the invasion have taken place, the six men would have sealed themselves in. Another thing caught my eye. All the tunnels that I knew had solid floors, but this one had loose gravel and soil. The military strategists had thought of everything – if one of the men had died, provision had been made for him to be buried without attracting attention and without causing problems for the remaining men inside the chambers.

The cultivation of the vine has a long history in al-Andalus

In the middle of the 20th century we were still exploiting the properties of limestone but we had come a long way from the hunter-gatherers who had used natural cavities in the rocks on which to paint 20,000 years earlier. Al-Andalus had been civilised. In the process we had destroyed forests, polluted rivers and learnt increasingly sophisticated ways of killing each other.

Monument commemorating the victory at Las Navas de Tolosa. La Carolina, near Las Navas, Jaén

MELTDOWN

CHAPTER FIFTEEN

Meltdown

AL-ANDALUS

On January 1, 1492, the Emir of Granada, Muhammad XII (popularly known as Boabdil), recognised that Granada could hold out no longer against a prolonged siege. He sent 500 hostages to the Catholic monarchs, Isabel of Castile and her husband Fernando II of Aragón and Sicily, who were encamped in Santa Fé on the plains west of Granada. He asked that, in return, they should send troops to the Alhambra to protect him from his own people. The following day Granada surrendered and four days later the Catholic kings entered the city and were handed its keys by Boabdil. According to legend, Boabdil then left the city and, as he crossed a mountain pass, looked back and wept. His mother is said to have remarked to him that he could now cry like a woman for what he had not been able to defend as a man. The pass, on the main road from Granada to the coast, is known today as the Suspiro del Moro, the Moor's Sigh. The capitulation of Granada marked the end of a spectacular 781-year period of Muslim rule over the territory that became known as al-Andalus. To understand how such a powerful state could have reached this dire end, we have to go back in time.

Even if we try to find an immediate cause for any historical event, the reality is rarely that simple and, as we dig deep, we realise that multiple causes, actions in other geographical areas and periods, and chance have had a bearing. This is clearly the case with regard to the fall of Granada and the Muslim rule in the Iberian peninsula. In its most immediate perspective it was Boabdil's decision to give in. At another level it was the pressure brought to bear for over a year by the Catholic kings who effectively blockaded the city. Even these events were dependent on preceding ones: the rise to power of Isabel, her union with Fernando, the fragmentation of the Muslim kingdom, Europe's crusading spirit and so on. I would argue that the events of 1492 had their origin 760 years earlier.

For a time it seemed nothing could stop the advance of the Muslims in the eighth century. Visigoth control had crumbled and Muslim troops had reached everywhere they chose to in Iberia. Then they made the fatal mistake of turning their attention to France. They reached Arles and Poitiers, but at Tours an army led by Charles Martel halted the Muslim advance and they withdrew into Iberia. It was the psychological moment: it showed that the all-powerful Muslim army was not invincible and it had reached as far is it ever would. The following 760 years are the history of a progressive shrinkage of the territory under Muslim rule, punctuated by short intervals of partial regaining of lands and even splendour, but within a bigger picture that was a downhill curve towards extinction.

If 732 was the marker, then the collapse of the Córdoba Caliphate in 1009 was the point of no return. Al-Andalus fragmented into small Muslim kingdoms or taifas. The distribution of the new taifas was largely determined by geography, with a dose of help from the individuals involved. The Badajoz taifa was based around the Guadiana Basin; Granada in Sierra Nevada; Zaragoza on the Ebro Basin; Toledo in the lands of the

CHAPTER FIFTEEN *Meltdown*

Tagus; Valencia was sheltered from the interior by the coastal mountains; and Sevilla and Córdoba tussled over the Guadalquivir basin.

Most taifas survived by paying tribute to the Christians in exchange for protection. The tribute became the main source of revenue for the Christians and it started a never-ending spiral of collapse for the taifas. The more tribute they paid the stronger the Christians became. Ironically, the first major conquests of the Christians were financed by the Muslim taifas.

By 1157, the Christians controlled the basins of the Ebro, Duero and Tagus rivers as well as Galicia and the coast of Portugal. Al-Andalus was confined to the basins of the Guadiana and Guadalquivir, the coast of the Mediterranean up to Tortosa by the Ebro delta and the southern Portuguese coast below the Tagus Estuary. The period of disintegration was concomitant with the psychological consolidation of a kind of common identity that linked Crown to land among the Christians. Alfonso VI The Brave (1065-1109) of Castile-León employed the title Totus Hispaniae Imperator (emperor of the whole of Spain). With this recognition of identity came a period of repopulation and conquest that advanced south from the Duero towards the Tagus. When Alfonso VI annexed the Toledo taifa in 1085 and Valencia shortly after, Castile-León became, for the first time, the largest kingdom in Iberia.

The advance had to be stopped and at this point we meet the first of the short-term reversals in the process of Muslim decline. All three developed on the same theme: help from brothers across the Strait of Gibraltar. All three came with a price tag. The fall of Toledo and Valencia brought the message to the southern taifas in Andalusia who overnight had the Christians on their doorstep. The Muslim kings, led by al-Mutamid of the Sevilla taifa, appealed for assistance to a new fundamentalist Berber empire. The Murabit (or Almoravids), with their power base in Marrakesh and the semi-nomadic Sanhaja Berber tribe behind them, had swept across North Africa and the Sahara as far south as Ghana in a wave of fundamentalist renewal.

They landed an army in Algeciras in the summer of 1086, marched north to Badajoz and defeated Alfonso VI at Zalaca in October of the same year. They then retired to North Africa and Alfonso to Toledo. For the next 20 years North Africans and Castilians battled for supremacy over al-Andalus, but the Muslims were unable to regain the lost lands of the north. In this period the North Africans made the most of the invitation extended to the Murabit, conquering the remaining taifas and annexing al-Andalus into their empire.

The North Africans did not only have to contend with the Castilians. There was also Aragón in the southern foothills of the Pyrenees. Its well-watered land along the Aragón river ran into the stark desert to the south, a situation akin to that of Cantabria and the plains of Castile. In addition to the desert, Aragón's expansion was hampered by the Zaragoza taifa, which was among the wealthiest and most powerful of all the Muslim kingdoms. Breaking southwards out of their mountain valley was problematic

Sunset across the Strait from a mosque in Gibraltar. Africa is across the Strait

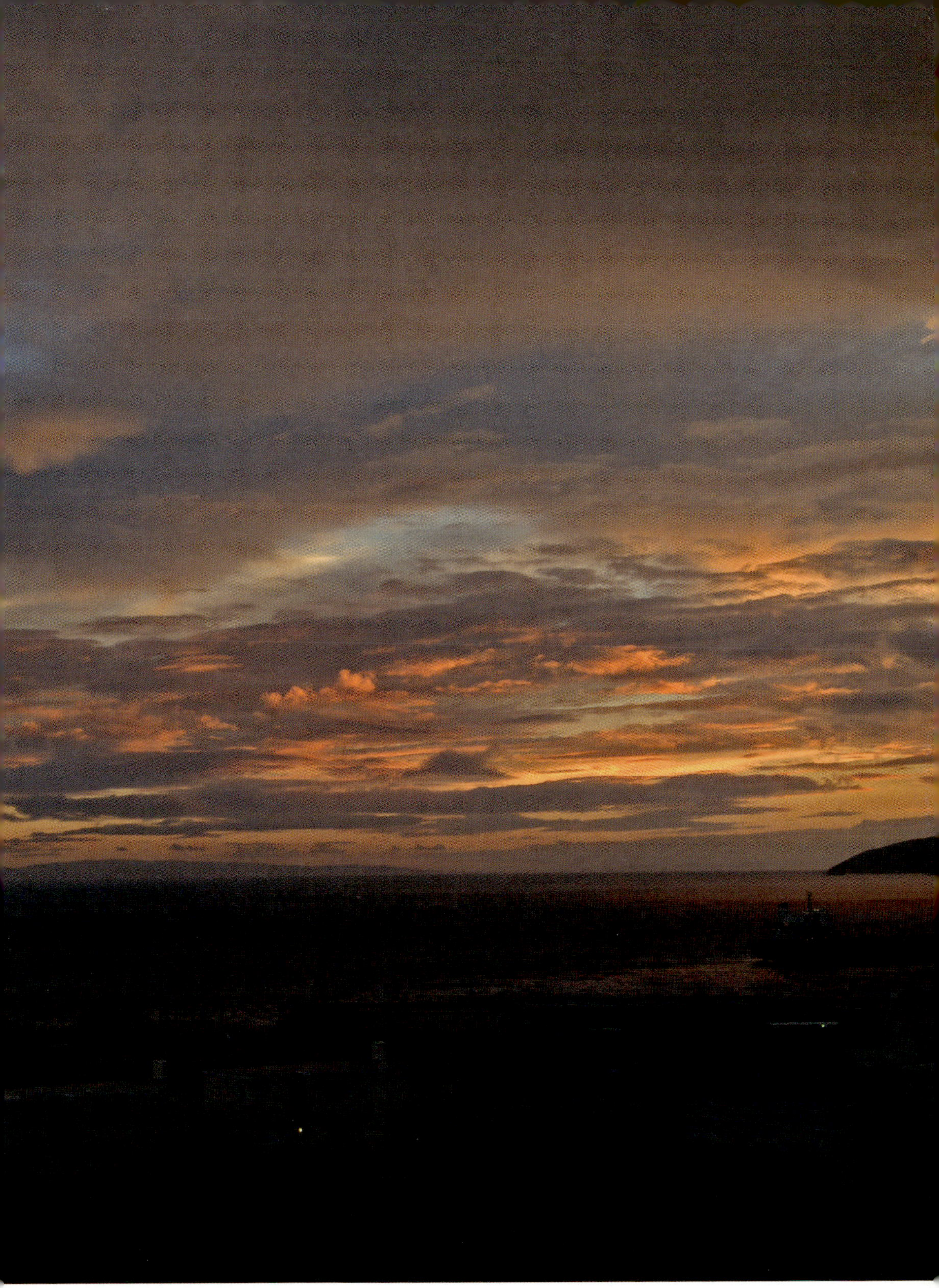

AL-ANDALUS

for the Aragonese, but their advantage lay in the mountain pass of Roncesvalles to the north which allowed contact with France.

Aragón made the most of the advantage from the northern connection and used French cavalry to support their expansion. They also developed a close relationship with the papacy which aided their crusading intentions. With this supporting combination they managed to break out and take Huesca in 1096. As on many other occasions on the long road to Granada, Christians and Muslims fought side by side. On this occasion the Aragonese had the French on their side but the Zaragoza Muslims drew on Castilian support. The Aragonese southward expansion was checked by the capture of Valencia by the North Africans in 1102.

To the east of Aragón small counties united by a language that was the ancestor of Catalan occupied small mountain valleys with rivers flowing from the Pyrenees. They were connected with the French north and combined a heritage that was a mix of Visigothic, Frankish and Mozarabic (Mozarab was the term used to define Christians who had lived under Muslim rule). The presence of Muslims in Zaragoza and Lérida in the south and west stifled Catalan expansion in those directions, so their interests moved northwards where they had a loose control over southern French territory. The presence of El Cid, the knight adventurer, in Valencia frustrated their ambitions regarding that city.

Rodrigo Díaz de Vivar, the legendary El Cid Campeador, is often mistakenly regarded as the archetypal Christian knight, who was largely responsible for defeating the Muslims in Valencia. In reality El Cid was a powerful mercenary who worked, at different times, for Christian and Muslim rulers. He was not dissimilar to the figure of Guzmán El Bueno. Having become chief general in King Alfonso VI's army, he was later forced into exile for mounting an unauthorised (but successful) expedition into Granada. Jealousy from king and rival nobles undoubtedly played its part.

El Cid turned mercenary for the Muslim king of Zaragoza. Seven years after his exile, he was back in Alfonso's court, having been recalled to help fight the invading North Africans. El Cid's story is not very clear at this point. Apparently he commanded a combined Christian and Muslim army in the area of Valencia and, when moving towards this city, he defeated and captured the Catalan count Ramón Berenguer II. Berenguer was ransomed by his son, who married El Cid's youngest daughter as a way of preventing future conflict. Valencia was ruled by an autonomous Muslim king, but North African influence caused an uprising. El Cid laid siege and, after two years, entered the city in 1094. Although in charge of Valencia in the name of the Castilian king, in reality he ruled an independent city state in which Muslims and Christians lived alongside. He died of natural causes in Valencia in 1099.

Hereditary disputes between Castilians and Aragonese, more than resistance from the Muslims, held up the Christian advance, which was only resumed after a series of truces brought pauses in the internal Christian squabbles. As a result, Zaragoza was

CHAPTER FIFTEEN *Meltdown*

taken by Aragón, with the help of the French, in 1118. The conquest of Zaragoza was hugely significant because it altered the Muslim-Christian balance of power in Iberia. Aragón doubled in size overnight and the absorption of new subjects boosted its small population of 125,000 to half a million. It was a landmark victory that opened up the way south.

The next few years were spent consolidating the new territory that had more Muslims than Christians. The Aragonese mounted raids into the south, in 1125 deep into Andalusia from where 10,000 Mozarabs were brought back to settle the newly conquered lands. It is an indicator of the tenuous hold on a land that was thinly populated, a common problem for Muslims and Christians when conquering new lands. Territorial conquests were also common among the Christian kingdoms. The Castilians, on the one hand, advanced and retook eastern Castile, the Rioja region and the Basque country. The Catalans, on the other, had been slowly emerging as a powerful force in the east and by 1137 they controlled French Provence and Zaragoza. The merger of Barcelona with Aragón then created the peninsula's second most powerful kingdom. Meanwhile, Navarra had remained an isolated kingdom in the mountains and struck peace with its neighbours in 1142. With the contemporary emergence of the Portugal in the west, Iberia now had four Christian kingdoms.

Portugal was isolated by the Castilians in the north and the North African Muslims in the south. The small kingdom occupied the coastal strip and river estuaries, the mountains to the east isolating it from the rest of the peninsula. The Portuguese took on the North Africans in the south of Portugal and defeated them at Ourique, in the Algarve, in 1139. Then in the north they defeated the Castilians on the Minho river in 1141. Here, once again, is clear evidence of territorial expansion that was unrelated to religious belief.

In the south the North Africans had another problem to contend with: the rise of a new fundamentalist sect in their homeland of North Africa. These were the Muwahhid (often referred to as Almohads from al-Muwahhid). Their founder and leader was Ibn Tumart who had undertaken a pilgrimage to Mecca and returned to Morocco with fresh fundamentalist ideas around 1120. They used strongholds in the High Atlas to attack the rulers of Morocco and seized power around 1145. The North African Murabit, increasingly stretched and weakened, were being attacked by fellow Muslims and under pressure in Iberia and the Maghreb. In al-Andalus new Christian incursions into Muslim territory became possible.

By 1142 the Castilians were in Coria, Extremadura and had led major raids into Andalusia. Two things were significant about a meeting of the kings of Castile-León, Portugal and Navarra in Valladolid in 1143. One was the absence of the Aragonese-Catalans and the other the presence of the papal legate. A co-ordinated Christian advance was planned to coincide with the second crusade and with the North African disarray. Córdoba was reduced to a vassal in 1146. The Murabit fortress of Calatrava

Jebel Musa, the southern Pillar of Hercules, from Ceuta. From here Tarik set up his assault on al-Andalus in 711

in La Mancha was taken the following year, protecting the route into Andalusia. Upper Andalusia was subdued with the assistance of Navarra. Meanwhile the Portuguese took Santarém and besieged Lisbon, which soon fell with the aid of an English, German and Flemish fleet that was on its way to the Holy Land. Almería fell to a joint force from Castile-León, Navarra, Aragón-Barcelona, Montpellier and Genoa. These latter events revealed the international dimension of the conflict and the importance of the navies of the maritime states in the conquest of major sea ports.

Meanwhile, the new rulers in North Africa had landed in Iberia in 1146. They subdued the Algarve in 1147 and raided as far as Badajoz and Sevilla. They took Córdoba in 1148, Málaga in 1154, Granada in 1156 and Almería in 1157. To protect the Strait's Mediterranean flank they built the first fortified city of Gibraltar in 1160, which was personally visited by their caliph who named it the Madinat al-Fath (City of Victory). Only Valencia and Murcia held out against the new Islamic wave from North Africa and support for them came from Castile-León, yet again Christian supporting Muslim against Muslim. The Christians failed to finish off the south, once again because of their own internal rivalries. It permitted the new North African power to regain control of ground lost by their predecessors. By 1174 they had retaken Trujillo.

Spectacular medieval castle at Molina de Aragon, Guadalajara

The shifting frontier, with raid and counter-raid, continued. Sometimes the Christians advanced when the North Africans had pressing troubles at home and other times Muslims advanced when the Christians busied themselves with internal dynastic rivalries. These rivalries meant that some of the Christian kingdoms actually supported the Muslims, as in 1196 when the North Africans attacked Castile with support from León and Navarra. The Christian solidarity of the second crusade had clearly dissipated. Papal intervention helped to renew the Christian offensive in 1210. The offensive opened in upper Andalusia in 1211, hitting at Baeza, Andújar and Jaén. A second Castilian offensive was launched the following year, this time supported by Aragón-Barcelona, Navarra and the French. A big clash was coming and it happened south of the pass of Despeñaperros, in the Sierra Morena. On July 16, 1212, King Alfonso VIII won a famous victory at Las Navas de Tolosa, routing the North African army. But the leaders of the two forces were dead within two years and the impetus of the advance subsided once more.

Ten years later Morocco was again in turmoil. The North African governors of al-Andalus took their chance and rebelled. Córdoba, Jaén, Baeza and Valencia declared their independence. They allied with the Castilians, who invaded Andalusia in 1225. Once

AL-ANDALUS

more, Muslims contributed to their own downfall by taking sides with the Christians and another nail had been driven into the coffin that would be sealed in Granada 267 years later. In a parallel advance the Leonese were taking the lands of Extremadura and encircling Trujillo, gaining control of the Guadiana in the process. What remained of al-Andalus was a series of small taifas: the Balearics, Valencia, the rest of Andalusia and Murcia. Aragón-Barcelona took Valencia and the Balearics shortly afterwards.

Castile and León were re-united in 1230 and the strengthened advance into Andalusia continued. The onslaught was ruthless. Úbeda fell in 1233, Córdoba in 1236, Jaén in 1246 and Sevilla in 1248. Murcia also recognised Castile-León while the Portuguese finished off resistance in the Algarve, taking Faro in 1249. Only Granada was left in Muslim hands when King Fernando III of Castile-León died in 1252.

It is during these difficult times that an opportunist Muslim adventurer declared himself king of Granada, Almería, Málaga and Jaén and founded the Nasrid dynasty that would rule the Kingdom of Granada until the fateful January day of 1492. He crowned himself Muhammad I of Granada, and ruled from 1238 to 1273. There would be 10 more Muhammads between him and Boabdil. When Jaén fell into Christian hands, Muhammad I agreed to become a vassal of the Christians. When he started construction of the immortal symbol of al-Andalus – the Alhambra – the Kingdom of Granada was already at the mercy of the Christians. The surprise is that it survived for another 250 years. This had partly to do with events across the Strait.

Something familiar was happening in Morocco. A new fundamentalist dynasty, the Merinids, was establishing itself and challenging the existing rulers. Occasionally employed as mercenary troops by their overlords, they soon became too powerful for them and conquered Marrakesh. It was a conflict between nomad and farmer, and the nomad won. The Merinids founded a new capital in the mountains of the Rif – Fez – and became the main force in North Africa until 1472, just 20 years before the fall of Granada.

We have reached the age of Alfonso X of Castile – El Sabio (the Learned) – whom we first encountered in Doñana. Conscious of the unrest that the Merinids were generating in North Africa, he pressed on with the reconquest, taking Cádiz in 1259 and Niebla (the county that would fall to the Medina Sidonias) in 1262. He carried the war into North Africa, sacking Salé on the Atlantic coast of Morocco. Muhammad I of Granada, worried about these developments, conspired with the Andalusian and Murcian population to spark a great Muslim insurrection in 1264 which the Aragonese had to put down in Murcia while Alfonso invaded Granada. Then came a reprieve thanks to personal ego. King Alfonso felt justified in claiming the title of Holy Roman Emperor and, instead of finishing off the last Muslim resistance, wasted time in France

In the Alhambra

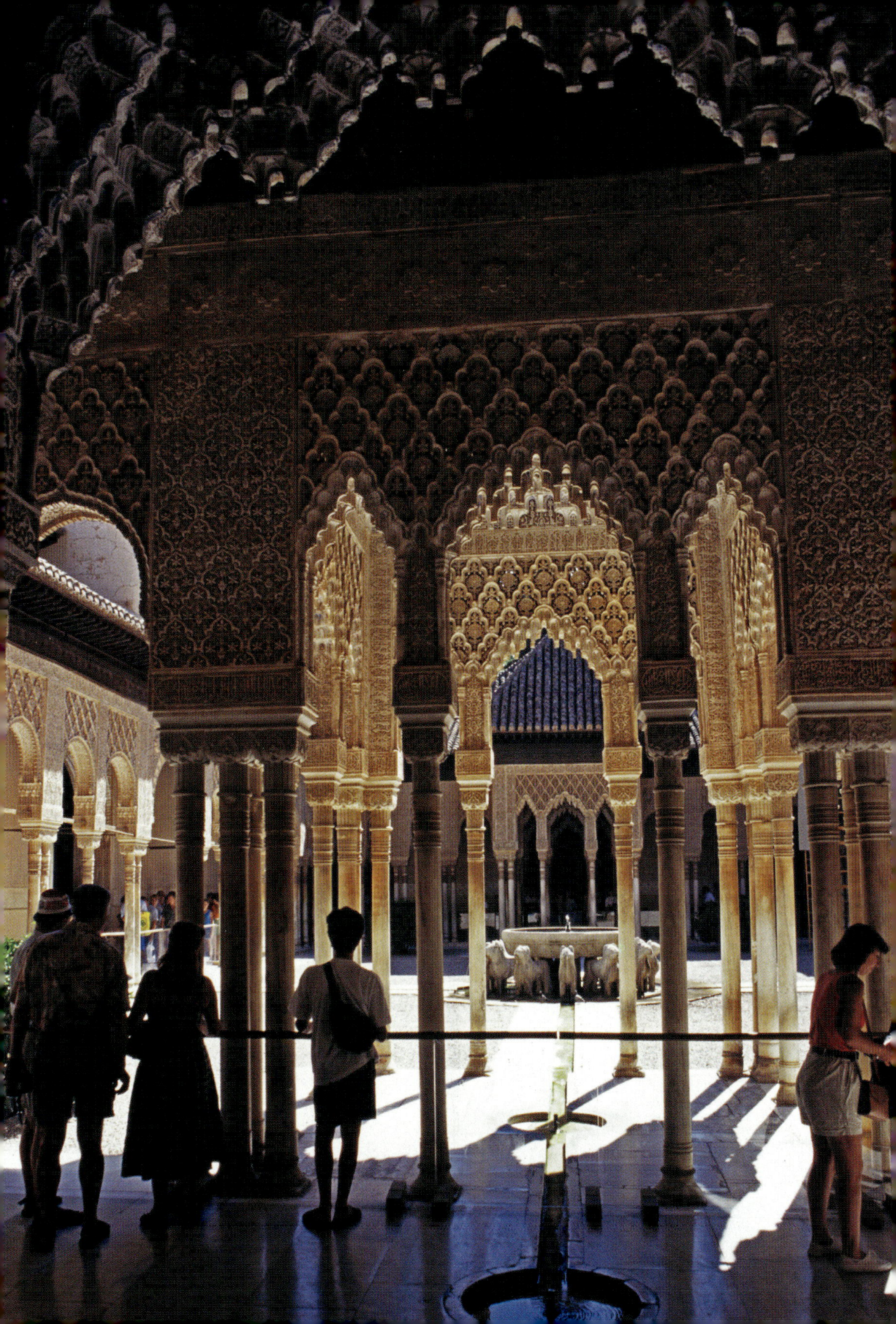

AL-ANDALUS

discussing with the Pope his unrealistic claims to the title.

It was the chance the Granada Muslims had been waiting for. In a move recalling al-Mutamid's invitation to the North Africans 189 years earlier, they ceded the ports of Tarifa and Algeciras in exchange for their support. The North Africans landed on the peninsula in 1275 and raided as far as Córdoba while the Granada Muslims threatened Jaén. The North Africans returned to Morocco with their booty but kept the Iberian ports for themselves. Now they controlled the two shores of the Strait of Gibraltar and the Battle of the Strait, the long period of fighting for control of the two shores involving all the Christian parties, North African and Granada Muslims and Genoese, had commenced. The North Africans returned to al-Andalus in 1277 and again in 1282. This was the time of the dynastic conflict between Alfonso and his son Sancho when Alfonso asked for help from North Africa. In desperation, the king who had done so much to push the Muslims out of Iberia, now invited his bitter enemy into his home. The North Africans, among them the mercenary Alonso Pérez de Guzmán, raided as far north as the Tajo. On his father's death Sancho IV came to the throne. What did he do? He called on the Muslims in Granada and his Aragonese allies to help him take Tarifa, which he did in 1292. The North African Muslims, with Granada Muslims supporting their enemy, had been kicked out of Iberia, but not for long. Two years later they returned, convinced of success by Prince Juan who was challenging Sancho, and the unsuccessful siege of Tarifa (made famous by the incident involving Guzmán's son) ensued.

In 1325, when King Alfonso XI had imposed his internal authority and reinforced the territories of Andalusia, the Granada Muslims once again called on their North African cousins for help. They retook Gibraltar, which had fallen into Christian hands, and held a territory that stretched up to Ronda while the Nasrids controlled Granada, Almería and Málaga. After the North Africans destroyed the Castilian fleet in the Strait in 1340, they crossed into Iberia with a great army, joined forces with the Granada Muslims and laid siege to Tarifa once more. The Castilians, with Portuguese support, came to the rescue and the opposing forces, for once Christian against Muslim, met at the Río Salado, south of Cádiz. The Muslims lost. The battle marked the end of the great African interventions in al-Andalus.

Two years later, Alfonso besieged Algeciras. He was helped by the Catalan fleet and crusaders attracted from far and wide, including the Earl of Derby. Chaucer chose to add the siege of Algeciras to the curriculum vitae of his knight in the prologue of the Canterbury Tales:

"...In gernade at the seege eek hadde he be
Of algezir..."

Paso de Moclin, Jaén – the gateway into Granada. The Sierra Nevada provides the backdrop

CHAPTER FIFTEEN *Meltdown*

The defending garrison used cannon, the first reported occasion when they were employed in Europe. With the fall of Algeciras, Gibraltar was left as the sole outpost of North African possessions on the northern shore of the Strait. By 1374 the weakened North Africans had left and Gibraltar went back to Granada.

Once again the impetus of Christian conquest lost energy. This was in part because Aragón was losing interest in Andalusia as it developed its Mediterranean empire that would include the Balearics, Sicily and Sardinia. The main reason the Aragonese had supported Castile in the siege of Algeciras was because they wanted to rid themselves of North African sea power that affected their maritime commerce. Meanwhile, Portugal was preoccupied with maintaining its independence and the periodic visits of the Black Death had huge demographic consequences on the population.

Granada was able to survive for a while longer by paying tribute to Castile and by playing Castile and Aragón against each other. The small kingdom had become swollen with refugees from areas conquered by the Christians. Its vital import and export trade depended on the Genoese, who had immunity at sea. Granada's inhabitants were supported by the kingdom's agriculture. By 1410 Antequera and its fertile plains were lost and much of the remainder of the kingdom, torn by internal rivalry, was in clear decline. Gibraltar fell in 1462 and the stage was set for the fall of Granada itself.

Toledo, the ancient capital of the Visigoths

Wheatear, a mountain refuge relic

CHAPTER SIXTEEN

Refuges and refugees

REFUGES AND REFUGEES

AL-ANDALUS

A poor water-carrier from Campillo de Arenas (in the Sierra Mágina of Jaén, west of the Sierra de Cazorla) was returning to his town carrying a load of skins full of vinegar on a skinny, bald donkey, half dead from starvation, when he met a stranger, who started to laugh when he saw the donkey.

"What joke is this, my friend?" exclaimed the stranger, "Is it carnival time for you to be walking like this?" "My friend," answered the sad water-carrier, "this poor animal, however ugly, earns me my bread, because I am poor and have no money to buy another." The stranger replied: "What, this filthy ass is what keeps you from starvation? Well, I don't think it will last you another week. Here, take this..."

The stranger handed a heavy bag to the water-carrier and said to him: "Go to the house of the old man Herrera, who is selling a good mule. Offer 1,500 reales for her. They are in this bag. Buy her today and don't leave it for tomorrow in case he changes his mind. If tomorrow I again find you on the track with this ugly donkey, I promise by my name, José María, that I will throw you and the donkey down the gully."

The 1,500 reales were indeed in the bag and, as the water-carrier knew what a promise from José María meant, he hurried to find Herrera and buy the handsome mule.

The following night Herrera was abruptly wakened. Shining a bright lantern in his eyes, two men thrust daggers against his chest. "Come on! Hurry! Your money!" they demanded. "Oh, poor me, I do not even have a quarter in the house," replied Herrera. "You lie. Yesterday a man from Campillo paid you 1,500 reales for a mule."

In this way the money returned to José María's hands.

This is one of many stories of the Robin Hoods of the southern Betic mountains and the Sierra Morena of 19th-century Andalusia. These bandoleros earned a reputation as violent highway robbers. The José María of our story was better known by the nickname El Tempranillo. He was born in Jauja, near Lucena in Córdoba, in 1805, and became known as "the King of Sierra Morena". Many others, like El Tragabuches, El Lero, or El Vivillo, robbed the wealthy, often as in our example to help the poor. The bandoleros rose to prominence in the context of rural Spain's extreme poverty. They became such a nuisance, and had such an impact on the economy, that Queen Isabel II was forced to create a new policing body, the Guardia Civil, founded in 1844.

The last bandolero, Juan Mingolla Gallardo, nicknamed Pasos Largos, was born in El Burgo, near Ronda, in 1874. He was killed in a shootout with the Guardia Civil on March 18, 1934, the year after the Casas Viejas uprising and two years before the start of the Spanish Civil War. For two centuries the bandoleros had terrorised waggon trains and cities. It was their knowledge of the terrain of the southern mountains of the Betic range and the Sierra Morena that allowed them their freedom. These mountains were their refuge.

In Chapter 11 we saw how the mountains of central and northern Iberia were refuges of species of plants and animals that were characteristic of temperate Europe and not the Mediterranean lands. These mountains, especially the northern ones of Cantabria

CHAPTER SIXTEEN *Refuges and refugees*

Inland stronghold of Alcalá La Real, where Queen Isabel waited for her camp to be built in Santa Fé

Bubión, a typical village of the Alpujarras

Maritime Pine forests and cliffs in Cazorla

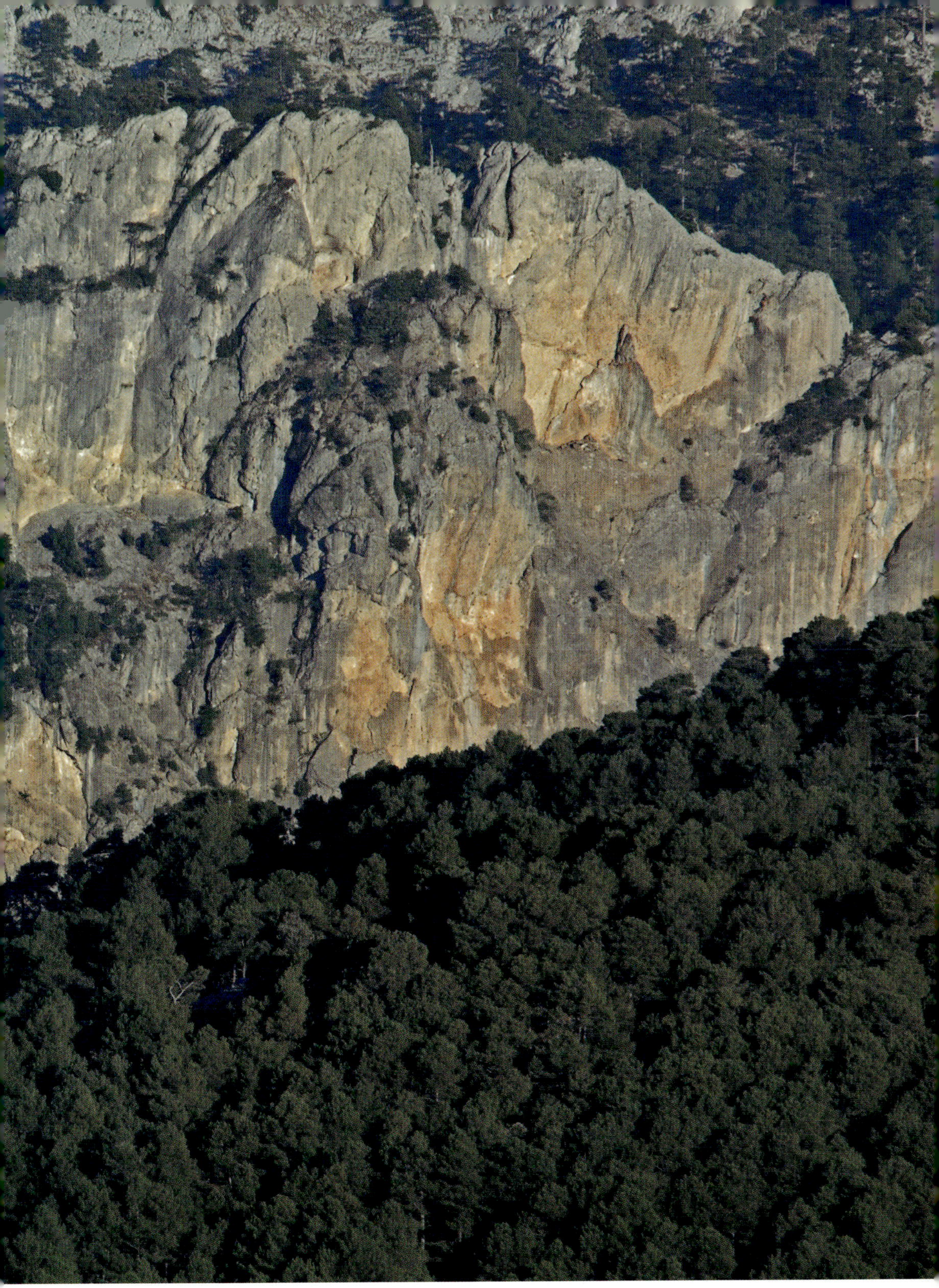

and the Pyrenees, were the stronghold of peoples who had kept their independence in the face of Roman, Visigoth and Muslim. In the south the mountain ranges are, in a way, the negative image of the northern ones. These mountains, between the Mediterranean and the Guadalquivir, form the Betic range, which runs from the limits of Andalusia with Murcia in the northeast down to the shores of the Strait of Gibraltar. They include the northeastern Sierra de Cazorla and the southwestern Serranía de Ronda. In between, master and lord of all the skies of the Iberian peninsula, is the Sierra Nevada with Mulhacén and Pico Veleta, peaks close to 3,500 metres high and loftier than any in the Pyrenees or Cantabria.

These ranges have been repeatedly isolated, as they are today, by climate. During colder periods, especially during the Ice Ages, the conditions became harsh and there were even small glaciers on the Sierra Nevada. Many species crept down the mountains and sought refuge at lower levels. In some cases they even reached the coast. In our work at Gorham's Cave we found that, during the short cold episodes between otherwise mild conditions were marked by the arrival of black pines. These trees are nowadays generally associated with the high mountains of the Betic range. In Cazorla they replace the maritime pine above 1,200 metres. Although this distribution may have something to do with human activities, there can be no doubt that their presence in Gibraltar, hundreds of kilometres from their present home and over a thousand metres lower, reflects a climatic cooling.

Once climate was warmer, these trees retreated up the slopes and remained to the present on their elevated islands. A classic example of such a restricted distribution is that of the pinsapo. This is a species of fir tree that is endemic to Andalusia, growing only on the cooler north-facing slopes above a thousand metres. Once it must have had a wider distribution across these sierras but, as the climate ameliorated, it went up the mountains and became cut off from other populations. The hand of man may have made matters worse, we do not know. The result is that the pinsapo is only found on three mountains in the Betic range, on the slopes behind Grazalema, in Cádiz province, in the Sierra Bermeja behind Estepona and in the Sierra de Las Nieves, southeast from Ronda. That is its world distribution. It is a jewel that has made it to the present-day but its existence is precarious. In an age of forest fires, imagine what would happen if an inferno raged across one of the pinsapo's haunts.

Sierra de Las Nieves is an excellent place to find some of these mountain jewels, among them some very interesting birds. Two, in particular, may seem unspectacular to the northern birdwatcher, but they are very special when we understand how they got here. They are the skylark and the wheatear. Both are very common birds in northern Europe. The skylark is a resident or partially migratory species while the wheatear is fully migratory, spending the winter in tropical Africa. In Andalusia you can see skylarks and wheatears almost everywhere, from the plains of La Janda to the valley of the Guadalquivir. The question is when do we see them there? The skylark is abundant

CHAPTER SIXTEEN *Refuges and refugees*

Mountain landscape on the southern slopes of the Sierra Nevada

Sunrise over the peaks of the Sierra Nevada

in the lowlands in the winter. These are skylarks that are escaping the cold of the European winter and they do very well in Andalusia. Come February and March, all these skylarks disappear back north and the fields are left empty. Not quite. If you go to the heights of Sierra de Las Nieves or Sierra Nevada you will hear the song of the skylark. Up here the birds find islands of habitat that are akin to their northern haunts and they stay to breed.

Something similar happens with the wheatear. You can find these birds almost anywhere in Andalusia during the migration seasons, but the birds do not stay. Go to the tops of the high Betics and you will find large numbers nesting in the company of the skylarks. Look closely and you will see that they are quite different from the European ones that you saw on migration. These are paler and appear to be genetically differentiated from their northern cousins. Isolation is drifting these birds in a direction that may, one remote day in the future, turn them into a new species.

These are two examples of the jewels that isolation in the mountains of the south has produced. Talk to the botanists and they will rattle a long list of plants that are unique to these mountains. Talk to the entomologists and they will tell you the same of butterflies, moths and beetles. There are even reptiles and amphibians that have made the jump to new species as a result of isolation on mountain islands.

Is it any surprise then that the last stronghold of the Muslims in al-Andalus should have been in these mountains? The historical process I described in Chapter 15 ended here. I gave political and military reasons why the course of conquest of these mountains took so long. My hunch is that the geography of the southern Betics, permitting people to maintain a rich agricultural economy and find myriad defensible refuges, had just as much to do with it. We have here almost a mirror image of the Cantabrian mountains. When the Arabs and Berbers got there in the eighth century, conquest was probably considered too difficult and not worth the effort. The presence of people willing to defend the land and with an intimate knowledge of the mountains sealed the decision and the Muslims moved on in another direction. Centuries later, the people who had originated in these northern mountains reached the south and faced a people who had lived in the southern mountains for a long time. These people were able to defend these strongholds and the risk and cost of taking them by storm was not worth the effort. Instead, an uneasy balance was struck. It was profitable for the attackers as they received economic benefit in the form of tribute. It was profitable for the defenders because it assured their autonomy. The final onslaught, much later, was prompted by over-riding issues of politics and religion.

A walk up the southern slopes of the Sierra Nevada, from the mountain village of Capileira towards the Mulhacén and Veleta peaks gives us an idea of the importance of this land. In the distance, to the south, the blue Mediterranean Sea is not that far away even as we pass the tree line and reach the snow fields. Within a relatively short distance we have a range of climates from the almost sub-tropical of the coast to the Alpine of

CHAPTER SIXTEEN *Refuges and refugees*

Part of the captive breeding programme of the Bearded Vulture in Cazorla

The Chough is a characteristic bird of the mountain refugia of Iberia. This bird is reaching its roost at sunset in the Tajo de Ronda

the peaks. This diversity in a short space is a treasure. For a rural community, like the Muslim one that lived here, it meant that a range of crops could be grown on the slopes. It also meant that the same crops could be grown in sequence on the slopes as the spring advanced, first as spring arrived in January on the coast and gradually upwards until it reached the high ground in July.

An inescapable sound as you trek up the slopes is that of running water. Deep water channels have been dug into the ground and trap the water from the melting snow in the spring. The water descends by gravity and is distributed to the terraced fields as required through secondary channels. A perfect example of efficiency, the waterways are used by the farmers of the Alpujarras, the southern slopes of the Sierra Nevada. The channels, made by the Muslim people of the Kingdom of Granada, have stood the test of time in a manner that few 21st-century engineering designs could hope to match. The slopes of the Alpujarras were the agricultural mainstay of the Nasrid kingdom. When Granada fell in 1492 many Muslims remained in the Alpujarras. They were allowed to stay because they had a knowledge that was useful to the conquerors but they had to do so at a price: conversion to Christianity. This was a new step as in Christian-conquered lands the Muslims (known as Mudéjars) had until then been allowed to practise Islam, albeit with limitations.

The Muslims had been promised freedom of religion by the Treaty of Granada, but when Cardinal Cisneros took over in Granada he introduced a much more fanatical and stricter approach than his predecessor. It included organised mass conversions and the burning of Arabic religious texts. This provoked an uprising in the Alpujarras in 1499-1500 which took until 1502 to quell. The Moriscos (a derogatory term meaning little Moors, replacing Mudéjar) were given the ultimatum to convert to Catholicism or leave the country. Forced with the choice, most converted but they continued to practise their faith under cover. Having nominally converted to Catholicism, they were now under the jurisdiction of the Inquisition.

Then in 1567 the relative calm of the preceding 65 years was broken when King Felipe II issued an edict that required the Moriscos to give up their traditions, including their Muslim names and dress and the use of Arabic. Even worse, they would be required to give up their children so that they could be educated by Catholic priests. The outcome was inevitably a second uprising in the Alpujarras and the Axarquía, the mountains west of the Alpujarras on the slopes behind Málaga in the area of Frigiliana, Bentomiz and Cómpeta, which lasted from 1568 to 1570. Part of the argument for the Catholic action was the supposed conspiracy between the Moriscos and the Ottoman Turks, so the entire episode had a wider geopolitical undertone.

Don Juan de Austria, half-brother of Felipe II, led the brutal repression, aided by many

The Fan Palm is the only native palm to Europe, having survived the Ice Ages in southern mountain refuges

CHAPTER SIXTEEN *Refuges and refugees*

nobles including the Duke of Medina Sidonia. A year after quashing the rebellion Don Juan led the Holy League's fleet to victory against the Ottomans and Barbary Corsairs at the Battle of Lepanto. The repression of the Alpujarras rebellion was brutal. Among the atrocities, in what amounted to a 16th-century ethnic cleansing on a massive scale, Don Juan slaughtered 2,500 Moriscos, including women and children, and then proceeded to raze the town of Galera and sprinkle it with salt.

The contemporary narrator Mármol Carvajal gives us chilling descriptions of what went on in the Alpujarras. The army distributed itself in loose bands with the orders to "…run across the land, cut down the wheat fields and do as much damage as possible to the enemy…to finish by wrenching them from the land so that they would not return, and to try to behead all those that they came across."

On September 22 they had "…brought to the country (of Cádiar) 1,100 women slaves and around 500 Moors were killed, having taken from them large quantities of cattle and baggage." Two days later, having razed the countryside across the Alpujarras, they "…brought back 200 Moorish women having killed 800 men." The following day an escort went to bring supplies from the Calahorra (defensive tower) and "…took away more than a 1,000 Moorish women, having beheaded another 400 men and done justice to 36."

In the last days of the uprising, even the Moriscos who had turned themselves in were killed. In a moving account of the outcome of these events in the Axarquía, the modern historian Antonio Navas Acosta described the scene at the end of the uprising: "The Morisco eradication from Bentomiz (the Axarquía) was truly a holocaust: the fields remained silent, the trees shattered, the roads broken, the towns dead and desolate. Many of them like Benescaler, Zucheila, Periana or the eminent Batarxis among others, never recovered their population; their ruins and walls remained for ever converted into ghostly places and its people persecuted to the very end."

It is estimated that around 80,000 Moriscos were forcibly resettled in other parts of Spain, mainly Valencia, and replaced by Christians who settled in the new lands south of Granada. It was the beginning of the end. By 1582 mass expulsion from Spain was being considered by Felipe II. Concern regarding the economic impact of such an expulsion, with the consequent loss of skills and agricultural manpower, delayed the eventual outcome, but it finally came in the reign of Felipe III.

In January, 1608, 116 years after the fall of Granada, a Council of State unanimously approved the expulsion of the Moriscos. The decree was signed by the king a year later. The order was announced on September 11, 1609, and the first galleons, laden with Moriscos, left Denia on October 2. It was the start of a humiliating and painful process. Many were taken to North Africa, others chose Genoa, yet others France, Sicily

Snowfall over a Pinsapo forest in Sierra Bermeja, Málaga

CHAPTER SIXTEEN *Refuges and refugees*

Dense woodland with relict Tertiary flora including Rhoddodendron. Sierra de Ojén, Cádiz

and Constantinople. They were not always welcome where they went and were often the subject of abuse, given their precarious circumstances. A contemporary Christian estimate put the figure of Moriscos who were killed resisting expulsion at 50,000 between October, 1609, and July, 1611. Another 60,000 died during the journey or on reaching their destination.

Estimates of the numbers expelled vary, but the figure of 600,000 is consistent with contemporary accounts. If so it represented around eight per cent of the entire population of Spain at that time. The desolation after the Alpujarras revolt paled into insignificance with the scene in many villages that remained uninhabited and the surrounding countryside that went fallow. Valencia lost a third of its population and almost half the villages were abandoned by 1638.

The architect behind the expulsion was Felipe's first minister, the Duke of Lerma, a man whose antiquated policies were based in feudal ideas. In 1607 the monarchy had declared itself bankrupt, but Lerma continued to pursue policies that would continue to sink the nation. The expulsion of the Moriscos was such a policy, which was based on political and religious motives without economic considerations. Behind Lerma was the Catholic Church of Spain. Among the chief instigators was the Archbishop of Valencia, Juan de

Semi-arid landscape, East Alpujarra, Granada

Ribera.

For Ribera, a major argument in justifying the expulsion was demographic. If Felipe III did not act with speed, he warned in 1602, Christians would soon be outnumbered by Moriscos. It was a line that was vigorously pursued until the king was convinced and the decision to expel the Moriscos was taken. Ribera's original intention, approved by the Council of State in 1609, had been to take all Morisco children under the age of 10 away from their parents and retain them in Spain (the age was shortly afterwards reduced to five). In this way they would be educated by priests or trusted Christians. The children would serve the Christians until they reached the age of 25 to 30 and would receive food, clothing and lodging in return. Ribera's policy also included that suckling babies were taken from their mothers and given to Christian wet nurses. Less than a year later, in 1610, the Catholic Church in Spain recommended that Morisco children over the age of seven should be sold as perpetual slaves to Christians, arguing that slavery was morally justified and spiritually beneficial. These actions seem to have been overlooked, or forgiven, when Juan de Ribera was canonised by Pope John XXIII in 1959...

Among the expelled Moriscos a number joined the ranks of the Barbary pirates, based in Salé on the Atlantic coast of Morocco, and participated in the raids on the Spanish

Grazalema (Cádiz) in the western betics has Spain's highest rainfall.

coast.
More than 100 years later the Catholic Church continued to influence government policy towards Moriscos and Jews. In Article X of the 1713 Treaty of Utrecht, marking the end of the War of Spanish Succession, the Catholic king of Spain ceded Gibraltar to the British Crown. A new power and a new religion, Protestantism, had entered the fray of Iberian politics. Emphasis was given to the restriction of Moors and Jews from living in Gibraltar, which was seen as a door they could use to re-enter Catholic Spain.

The relevant passage of the treaty is worth reproducing here: "And Her Britannic Majesty, at the request of the Catholic King, does consent and agree, that no leave shall be given under any pretence whatsoever, either to Jews or Moors, to reside or have their dwellings in the said town of Gibraltar; and that no refuge or shelter be allowed to any Moorish ships of war in the harbour of the said town, whereby communication between Spain and Ceuta may be obstructed, or the coasts of Spain be infested by the excursions of the Moors.

"But whereas treaties of friendship and a liberty and intercourse of commerce (exist) between the British and certain territories situated on the coast of Africa, it is always to be understood, that the British subjects cannot refuse the Moors and their ships entry

In the extreme west, the Betic Mountains face the Atlantic Ocean

into the port of Gibraltar purely upon the account of merchandising. Her Majesty the Queen of Great Britain does further promise, that the free exercise of their religion shall be indulged to the Roman Catholic inhabitants of the aforesaid town."

In the years to come Moors and Jews became the trading lifeline of Gibraltar's British garrison and many Sephardic Jews, in particular, settled there, back in a tiny refuge on the peninsula from which they had been expelled. They have lived there to the present day.

Fallow Deer are introduced into Iberia where they thrive in forested environments

EDEN LOST

CHAPTER SEVENTEEN

Eden lost

AL-ANDALUS

At the start of this book I put forward a paradox. Using the wolf as an indicator, I asked how could present-day al-Andalus be so ecologically rich and yet so poor at the same time? The answer lies within these pages and it is time to bring it all together to seek an answer to my question.

As far as we are able to tell, the wolf has been a part of the fauna of the Iberian peninsula for a very long time. It was one of a diverse group of carnivorous mammals that thrived in the savannahs and woodlands of prehistoric Iberia. We find the wolf, along with spotted hyena, leopard, brown bear, Spanish lynx, wild cat and fox in the ancient archaeological levels at Gorham's Cave in Gibraltar that reach back to 120,000 years ago. This was a modern fauna, with species still around today, which had gradually emerged out of an ancient world of mega-mammals that lived across Eurasia more than a million years ago. These carnivorous mammals were very widely distributed. They tolerated large changes in climate as long as there was food, and there certainly was no shortage of that in those early woodlands of Europe. Their ancestors predated the arrival of the first humans in Europe around 1.8 million years ago and in the Iberian peninsula, the future al-Andalus, around 1.2 million years ago. When our ancestors arrived in Iberia for the first time, wolves, of some description, were already roaming across the pristine countryside.

The food these carnivores hunted and scavenged was in the form of large packages of meat, weighing anything between 100 kilograms to more than a ton. These were the mega-herbivores of Eurasia and they were more sensitive to climate change than the carnivores. There were those that lived in the treeless tundra, like the reindeer and the musk ox; there were those that lived in the dry steppe, like the steppe bison and the saiga antelope; and there were those that lived in the warm savannahs of temperate Europe, like the red deer and the wild boar. The violent and rapid climate changes of Pleistocene Europe, the long period between 2,000,000 and 10,000 years ago, certainly make the current climatic worries appear minor in comparison.

It often became very cold across Europe. Ice sheets reached southern England and much of France eastwards was a barren waste of frozen ground with, at best, a cover of short, seasonal, growth that has been described as tundra-steppe. In this environment the kings of the herbivores, the woolly mammoths and woolly rhinos, thrived. The tundra-steppe penetrated into the Iberian peninsula when it got really cold and the animals followed. Our fossil evidence, and that from identifiable animals painted by prehistoric people in cave walls, tells us that the mammoth, the rhino, the reindeer and others reached deep into the heart of the high tablelands north of present-day Madrid. The high altitude and northerly position of these lands permitted the European Ice Age intrusion into Iberia but it went no further.

The Barbary Macaque, or Rock Ape, was introduced into Gibraltar by the British in the 18th century

CHAPTER SEVENTEEN *Eden Lost*

The Mediterranean Chamaleon is an introduced species that survives in the warm coastal strip of Iberia

To the south, especially along the coasts of the southwest, heat-loving animals and plants survived the onslaught. In the drier southeast, around present-day Almería and Murcia, plants able to cope with aridity fared best. Among the survivors were humans, the Neanderthals, who managed to stake out an outpost in Gibraltar and the surrounding areas. The mildness of the climate and the consequent ecological richness of these lands allowed the extension of the Neanderthal lineage by several thousand years after they had disappeared from the rest of the continent.

Climate and climate change are then the first factors to take into account. The violence and speed of change of the Pleistocene caused massive redistribution of species and many extinctions. The scale of these rearrangements and losses fell dramatically from 10,000 years ago when the climate warmed up.

We have not known a full-blown Ice Age, medieval Little Ice Age apart, since then. Climate caused the extinction of the woolly mammoth and the woolly rhinoceros just as it had caused other extinctions in earlier Ice Ages, but many animals remained. Some, like the reindeer, simply abandoned Iberia for the Arctic, but many stayed to form part of the typical Iberian fauna, including the wolf and all the other carnivores. Yes, the spotted hyena, the leopard and probably the lion were also part of that fauna.

The Iberian Wall Lizard is an endemic of Iberia

Once the climate settled around 10,000 years ago, the regime we have observed across Iberia was established. With the exception of Cantabria and the Pyrenees in the north, the Iberian climate was Mediterranean with its characteristic summer dry season. This climate was modulated by the second factor that we need to take into account: geography. The pressure that the African tectonic plate put on this peninsula, as it pushed north and collided with Europe, was great. Although settled by now to some degree, this process has by no means stopped altogether. As an example, the Rock of Gibraltar is still rising, albeit at a much slower rate than a million years ago, as the continents continue their geological conflict. The result of this pressure has been the elevation of land that was formerly sea-bed to form great limestone mountain chains. These relatively young and un-eroded mountains reach great heights. The range of altitude in Iberia is second to none in Europe. It is responsible for the climatic and ecological diversity to be found over short distances.

The topographic heterogeneity of Iberia, superimposed on the latitude range in what is effectively a mini-continent, has generated a land that is ecologically rich and diverse like no other in Europe. The distribution of the high mountains was also responsible for another feature that became important for wildlife and human affairs. This was the

AL-ANDALUS

alignment of its major rivers. Four of the five great Iberian rivers flow west, traversing great distances to reach the Atlantic. They are blocked from flowing into the nearby Mediterranean by the high mountains that run northeast from the Strait of Gibraltar to Cazorla and then north along the Mediterranean coast to the very doorstep of the Pyrenees. The rivers that break into the Mediterranean travel very short distances across steep gradients which make them un-navigable. The exception is the Ebro that broke through from the northern Cantabrian mountains and generated the only major Iberian delta with its rich ecology. The others flowed westwards and contributed to the ecological richness of this land, generating large inland shallow lakes, as in the Tablas de Daimiel, when the shallow gradient of La Mancha combined with the winter rains to promote overspill.

The peculiar mix of climate and geography in a large peninsula thus created an ecological paradise without rival in Europe. Its geographical and climatic isolation from Europe north of the Pyrenees promoted the formation of unique endemic forms of life. Let us take a look at the vertebrate animals to illustrate this richness and uniqueness. The birds are the best studied and we can look at these in some detail as population estimates are available for the whole of Europe. The main species are listed in Appendix 1 at the end of the book.

One hundred and seventy species have Iberian breeding bird populations that place them in the top 10 in Europe. Of these, the size of the breeding populations of no fewer than 107 species (16 of which are found nowhere else) ranks them number one in Europe. Iberia is truly a reservoir of bird diversity and of some of the largest populations in Europe. The species with their strongholds here reflect the peninsula's ecological diversity. Let us look at the top 106 in a little more detail.

Birds that nest in rocky habitats, sand banks or in the urban environment dominate. They account for 32 species, of which four are exclusive to the peninsula. A similar number of species (three of them exclusive to Iberia) nest in trees, either in forests or the more open woodland including the dehesas. Some way behind are the birds of the plains and desert regions with 19, including three unique to Iberia. Next are species that nest in wetland and coastal aquatic environments with 13 species, of which four are unique. Finally, we have birds of shrublands with 11 species, including two unique ones. In sum they represent the ecological diversity of Iberia that we have discovered throughout the chapters of this book.

The main species of other vertebrate groups are listed in Appendix 2. Some species are unique to the peninsula and show a highly localised distribution. Here I include seven species of freshwater fish. Five of them are localised along the major rivers that run west into the Atlantic while the other two are coastal in eastern Spain. For these species,

The Moorish Gecko is an introduction from Morocco that has thrived in the warm climate of southern Iberia

CHAPTER SEVENTEEN *Eden Lost*

the major rivers, separated from each other by vast tracts of land, have been islands with the only possible contact being along the coasts. There are four localised amphibian endemics, five reptiles and four mammals.

Other endemics are more widespread and occupy larger areas of Iberia. They are a river fish, three amphibians and five reptiles. Similar to this group is one that has species that are almost totally Iberian but with populations that have managed to filter into Mediterranean areas of France. They are two freshwater fish species, five amphibians, six reptiles and three mammals. The contrast is provided by the European fauna that manages to penetrate into the Euro-Siberian areas of the Pyrenees, Cantabria and, in some cases, mountain peaks further south. They are six freshwater fish, five amphibians, 10 reptiles and 22 mammals. Where European and Mediterranean species meet, at the interface of major bioclimates as on the edge of the Cantabrian mountains or in the Gredos, the local ecological diversity is impressive.

Another factor comes into play in producing diversity, an unexpected one. It is Man who has added to the diversity by introducing species from outside which had not reached the peninsula but were perfectly capable of living in its climates. The process was especially prominent in Roman and Muslim times. Among the most obvious introductions, that have become widespread and successful, are the spur-thighed tortoise, Moorish and Turkish geckoes, Mediterranean chameleon, Algerian hedgehog, Egyptian mongoose, genet and fallow deer. Perhaps the best known of all is the Barbary macaque, a tailless monkey that has been misnamed Rock ape. It once roamed as far north as Germany and the British Isles but went extinct as the climate of the Ice Ages left it only in the milder parts of North Africa. The present population of Gibraltar macaques was introduced from Morocco by the British as pets during the 18th century. Some escaped and their descendants live in a semi-wild state on the Rock.

Unfortunately, Man's activities have had more to do with the deterioration of Iberia's ecological richness than its enrichment. He has become the main agent of large-scale ecological change in the past 10,000 years, causing huge alterations in habitat and loss of species that can only be compared to the massive changes of the Ice Ages. The speed of this activity has been unprecedented. Having answered the first part of the paradoxical question, why Iberia is so ecologically rich, I now turn to the other part: why has it deteriorated to the degree that the wolf is now practically absent from most of its former territories?

It all started around 7,500 years ago when the Neolithic culture, with its production economy based on agriculture and farming, reached the Iberian peninsula from the Middle East. The Neolithic people that lived along the coast around 5,400 BC, as in Gibraltar, continued the fishing traditions of their Palaeolithic predecessors. Theirs was a subsistence economy based on the carrying capacity of the environment, and it was sustainable. Others were living from a hunting economy based around the rich wetlands of La Janda, catching birds and mammals that were attracted to these special habitats,

CHAPTER SEVENTEEN *Eden Lost*

The Thekla lark is an Iberian endemic that evolved in isolation during the Ice Ages

The woodchat shrike is a typical trans-Saharan migrant that breeds in Mediterranean in the spring

AL-ANDALUS

and painting the animals that they saw on the walls of the Tajo de las Figuras. At about the same time people were beginning to farm inland, as in the Sierra de Baza, marking the beginning of Man's impact on the environment of the future al-Andalus.

By the fourth millennium we find clear evidence of human activity on the landscape. At Gorafe people were building large megaliths. Between 3,800 and 2,700 BC climate changed from a humid period to an increasingly arid one and suspicion grows that all was not due to natural climate change.

Man's impact is clear by 3,000 BC as a result of large-scale mining in the Tinto and Odiel rivers in Huelva. A new dimension is the possible first contact of Bronze Age eastern Mediterranean mariners with local Iberian people, as suggested by the presence of foreign amber in Gibraltar some time between 2,265 and 1,505 BC. There is evidence of the intensification of agriculture around 2,100 BC and the increasing impact of spreading forest fires probably associated with land clearance as the Argaric culture developed locally in the southeast. This culture collapsed around 1,500 BC and was followed by a period of large-scale mining and the development of large towns by the Iberians between 1,300 BC and the arrival of the Romans in the third century BC. During this period, from the eighth century BC, the coastal people of Iberia established direct contact with Phoenician, and later Carthaginian, mariners from the east. It was a time of commercial intensification and absorption of new ideas and technologies brought by sea from the eastern Mediterranean. The mining kingdom of Tartessos, by the estuaries of the Tinto and Odiel, profited from the exchange and we can assume that the new demand for precious metals was the catalyst of the mining process. By the time the Romans reached Iberia, there were evident signs of human modification of large areas of the landscape.

On the rich coasts of the Strait the early commercialisation of fish reached industrial proportions with the Romans and the establishment of factories for the large-scale processing of fish and the manufacture of garum, along with the allied industries of salt extraction and the manufacture of amphorae. The industrial exploitation of the sea carried on into the sixth century AD. It never disappeared altogether under Muslim rule. By the end of the 13th century Fernando IV granted Guzmán the right to exploit the fisheries between the border with Portugal and the Strait of Gibraltar. It marked the start of the almadrabas of the successive Dukes of Medina Sidonia.

The deforestation and exploitation of the tablelands was a gradual process. Between 748 and 754 AD a series of famines caused depopulation of vast areas of meseta which probably slowed down the process of human impact on the landscape. Between the 10th and 14th centuries the growing but landlocked Castilian kingdom, without access to the sea, developed the industrial exploitation of salt mines in the lakes around Villafáfila.

Spring starts early in the extreme south. The paper-white narcissus flowers at Christmas

CHAPTER SEVENTEEN *Eden Lost*

The 14th century was a period when industrial exploitation of natural products seems to have intensified. The exploitation of salt came under royal monopoly in Castile and the Portuguese started to exploit the cork oak for the tanning industry. Even so, herds of semi-wild cattle roamed the forested Guadalquivir valley, providing ample food for its wolves.

Things took a definite turn for the worse between the 16th and 18th centuries. This period marked the fragmentation of the forests of the Guadalquivir valley to be replaced by treeless expanses devoted to cereals and other agriculture. The forests of the sierras were cut back to build galleons; much of the Invincible Armada of 1588 was made from the broad-leafed woods of central and southern Spain. It was during this time that we can measure the impact of human action on a species. In the 16th century the greater flamingo abandoned the Ebro delta as a breeding ground and the mid-17th century saw the massive deforestation of Doñana, but there was also concern over the conservation of hunting grounds. King Felipe II visited Daimiel in 1575 and urged its protection. Active measures towards reforestation took place during the 18th century. The systematic plantation of the stone pine started in Doñana in 1737. The cork stopper industry developed from 1750 and took off during the second half of the century, reaching Extremadura in the 1830s and Andalusia in the 1840s. Inadvertently, the cork oak forests gained protection because of their economic importance. Despite this protection, large areas of cork oak forest were still being wiped out in the Serranía de Ronda at the end of the 19th century to supply the tanning industry. Large tracts of woodland also went in the Sierra Morena to supply charcoal and the mining industry. On a local scale, the end of the 18th century marked the start of a different form of mining, this time by the excavation of galleries for the placing of artillery pieces inside the Rock of Gibraltar. The success of the enterprise promoted the large-scale tunnelling inside the Rock during the Second World War.

The first attempts to drain Spain's largest lake, La Janda, began between 1825 and 1838. It marked the start of a bleak period of drainage of wetlands that intensified during the 20th century and ended with the loss of many lakes and marshes and that of La Janda in the 1960s. On a par was the dire situation in Daimiel which, despite Felipe II's 16th-century plea, suffered greatly from drainage schemes – to the point of almost no return at the time of writing these lines.

The mountains fared better for a time, in spite of the deforestation, but hunting pressure killed off the Pyrenean and Portuguese forms of ibex by 1900. Over-hunting pushed many species to the brink of extinction. The use of poisoned baits spelled the end of the wolf, already on its knees because of habitat loss and persecution, during the first decades of the 20th century. The bearded vulture suffered the consequences of this activity and just managed to hang on in the mountain refuge of the Pyrenees. The great bustard, once abundant on the southern plains of Andalusia, was lost there when the last surviving male hit an electric pylon in La Janda on April 10, 2006.

The Spanish festoon is a beautiful Iberian butterfly

Wetland species suffered the worst fate and many disappeared from the Iberian lakes altogether during the 20th century. One species, the white-headed duck, was on the edge of the precipice in the 1970s but managed to recover because of protection of its lake habitat in Córdoba. Its case gives us optimism in an otherwise painful story of destruction, showing us that the efforts of a few caring individuals can make a difference. The first example of such selfless efforts was the protection of the remaining populations of the Spanish ibex in Gredos and the southern ranges.

So now we have the answer to the second part of the question. The deterioration of al-Andalus is a millennial story, starting 7,000 years ago, in which humans have played a central role. The size of Iberia, its many high mountains and the richness of its coastal waters have permitted the survival of many species despite the attrition they have suffered over such a long time. So the peninsula remains a rich land but, in comparison with the Iberia of times past, it is highly impoverished. The faint hope for the future comes from the efforts of individuals and collectives, but they work against the tide of development and economic growth…

On a visit to Cazorla I am greeted by a biologist who is going to show me something special. A 10-kilometre drive along forest track brings us to a mountain glade, the Nava de San Pedro, where we leave our vehicle and walk along a small path through the woods. A dog barks in the distance and we see a fence and some discrete buildings within the trees. The friendly dog greets us as we climb towards a complex of large wooden aviaries. Looking towards the covered end of one such cage, I sigh in awe. Two gigantic bearded vultures sit quietly in the shade, staring at me with those penetrating eyes that have captivated naturalists for centuries.

This is the site of a successful breeding programme and the cages have a number of bearded vultures of all ages. The programme, based on sound conservation practice, does not aim to release birds before solving the problem that caused their extinction from these mountains in the first place. In parallel with the captive breeding programme, members of the Gypaetus Foundation have pursued an active public campaign aimed at increasing awareness of the species and preventing the continued use of poisoned baits by goatherds. In 2006 the first three young bearded vultures were released into the wild. Two more were released in 2007. In this time one made it to the population of the Pyrenees and one from the Pyrenees reached the Cazorla group, showing the scale on which these birds operate and the opportunities for birds of the two populations to breed. It gives us hope for the future of the bearded vulture. It gives us hope for the future of wild al-Andalus.

Clash of religions in the Córdoba mosque-cathedral

ORIGINAL SIN

CHAPTER EIGHTEEN

Original sin

AL-ANDALUS

When we began this journey through al-Andalus, I described the drive from the forests of Cazorla down to the olive deserts of Jaén. In my desperation I turned back and sought refuge in the mountains. There, amid the incessant trill of the Bonelli's warbler and the reassuring silhouettes of the griffon vultures overhead, I felt comfortable and safe. I was in an island surrounded by encroaching civilisation. I reflected on how many times plants, animals and people had found serenity in these mountains – and a home.

In Chapter 1 I asked what the story of al-Andalus could tell us about ourselves and the situation we face today? I have answered this in part in the previous chapter. Here I want to analyse our own nature and how it has changed, if at all, through time. To do so I will pick from examples in the preceding chapters.

The young Cambridge students, Atkinson & Co. embodied the adventurous, carefree spirit of humankind. It is the innate spirit of the hunt, evolved into our genes over millions of years. Within it is a deep sense of reverence for the prey, be it an animal actually hunted or one that was simply, as in their case, to be photographed. We also see it in the boundless, child-like energy of Abel Chapman or Willoughby Verner. Imagine the conditions of Spain just before the Civil War. Yet here were three young men, unable to speak Spanish and knowing nothing of local customs, willing to go to any extreme to be the first to photograph a vulture. There was no gain to be had from the venture except for the glory of the achievement. It is a refreshing contrast to other aspects of human nature that has dominated the greater part of the story of al-Andalus.

Prejudice has all too often dictated human action and it has often had dire consequences. The widespread poisoning of the wolf may have found its justification in the loss of a few lambs and the carnivore's reputation, which even finds its way into our fairy tales. Much of this reputation was unfounded or caused by our invading its lands and exposing our naïve domesticates to an intelligent predator, but was this sufficient reason for us to wipe it out from almost every corner? Worse still, in the process or directly through unfounded intolerance, we poisoned the majestic bearded vulture out of existence in our skies. A poor, harmless scavenger was eliminated on account of its supposed predatory habits and killing of lambs. It was totally without basis, but we have been left to pick up the pieces of this crime. Do we learn? It seems not. After all why is the equally harmless Egyptian vulture heading for extinction in 21st-century Iberia for similar reasons to the bearded vulture 100 years ago?

Chance and historical contingency have been responsible for many stories unravelled in this book. Had the Irishman William Garvey Power not decided to come to Jerez in the 18th century and had Guzmán El Bueno not defended Tarifa at the expense of his son's life, then the 19th Duke of Medina Sidonia would not have owned Doñana and been in

Synagogue in Córdoba. At the height of its splendour, Muslim, Christian and Jew lived side by side in Córdoba.

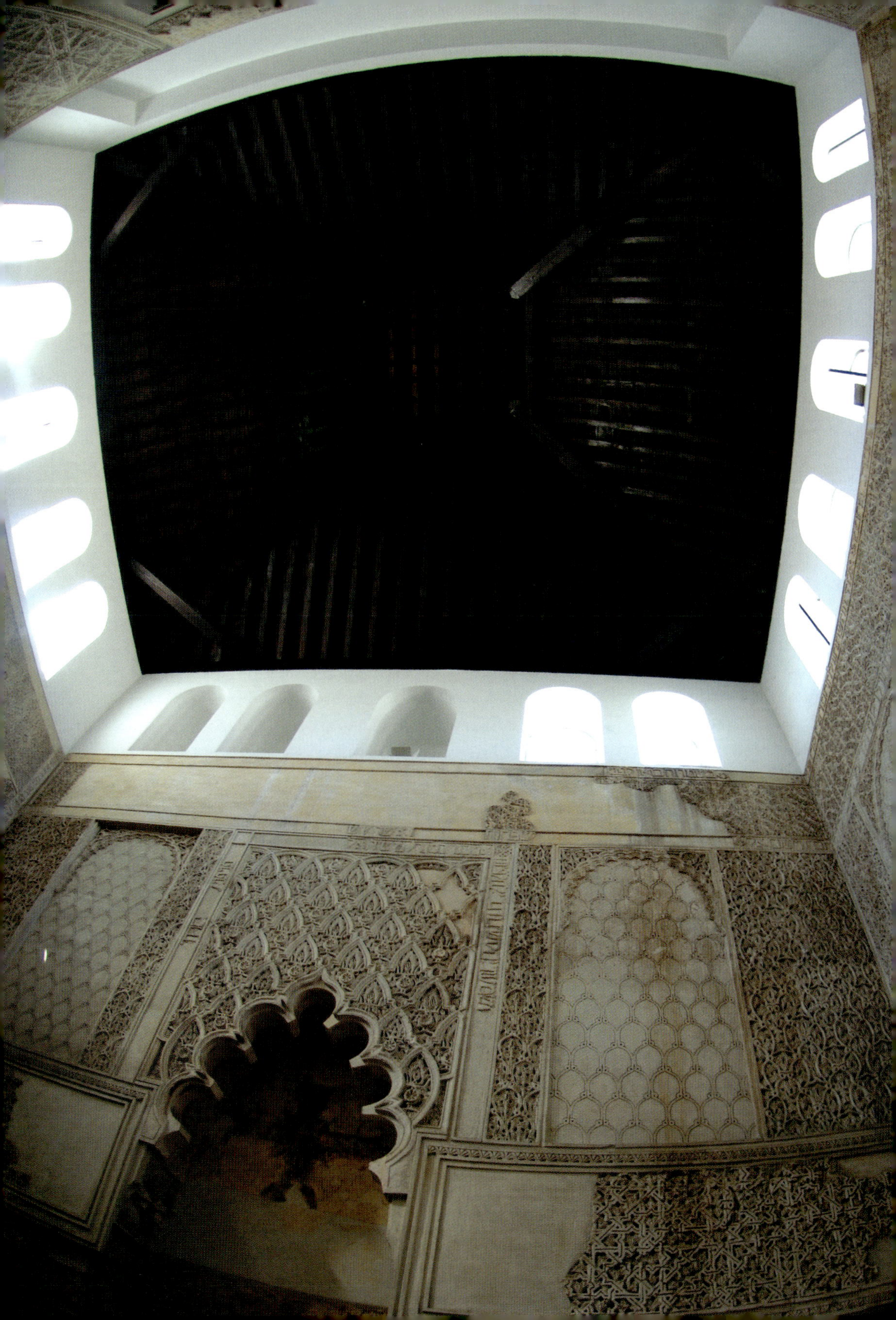

a position to sell it to Garvey's grandson in 1900. Had Abel Chapman not met Garvey, his work in Doñana may never have flourished and, maybe, its importance never realised. Perhaps we would never have had the chance to study its wildlife in the 1990s. Had Chapman not met the members of the Spanish aristocracy in Doñana, quite possibly the Gredos mountains would have lost their ibexes.

Chance or unplanned actions have also played an important part throughout the history of al-Andalus. Some have had positive outcomes along unexpected lines. The increase in cattle farming in parts of Spain during the 20th century had a purely economic basis. No farmer was selflessly thinking of griffon vultures when he took the decision to increase his stock of cows or bulls. The coincidence of the practice with the move towards greater protection of natural areas where the vultures nested contributed in large measure to the success and recovery of the griffon vulture population. Had markets dictated less ranching, we might be facing a very different situation today. What this example does show is how vulnerable a species like the griffon is to outside forces and how quickly its situation can change. It may be changing as I write these lines. Pressure to close feeding sites and to prevent carcasses being left out in the open, as a result of stricter measures to prevent the spread of disease among livestock, could rapidly change the panorama for the griffon vulture.

Another example of fortuitous conservation has been that of the cork oak forests. Had the removal of cork oaks for tanning and charcoal proceeded at the 19th-century rate, we would probably have few such forests left today. The mass removal of cork oak forests before the wine stopper industry developed, is an example of the degree of wanton destruction we are prepared to inflict on nature to serve our purposes. Had evolution not blessed the tree with a fire-resistant bark, then this tree would not have had economic value. Once we discovered the usefulness of cork to the wine stopper industry and that the trees' regenerative nature allowed them to survive the removal of their bark, a chance balance was struck. It was pure luck. What would have happened to the wine industry had there been no cork? What will happen to the cork oak forests now that plastics and aluminium screw tops have invaded the market?

The industrial exploitation and commercialisation of tuna owes its origin to historical contingency too, this time to Hannibal and his elephants. His attack on Saguntum and later Rome forced the latter to retaliate and carry the battle to its origin, Spain. Once in the Iberian peninsula, having expelled the Carthaginians, the Romans understood its richness and proceeded to colonise it. They reached the shores of the Strait of Gibraltar and soon latched on to the Carthaginian idea, learned from their Phoenician ancestors, of exploiting the tuna migrations. The industry may not have developed at all had the Phoenicians not set sail, under Assyrian duress, from the other end of the Mediterranean in search of metals. Had the source of metals been somewhere else, the Phoenicians may never have discovered the migration through the channel. They did discover it and Rome took the idea and improved it.

CHAPTER EIGHTEEN *Original sin*

Adaptation for the snow – chimneys in the Alpujarras

Countryside abandonment – Llanos de Santa Ana, Jaén

AL-ANDALUS

Chance also had its hand in the conquest of another world. Had Pelayo not started his small eighth-century territory in the mountains of Asturias and the Muslims not kept away from it, the chain of events leading to the fall of Granada seven centuries later might have been very different. Had the unproductive lands of Extremadura not been Christianised at such an early stage in the process, the crusading knights may not have got so easily bored once peace arrived. Had Columbus' ambition not found its perfect opportunity in the Granada of 1492, the New World may not have been discovered at that time. This opened the door to the crusading spirit's extension to another continent against new people. Otherwise, Pizarro and Atahuallpa might never have met each other and the world would be a different place.

Just as the road to hell is paved with good intentions, many well-meaning environmentalists can cause more damage than good. There are many paradoxes in this world and, if we are unable to understand the complexity of ecological systems, our simplistic approach can do a great deal of harm. One such paradox is provided by another fortuitous outcome. Take the case of bull-fighting, an al-Andalus tradition. I am not going to defend cruelty to animals but I can step back and see the wider picture. What I see is a great number of wild plants and animals that have survived in large estates of open grassland or dehesa where fighting bulls are reared. Much of the flat, low-lying, ecology of al-Andalus has been turned over by the plough and these large bull ranches are islands of precious habitat for many species. Before damning the cruel loss of a few purpose-bred domesticates each year we should at least consider the alternatives. Our good intentions can cause a great deal of harm.

In 2005, after years of battling, fox-hunting was banned in the United Kingdom. You might expect that, as a committed ecologist and conservationist, I would approve. However, as with bull fighting, it seems to me that the wider picture has been missed. Undoubtedly, if we focus exclusively on the suffering of foxes, the move is to be welcomed, but let us take a broader view. The fox-hunting tradition that the Duke of Wellington and, later, Lord Kitchener used to train their cavalry spread across the British Empire and other parts of the world. Some of the characters involved did much more to conserve species and habitats than the average environmentalist would expect to achieve in a lifetime. Take Pablo Larios. Through conservation and management of fox-hunting lands he preserved wild habitats and species until agriculture encroached irreversibly.

Hunting is also criticised as anti-conservationist. Indiscriminate, out-of-control, large-scale hunting like the shooting of great bustards from light aircraft or the commercial pursuit of tuna via satellite and helicopter is certainly deplorable and no justification can be found for it. It can and does cause population, even species, extinctions. Let us not

Don Quixote, Puerto Lapice, La Mancha

CHAPTER EIGHTEEN *Original sin*

throw out the baby with the bathwater. The naturalists and hunters we have met in this book were actually great students and lovers of nature and the countryside. They would admonish us if they returned and saw the state of our planet. Chapman was largely responsible for saving the Gredos race of the ibex and Larios for those in the southern mountains. These people shot animals but they saw nature from the inside, having spent many hours in the field. They knew the lives of their prey, enjoyed watching and studying them and knew when not to kill them. None of them ever threatened a species to extinction. They always showed them respect.

What amazes me about the 21st century and the conservation and animal rights banners is their randomness. By all means tackle the hunting of foxes with vigour, but much graver issues are escaping our attention. Habitats, ecosystems and thousands of species are under threat throughout the world. I would sacrifice a few foxes any day in return for saving a species from extinction. The two are, of course, possible but somehow, cosmetically, we only choose the soft and cuddly options. Meanwhile, the world of spin continues to spin towards the abyss…

The main cause of deterioration is the prolonged historical impact on the land. Very often self-styled conservationists disregard and misunderstand scale. By becoming excessively concerned with the local the large-scale situation facing many species is forgotten. We have seen how waterbirds come and go between Doñana and African wetlands and how vultures move with impunity across Iberia and North Africa. The drainage of Iberia's wetlands like La Janda and Daimiel, the shrinkage of Doñana and the Ebro delta and the loss of countless small, anonymous lakes and lagoons in less than 100 years cannot be ignored as if nothing had happened. Today, few seem willing to consider the regeneration of La Janda. Instead, a costly cosmetic exercise declares the sterile man-made reservoirs of the Barbate river to be its "wetlands". The human ability to generate endless spin carries on, but it does not bring the birds back. These wetlands cannot be considered in isolation. On the scale at which waterbirds operate, they were part of an integrated system which included wetlands in Morocco and in West Africa. Many of those have gone too. Is it any wonder that so many species have disappeared? The gallant efforts to save the white-headed duck offer hope but are a lone cry in the wilderness. Protection of large tracts of habitat and networks are the solution. When we have applied the formula, it has worked. Audouin's gull and greater flamingo in the Ebro delta (and ibex in Gredos) are examples. Species re-introductions are less successful unless we are able to stop the cause of the initial decline. The bearded vulture may yet provide us with a model example. The antithesis – large-scale habitat fragmentation and loss and commercial exploitation – has always been the recipe for extinction, from Neanderthal to the last breeding cranes of La Janda.

If we had not come on the scene with our new inventions of agriculture and domestication of animals, today's world would resemble that of 10,000 years ago. Climate has not changed dramatically enough in this period to have caused major

CHAPTER EIGHTEEN *Original sin*

Wind sports, Tarifa, with North Africa beyond

Muslim, Christian and Jew have lived side by side in Gibraltar for over three centuries

alterations. In al-Andalus luck – in the form of a large, southern, topographically varied land (some would call it environmental resilience) and a particular history that diverted activity to another continent (America) for a long time after 1492 – has helped to slow the rot. We can detect this resistance as far back as the Neolithic. Even though many people were changing over to agriculture, the ecological richness of coast and mountain delayed the process as others kept hunting, fishing and gathering. It is another important lesson about our nature and our evolution: if something works, it is best not to change. Certainly, the al-Andalus that reached the 21st century, though impoverished, was ecologically healthier and richer than much of the rest of Europe.

The history of al-Andalus can teach us many lessons for the future. Our minds do not seem to fully take on board even the present concern about climate change. It is as if we know a change is coming but will somehow be exempt from its effects, imagining it will be a slow process that will affect us only gradually and that we will adapt. Prepare to be surprised. Let us remind ourselves of the speed with which the Mediterranean filled up – 36 years, equivalent to a single human generation. Perhaps sea-level change will convince us. In the Pleistocene sea levels on the al-Andalus coasts swung between 120 metres below present levels and eight metres above, a range close to 130 metres, but still we build on low-lying coasts and on flood plains. Severe climate change has had huge impacts on past human populations so why should we be exonerated? In some cases, it even caused the extinction of a lineage – the Neanderthals – but we continue trying to comfort ourselves with mistaken preconceptions. We still think that the Neanderthals were a bunch of idiots and that it was our superiority that wiped them off the face of the Earth. Even if that were true, which it is not, it hardly seems something to be proud of. The evidence to the contrary stares us in the face, but we choose to explain it away. What does the story of al-Andalus tell us about our own nature and how we behave towards each other? To me it speaks of a built-in nature that is Machiavellian but generous at the same time, capable of indescribable cruelty and great acts of heroism. What has changed with time has not been our nature but its cultural context, dramatically seen in al-Andalus with the waves of peoples who arrived and settled here: Phoenician, Greek, Carthaginian, Roman, Vandal, Suevi, Alan, Visigoth, Byzantine, Arab, Berber, even British.

At the heart of that nature is territory in its widest sense. By that I mean land, resources, other people, money… The story of al-Andalus is the story of the struggle for territory. How was this articulated? Let us take the various expressions that we have found throughout this book.

The story of al-Andalus talks to us, among many other things, about contact between people from distant lands. In its earliest expression we may have the diffusion of ideas

In the name of a better environment

CHAPTER EIGHTEEN *Original sin*

about agriculture from the Middle East 7,000 years ago, but it is the arrival of ancient eastern mariners in the Bronze Age, maybe as early as 3,500 years ago, that marks what we could describe as history's first example of globalisation. If we return briefly to the painted sailing ships of the Laja Alta, we can form an image of the kind of awe that local people would have felt when confronted with such god-like technology. A parallel would have been the mesmerised submission of the Inca to an illiterate Extremaduran pig-herder who had guns. The outcome seems to have been less catastrophic for the Bronze Age Iberians than for the poor Inca.

The Phoenicians gradually settled in southwestern Iberia but do not seem to have taken advantage of their advanced technology to wipe out the natives. Instead, they apparently thrived by trade and exchange, certainly a more sophisticated approach than that of the treasure-grabbing conquistadores 23 centuries later. The Phoenicians had one very human ability: to keep what they had from others. In Tartessos they had literally hit the jackpot. They seem to have cleverly exploited myth and religious belief to perpetuate the idea of a dangerous sea, the end of the world, beyond the Pillars of Heracles. By doing so they kept the monopoly of the Atlantic market.

In the case of Pizarro and Atahuallpa it was the technological differential that marked the difference between otherwise similar people only separated by different cultural backgrounds and histories. We find this form of dominance, imposed by weapons, among kings, nobles and peasants. Technology did not always win the day. The clearest example of its failure was the attack of the floating batteries on Gibraltar in 1782. In this case the most powerful machines of the day were defeated by ingenuity. The practice of heating cannon balls and firing them red-hot stopped the gigantic machines. It was the exception.

Human inventiveness seems to have been expressed mainly under two very distinct circumstances. On the one hand we have war. Would the ingenuity needed to come up with the red-hot shot have been expressed in times of peace? Would the excavation of gun batteries inside the Rock of Gibraltar in the 18th century, or the construction of a city inside the same Rock during the Second World War, have happened had it not been for a pressing need in time of war?

On the other hand we find excellent examples of inventiveness when there was money to be made. The amazing development of techniques for capturing tuna and other fish by the Romans, their commercial and business acumen, and their ability to bring together isolated industries (such as salt extraction with fishing to produce salted fish) were at the service of profit. When commercial gains were to be made, otherwise territorial humans joined forces and co-operated. The success of the Roman salted fish and garum trade was due, in no small measure, to the collective effort embodied in their Societas.

The example illustrates another human achievement that started with agricultural technology. Once you begin to produce a surplus you need to find ways of storing it.

Sunset and telephone lines, Gallocanta, Teruel

In the case of tuna the surplus was produced by the passage of thousands of fish in a very short period. The solution was to salt the fish to preserve it. Once that had been achieved, commercial exploitation was possible as the fish could be transferred across large distances without fear of deterioration. It became big business.
The tuna industry was certainly big business for the Dukes of Medina Sidonia. Their ancestors' achievements gave them the tuna monopoly and they became almost omnipotent for a time, a third of their revenue coming from this business. It was another way of gaining power. The dukes became almost second-tier kings, commanding armies of fishermen and a hierarchy within their own mini-kingdom that nobody could challenge.
People have shown themselves capable of many things for a price. In al-Andalus we see this in the way people were willing to fight, at a price, for any master. Guzmán El Bueno's story is a classic example of someone who built wealth as a mercenary and who fought for different masters, even of different religious faiths. Many others did the same. Remember, for example, El Cid or Abd al-Rahman III's army, which was a mix of Muslim Berber and Christian Slav? It is difficult to understand the context of the world of al-Andalus but some things could equally be out of our own time. How could

AL-ANDALUS

Guzmán El Bueno, exiled in Morocco for fighting against Prince Sancho, buy lands in Spain from the wealth secured through his fighting? Money talked…

At a time and in a land when versatile people were few and far between, alliances often switched out of need. A good example was Prince Sancho's invitation, once he had become king, to his former enemy Guzmán to defend Tarifa for him. Sancho was clearly limited in his choice and Guzmán was available, for a fee.

Incidentally, the Catholic Aragonese and the Granada Muslims fought together on the side of Sancho in the capture of Tarifa. This was not a rare situation and the story of al-Andalus is full of such examples. The very conquest of Iberia by Tarik stemmed from internal rivalries among Visigoths; Catholic Portuguese separately fought North African Muslims and Catholic Castilians; Catholic Navarra and León supported Islamic North Africans against Catholic Castile; the Muslims of al-Andalus supported the Catholic King Fernando III of Castile against Islamic North Africans; Muslim Merinids waged war on Muslim Muwahhid; Catholic Spanish and French fought Protestant British at Gibraltar and Trafalgar but shortly after British and Spanish fought French across Iberia. It was a long and complicated story…

When rival powers were evenly balanced, an unstable equilibrium persisted, so long as interests could be kept separate. For a long time this is what happened between Castile and Aragón. Each pursued its own separate crusade, Castile into Andalusia and Aragón developing its Mediterranean state. So long as the interests did not overlap, all was fine. When they did, war usually outshone diplomacy. In the end, it was the tried and tested method of gene-mixing, intermarriage of lineages, that resolved conflict and created bigger and more powerful states.

Religion has played a major, central, role in human affairs. For a long time the Catholic Church vied with the Crown for power. At the same time, it often suited the Crown to have bands of monks and friars establishing enclaves of religious passion, in otherwise unpopulated territory, as in Guadalupe, as a means of fighting a war and consolidating conquest. Religious symbolism also helped validate power. This was the case with the "discovery" of the remains of St James during the early Christian expansion in the north.

The Catholic Church influenced the course of history and imbued the crusading spirit of the later periods of conquest. As Grand Inquisitor, Tomás de Torquemada wielded authority that was able to shape Queen Isabel's policy towards Jews and Muslims. The fervour of the Grand Inquisitor and his queen was matched by the fanaticism of the various Berber Muslim dynasties, Murabit, Muwahhid and Merinid, which brought austerity and repression into al-Andalus. It was all a far cry from the tolerance in the 10th-century secular court of the Caliph of Córdoba or in 13th-century Catholic Trujillo.

The role of religion has transcended the spiritual and has woven political networks, which allowed some men to succeed while others were put to the sword or burned at the

CHAPTER EIGHTEEN *Original sin*

stake. Some have gone to great lengths to achieve absolution. In the paranoid world of the Inquisition, it seems that even the powerful Duke of Medina Sidonia sought to deny his North African heritage and his wife's Jewish one by buying a respectable Leonese lineage that would keep him in favour.

A more institutionalised way of wiping out history was to transform places of worship. When the first Duke of Medina Sidonia finally recovered his father's remains after Gibraltar had been taken in 1462, he gave them rest in a Catholic chapel that replaced the Muslim mosque within the castle itself. A more acute example was the building of a cathedral within Córdoba's Great Mosque. In its most extreme form, at state level, it took the shape of ethnic and religious cleansing as with the expulsion of the Sephardic Jews in 1492 and the Muslims in 1609, or the destruction of Carthage centuries earlier.

The quest for political power sometimes over-rode religious fervour or even kinship. We have seen a number of examples of Muslim siding with Christian against Muslim or against Christian. In such cases even members of a blood line came into conflict with each other. The great Alfonso X, staunch Catholic conqueror, made a pact with the Muslim fundamentalist Yusuf to help him defeat his own son, Sancho. Later, Prince Juan allied with the Muslim Merinids to try and take Tarifa from his brother, King Sancho IV. Dynastic battles reflected rivalries for power, usually among kin, in situations when the line of succession was unclear or when the balance of power between rivals could not determine a clear outcome. Such was the case in the struggle between King Pedro the Cruel and his half-brother, Enrique de Trastámara, who killed him to take the throne of Castile. Chance, once again, came into play in this particular conflict. The Guzmáns had openly supported the Trastámara lineage and this led to their descendants acquiring the dukedom of Medina Sidonia. Had events gone against the Trastámaras, would the Medina Sidonias have developed their tuna industry, kept Doñana, captured Gibraltar in 1309 and again in 1462, or commanded the Invincible Armada in 1588?

In the same way as unclear dominance among contenders to the Crown led to conflict, when the power of monarch over noble was weak, we find monarchs who were more willing to compromise in return for support. Nobles were able to secure great benefits in return and even contested the monarch's authority. The Medina Sidonias repeatedly challenged the Crown for ownership of Gibraltar. Queen Isabel, needing Medina Sidonia's support in her campaign in North Africa, allowed him to keep the territory. Once the all-powerful queen found that she could claim it without fearing for her own position she kicked the duke out. By the 16th century, the monarchy was so powerful that in 1588 the poor 7th Duke of Medina Sidonia did not dare contest the great King Felipe II's order to launch the Invincible Armada, despite his misgivings about the enterprise.

This type of conflict between monarch and noble was frequent, especially as newly conquered lands had to be controlled and repopulated. One usual way of rewarding loyal supporters was through the transfer of lands or other economic concessions, like the award of the tuna monopoly to the Guzmáns. The award of titles and incorporation into the nobility was another way. It is how the Guzmáns climbed up the ladder, becoming first Counts of Niebla under King Enrique IV, then Dukes of Medina Sidonia under King Juan II, and finally Marquises of Gibraltar under Isabel.

At the other end of the spectrum we find situations in which the conquest or defence of conquered land became too difficult and wasteful and losses were cut rather than indulge in further fruitless expenditure. The Muslim decision not to pursue a long-drawn conflict in the Cantabrian mountains is a case in point. Another was the sale of Algeciras and Gibraltar by the Fez Merinids back to the Granada Nasrids (Muslim to Muslim) in 1294 after their failure to retake Tarifa. The 200-year delay in the conquest of Granada may well have been another.

An alternative strategy was to switch sides. The first Duke of Medina Sidonia took sides with the powerful faction supporting Prince Alfonso against King Enrique IV of Castile. Medina Sidonia secured a warrant from the prince that allowed him to storm Gibraltar and regain possession for his family in 1467. Following the death of the prince and the duke, Medina Sidonia's son and King Enrique made their peace and Medina Sidonia kept Gibraltar. Medina Sidonia gained the territory and the king a powerful ally and guardian in the lands of the south.

In such a cut-throat world it is surprising to find extreme acts of loyalty and chivalry. It is hard to understand Guzmán's stand at Tarifa in 1294 when we know how he had changed allegiance several times before without apparent qualms. Yet his loyalty towards his former enemy, King Sancho, was so strong that he was even prepared to sacrifice his own son and not betray his new master. Of course, we have to be aware of a very human trait which is the enhancement of stories that, with the passage of time, begin to take on legendary status. As David Lowenthal argued many years ago, the past is indeed a foreign country. Can we really put ourselves in the setting and the minds of the people of 1294?

Conflict brings out the worst in humans but it also brings allies closer together and produces acts of extreme altruism. Such was the case when, in 1436, Enrique de Guzmán returned to the beaches of Gibraltar to try and save his stranded knights, drowning in the process. Its antithesis was the cruelty and lack of compassion shown by the Nasrid defenders of Gibraltar at the time. In a story reminiscent of Hector's death in Troy, they decapitated Guzmán's body then hung it outside the city walls. Such terrible gestures were, in the context of their day, a way of showing power and might and, ultimately, of self-preservation.

For much of the history of al-Andalus conflict was between closely matched classes of nobles and kings, which is where the power resided. On occasions there were popular revolts, as when the Berbers staged their uprising against the Arab minority in 740. It happened when sheer numbers overwhelmed the powerful few, but it was rare. More often than not the combination of monarchy, nobility and religion imposed an unjust

CHAPTER EIGHTEEN *Original sin*

order on the rest. In more recent times the continuation of feudal practices and extreme poverty in the rural population invited new anarchic and communist political systems and the rise of the bandoleros. The only solution for the feudal overlords was repression, either through spin (as in the case of the Mano Negra) or indescribable cruelty (as in Casas Viejas).

It does not always have to be this way. Something deep in our psyche allows us to connect and share experiences that we may not have lived directly. I think that it is a built-in feature in our system that goes back to the days when groups of hunter-gatherers first had to split into smaller groups to find prey. When that happened for the first time and the groups met after a few days, the experiences of one were transmitted to the other by words, song or through painting. We experienced what we had not seen first-hand. In the same way, when we read accounts written in another time that are familiar because of our own experiences, we connect with those who wrote those lines even if they are long departed. My experiences with young griffons in Laja Aciscar brought me closer to Verner and those with cranes in Gallocanta closer to Irby.

In the same way, people with such diverse origins as Verner and Larios shared a common spirit; Jews, Muslims and Catholics were able to live in harmony in Córdoba and Trujillo; Jews, Muslims, Catholics, Protestants, Hindus and all others, including non-believers, still do today in the cosmopolitan world of Gibraltar. Our minds have changed little from those of the first farmers of 10,000 years ago, but the context has shifted at a pace that has not always allowed us to remove rationally the shackles imposed by "territory". The process has been one in which destruction of plants, animals, people and places has been the dominant and unfortunate theme. The exceptions provide the basis for optimism. They are the examples that show the possible. We will only become fully human the day we are able to detach the territorial animal from the compassionate being within…

Back in Cazorla, I sat under the shade of the tall maritime pines and looked across the valley where the Guadalquivir was starting its long journey towards the distant Atlantic. A myriad butterflies flitted busily in the small prairie below me. A small group of fallow deer grazed nervously in the dappled light of the forest behind. Raucous carrion crows argued over a scrap of food while a red squirrel raced down a tall pine trunk to the grassy floor. Looking around nervously, it selected a special cone out of hundreds on the ground and returned to the haven of its favourite tree. When I looked up at the tree, my attention was drawn to several birds, a mix of crimson, orange, green and brown, which were dissecting cones from the outer branches. They were crossbills, finches specialists in eating pine seeds.

On the horizon another thermal of griffons started to wheel into the skies. One looked an odd shape and was much darker. Its outline reminded me of the bearded vultures that had once lived in this sierra, but it could not be – they were long gone. I focused my binoculars on the strange silhouette. I could sense the bulk of the bird. It turned on the thermal and the sight of a diamond-shaped tail made me jump for joy. Yes, it was a bearded vulture! This was one of the young birds that had been released last year and it was back – and free – in its natural home. Maybe it would be some time before I would hear the howl of a wolf in these mountains, but I was happy that, with our help, some of the natural jewels of al-Andalus were starting to return home.

Sta Luzia church, Portugal, at night. Christianity eventually came to dominate al-Andalus.

CHAPTER EIGHTEEN *Original sin*

Appendix One

Bird species of special importance in the Iberian peninsula in Europe

① Species unique to Iberia
Balearic shearwater
Marbled duck
White-headed duck
Crested coot
Spanish imperial eagle
Andalusian hemipode
Black-bellied sandgrouse
Red-necked nightjar
White-rumped swift
Little swift
Lesser-crested tern
Dupont's lark
Thekla lark
Black wheatear
Azure-winged magpie
Trumpeter finch

② European species with largest populations in Iberia
Cattle egret
Spoonbill
Red-crested pochard
Purple gallinule
Baillon's crake
Black-shouldered kite
Black kite
Bearded vulture
Egyptian vulture
Griffon vulture
Black vulture
Short-toed eagle
Golden eagle
Booted eagle
Bonelli's eagle
Lesser kestrel
Peregrine
Red-legged partridge
Quail
Little bustard
Great bustard
Pin-tailed sandgrouse
Great spotted cuckoo
Little owl
Scops owl
Pallid swift
Roller
Bee-eater
Hoopoe
Black-winged stilt
Stone curlew
Collared pratincole
Kentish plover
Audouin's gull
Yellow-legged gull
Gull-billed tern
Calandra lark
Short-toed lark
Lesser short-toed lark
Crested lark
Crag martin
Red-rumped swallow
Tawny pipit
Alpine accentor

AL-ANDALUS *Appendix One*

Rufous bush robin
Stonechat
Black-eared wheatear
Blue rock thrush
Cetti's warbler
Fan-tailed warbler
Melodious warbler
Marmora's warbler
Dartford warbler
Spectacled warbler
Subalpine warbler
Sardinian warbler
Orphean warbler
Bonelli's warbler
Firecrest
Crested tit
Short-toed tree creeper
Wall creeper
Southern grey shrike
Woodchat shrike
Chough
Raven
Spotless starling
Rock sparrow
Citril finch
Snowfinch
Serin
Cirl bunting
Rock bunting
Ortolan bunting
Corn bunting
Rock dove
Turtle dove
Barn owl
Nightjar
Kingfisher
Woodlark

Sand martin
House martin
Mistle thrush
Long-tailed tit
Coal tit
House sparrow
Tree sparrow
Goldfinch
Linnet
Iberian chiffchaff

❸ **European species with important populations in Iberia** (ranked 2nd to 10th in population size in Europe)

Squacco heron
Little egret
Purple heron
Greater flamingo
Red kite
Montagu's harrier
Eleonora's falcon
Wryneck
Avocet
Nightingale
Black redstart
Penduline tit
Red-backed shrike
Alpine chough
Water rail
Cuckoo
Green woodpecker
Little tern
Wheatear
Jackdaw
Greenfinch

AL-ANDALUS *Appendix One*

Glossy ibis
Alpine swift
Slender-billed gull
Whiskered tern
Rock thrush
Moustached warbler
Golden oriole
Crossbill
Wood pigeon
Skylark
Blackbird
Blue tit
Jay
Cory's shearwater
Little bittern
White stork
Kestrel
Bluethroat
Moorhen
Tawny owl
Whitethroat
Spotted flycatcher
Great tit
Nuthatch
Blackcap
Magpie
Hen harrier
Eagle owl
Olivaceous warbler
Spanish sparrow
Garden warbler
Night heron
Honey buzzard
Goshawk
Black-necked grebe
Yellow wagtail
Shag

Black stork
Capercaillie
Ring ouzel
Guillemot
Savi's warbler

Appendix Two

(ssp denotes sub-species)

❶ Species endemic and widespread in Iberia

Freshwater fish
Iberian nase (western Iberian rivers)

Amphibians
Sharp-ribbed salamander (southern 2/3)
Bosca's newt (western half)
Painted frog (SW 2/3)

Reptiles
Spiny-footed lizard (southern 2/3)
Bedriaga's skink (southern 2/3)
Amphisbaenian (southern 2/3)
Horseshoe whip snake (southern 2/3)
Lataste's viper (Mediterranean bioclimates)

Butterflies
Purple hairstreak ssp
False ilex hairstreak ssp
African grass blue ssp
Brown Argus ssp
Spanish chalk hill blue
Marsh fritillary ssp
Spanish fritillary ssp
Marbled white ssp
Esper's marbled white ssp
Western marbled white ssp

Dragonflies
Damselfly sp (Ischnura graellsii)

❷ Species endemic and localised in Iberia

Freshwater fish
Portuguese roach (lakes and lowland rivers in Portugal)
Pardilla roach (western Iberian rivers)
Calandino roach (western Iberian rivers)
Spanish minnowcarp (Guadiana only)
Iberian toothcarp (SE Spain, coastal)
Valencia toothcarp (SE Spain, coastal)
Iberian barbel (Tagus, Guadiana, Guadalquivir)

Amphibians
Golden-striped salamander (NW)
Pyrenean brook salamander (Pyrenees)
Iberian midwife toad (middle west)
Iberian frog (NW)

Reptiles
Spanish algyroides (mountains SE La Mancha)
Schreiber's green lizard (NW)

Iberian rock lizard (north and central mountains)
Bocage's wall lizard (NW)
False smooth snake (southern 1/3)

Mammals
Pyrenean desman (mountains of NW)
Cabrera's vole (C and SE mountains)
Lusitanian pine vole (NW)
Spanish lynx (C and SW)
Spanish ibex (C and S)

Butterflies
Green-striped white (C and S)
Sooty orange-tip (E half)
Desert orange-tip (S)
Scarce copper ssp (C and N)
Lorquin's blue (SW)
False baton blue (C and S)
Zephyr blue ssp (C)
Silver-studded Blue ssp (S)
Mountain Argus ssp (C and E)
Spanish Argus (C and E)
Glandon blue ssp (S)
Gavarine blue ssp (N)
Oberthur's anomalous blue (NE)
Agenjo's anomalous blue (NE)
Forster's furry blue (N)
Furry blue ssp (N)
Mother of pearl blue (C and E)
Chalk hill blue ssp (C and N)
High brown fritillary ssp (C and S)
Shepherd's fritillary ssp (C and N)
Knapweed fritillary ssp (C and S)
Aetherie fritillary ssp (SW)
Lesser-spotted fritillary ssp (NW and SE)
Southern hermit (C)
Yellow-spotted ringlet ssp (N)
Silky ringlet ssp (N)
Spanish brassy ringlet ssp (N and SE)
Water ringlet ssp (N)
Lefebvre's ringlet ssp (NW and NE)
Zapater's ringlet (N)
Chapman's ringlet (NW)
Oriental meadow brown ssp (SE)
Sandy grizzled skipper ssp (C)

Dragonflies
Dragonfly sp (Paragomphus genei, S)
Dragonfly sp (Onychogomphus costae, C and S)
Skimmer sp (Orthetrum trincaria, S)
Skimmer sp (Orthetrum chrysostigma, S)
Skimmer sp (Orthetrum nitidinerve, S)
Darter sp (Diplacodes lefebvrii, S)
Darter sp (Brachythemis leucosticta, S)
Darter sp (Zygonyx torrida, SE)
Darter sp (Trithemis annulata, S)
Darter sp (Selysiothemis nigra, E)

❸ Mainly Iberian species that reach southern France

Freshwater fish
French nase
Sandsmelt

AL-ANDALUS *Appendix Two*

Amphibians
Marbled newt
Midwife toad
Western spadefoot
Parsley frog
Stripeless tree frog

Reptiles
Large psammodromus
Spanish psammodromus
Ocellated lizard
Iberian wall lizard
Ladder Snake
Viperine snake

Mammals
Mediterranean pine vole
Southwestern water vole
Algerian mouse

Butterflies
Scarce swallowtail ssp
Spanish festoon
Portuguese dappled white
Moroccan orange-tip
Mountain clouded yellow
Spanish purple hairstreak
Provence hairstreak
Black-eyed blue
Panoptes blue
Escher's blue ssp
Provence chalk hill blue
Provençal fritillary
Meadow fritillary
Striped grayling
Black satyr
False grayling ssp

Spring ringlet
Spanish gatekeeper
Dusky heath ssp

Dragonflies
Demoiselle sp (Calopteryx xanthosoma)
Damselfly sp (Platycnemis acutipennis)
Damselfly sp (Platycnemis latipes)
Yellow club-tailed dragonfly
Dragonfly sp (Gomphus graslini)
Splendid emerald

❹ North European species that reach northern Iberia

Freshwater Fish
Minnow
Bullhead
Roach
Rudd
Barbel
Perch

Amphibians
Alpine newt
Palmate newt
Yellow-bellied toad
Common frog
Agile frog

Reptiles
Green lizard
Sand lizard
Viviparous lizard

Common wall lizard
Slow worm
Western whip snake
Aesculapian snake
Smooth snake
Adder
Asp viper

Mammals
Millet's shrew
Pygmy shrew
Alpine shrew
Water shrew
Miller's water shrew
Lesser white-toothed shrew
Whiskered bat
Bechstein's bat
Common long-eared bat
Red squirrel
Fat dormouse
Hazel dormouse
Bank vole
Field vole
Common vole
Northern water vole
Yellow-necked mouse
Harvest mouse
Brown bear
Stoat
Pine marten
Chamois

Butterflies
Clouded Apollo
Brown hairstreak
White letter hairstreak
Black hairstreak
Sooty copper
Short-tailed blue
Alcon blue
Large blue
Dusky large blue
Silvery Argus ssp
Meleager's blue
Duke of Burgundy fritillary
Purple emperor
Lesser purple emperor
White admiral
Camberwell beauty
Peacock
Map butterfly
Small Pearl-bordered fritillary
Pearl-bordered fritillary
Weaver's fritillary
False heath fritillary
Heath fritillary
Pearly heath
Chestnut heath
Woodland brown
Chequered skipper

Dragonflies
Demoiselle sp (Calopteryx splendens)
Damselfly sp (Platycnemis pennipes)
Damselfly sp (Ischnura elegans)
Red-eyed damselfly
Club-tailed dragonfly
Hairy dragonfly
Dragonfly sp (Aeschna juncea)
Dragonfly sp (Aeschna grandis)
Dragonfly sp (Cordulegaster bidentatus)
Dragonfly sp (Cordulea aenea)

AL-ANDALUS *Appendix Two*

Dragonfly sp (Somatochlora metallica)
Dragonfly sp (Somatochlora flavomaculata)
Skimmer sp (Orthetrum albistylum)
Darter sp (Sympetrum danae)
Marshland darter
Darter sp (Sympetrum vulgatum)
Darter sp (Leucorrhinia dubia)
Darter sp (Leucorrhinia pectoralis)

❺ Species introduced by man

Reptiles
Spur-thighed tortoise (south)
Moorish gecko (Mediterranean bioclimates)
Turkish gecko (south)
Mediterranean chameleon (south)

Mammals
Algerian hedgehog (SE/E)
Egyptian mongoose (SW)
Genet (Iberia and SW France)
Fallow deer
Barbary macaque (Gibraltar)

Appendix Three

Chronology of al-Andalus (based on this book)

(global events in red)

BP (Before Present — generally applied prior to 10,000 years ago)
1.8 million	First Europeans in Dmanisi, Georgia
1.2 million	First people in Orce and Atapuerca
780,000	Homo antecessor in Atapuerca
120,000	Neanderthals in Gorham's and Vanguard Caves, Gibraltar
24,000	Last Neanderthals on the planet in Gorham's Cave, Gibraltar
18,500	First modern humans in Gorham's Cave, Gibraltar

BC
5,400	Neolithic fishermen in Gibraltar
5,400-3,700	Neolithic farmers in Sierra de Baza
around 5,000	Neolithic people in La Janda paint Tajo de las Figuras
4,236	First date of Egyptian calendar
4,000	Rice farming in China
around 3,900	Megalith building in Gorafe
3,800-3,600	Humid period in Sierra de Baza
3,760	First date in Jewish calendar
3,300-2,700	Aridification in Sierra de Baza
3,000	Major mining impact in Tinto and Odiel rivers
2,800	Foundation of Old Kingdom of Egypt
2,500	Founding of Knossos in Crete
2,350	Sumerian Empire founded
2,265-1,505	Bronze Age people in Gibraltar and possible contact with eastern/central Mediterranean
2,100	Increase in fires in Sierra de Baza
1,570	New Kingdom of Egypt
1,500	Collapse of Argaric Culture
1,300-220	Iberian culture in south-eastern Spain

AL-ANDALUS *Appendix Three*

1,193	Troy destroyed by the Greeks
961	Death of King David and succession of Solomon
800-410	Phoenicians arrive from the eastern Mediterranean
776	First Olympic games in Greece
509	Foundation of Roman republic
336-323	Reign of King Alexander the Great
219	Hannibal attacks Saguntum
218-201	Second Punic War
171	Foundation of Carteia
45	Caesar becomes dictator of Rome

AD

30	Crucifixion of Jesus
77	Roman conquest of Britain
370	Huns invade Europe
410	Goths sack Rome
476	End of western Roman Empire
527	Justinian becomes Byzantine emperor
533-534	Byzantines conquer the coasts of the Strait of Gibraltar
620	Vikings invade Ireland
632	Death of Muhammad
711	Tarik lands in Gibraltar in April
711	Tarik defeats Rodrigo in the Battle of the Guadalete on July 19
712	Musa lands in Algeciras
713	Siege of Mérida
718	Battle of Covadonga
732	Defeat of Muslims by Charles Martel
740	Berber revolt
748-754	A series of famines across the Meseta. King Alfonso I captures León, Astorga and Braga
750	Abbasids overthrow the Umayyads in Damascus
756-788	Abd al-Rahman I rules from Córdoba
771	Charlemagne becomes king of the Franks
830	Discovery of Saint James' remains
881	Conquest of Villafáfila by King Alfonso III of León
~900-1300s	Industrial salt extraction in Villafáfila

AL-ANDALUS *Appendix Three*

981	Vikings settle in Greenland
1002	Leif Eriksson reaches North America
1031	Umayyad dynasty collapse in Córdoba
1085	King Alfonso VI of Castilla annexes the Toledo and Valencia taifas
1086	Murabit land in Algeciras in the summer
1086	Murabit defeat King Alfonso VI of Castilla at Zalaca
1096	First crusade
1096	Aragonese take Huesca
1096	Princess Teresa and the Count of Burgundy entrusted with the County of Portugal
1099	Crusaders capture Jerusalem
1100	Aragonese take Barbastro
1102	Murabit take Valencia
1104	Catalans capture Balaguer
1106	Death of Murabit Emir Yusuf ibn-Tashfun
1117	Series of truces between King Alfonso I of Aragón and Urraca
1118	King Alfonso I of Aragón takes the Zaragoza taifa
1125	Alfonso I raids deep into Andalusia
1130	Ibn Tumart killed in battle
1130	Rise to power of Murabit Abd al-Mumin
1139	King Alfonso Enríquez of Portugal defeats the Murabit at Ourique
1141	King Alfonso Enríquez defeats the Castilians at the Minho river
1142	Kingdom of Navarra strikes peace with Aragón-Barcelona
1142	King Alfonso VII of Castile takes Coria
1143	Kings of Castilla-León, Portugal and Navarra and the papal legate meet in Valladolid
1146	Córdoba reduced to a vassal of Castile
1146	Muwahhid land in Iberia
1147	Second crusade
1147	Muwahhid subdue Algarve
1147	Fall of Calatrava
1147	Fall of Santarém
1147	Siege and fall of Lisbon

AL-ANDALUS *Appendix Three*

1147	Fall of Almería
1148	Muwahhid take Córdoba
1151	Muwahhid take Algiers
1154	Muwahhid take Málaga
1156	Muwahhid take Granada
1157	Death of King Alfonso VII of Castile
1157	Muwahhid take Almería
1160	al-Mumin builds Madinat al-Fath
1162	Muwahhid push Normans out of Tunisia
1169	Reign of Saladin
1174	Muwahhid take Trujillo
1189	Third crusade
1196	Muwahhid attack Castile
1202	Fourth crusade
1204	Crusaders capture and sack Constantinople
1211	King Alfonso VIII of Castile attacks Baeza, Andújar and Jaén
1211	Muwahhid take Salvatierra
1212	Alfonso VIII wins Battle of Las Navas de Tolosa on July 16
1214	Death of Alfonso VIII
1215	Magna Carta
1217	Fifth crusade
1224	Muwahhid Yusuf II dies sparking rebellion in al-Andalus
1225	King Fernando III of Castile invades Andalusia
1225	King Alfonso IX of Aragón takes lands of Extremadura to control the Guadiana
1228	Sixth crusade
1229	Fall of Cáceres
1230	King Alfonso IX dies and Castile and Aragón unified under Fernando III
1230	Fall of Badajoz, Mérida and Montánchez
1233	Fernando III takes Úbeda
1233	Fall of Trujillo
1234	Fall of Medellín, Santa Cruz and Alanje
1236	Fernando III takes Córdoba
1238-1273	Muhammad I rules in Granada
1246	Fernando III takes Sevilla

AL-ANDALUS *Appendix Three*

1248	Seventh crusade
1248	Fall of Sevilla
1249	Portuguese take Faro
1252	Death of Fernando III
1258-1286	Rule of Abu Yusuf Yakub and the foundation of Fez
1259	King Alfonso X of Castile takes Cádiz
1262	King Alfonso X takes Niebla
1264	Muslim insurrection in Andalusia
1264	King Alfonso X captures Benalup
1269	Merinids take Marrakesh
1271	Marco Polo visits Kublai Khan
1275	King Alfonso X's eldest son, Fernando de la Cerda, dies creating a dynastic struggle
1275	Merinids land in Iberia
1276	Truce struck between King Alfonso X of Castile and the Merinid Emir Yusuf
1277	Merinids land in Iberia a second time
1278	Blockade of Algeciras by King Alfonso X of Castile
1282	Merinids land in Iberia a third time
1284	Accession of King Sancho IV to the throne of Castile
1284	Alonso Pérez de Guzmán exiled in Morocco on the accession of Sancho IV
1291	Saracens capture Acre, marking the end of the Crusades
1292	King Sancho IV of Castile captures Tarifa and Pérez de Guzmán is awarded its tenancy and defence
1294	Prince Juan besieges Tarifa with Merinid support. Guzmán's son is murdered in front of his father
1295	King Fernando IV ratifies Guzmán El Bueno's fishing rights from Portugal to Gibraltar
1300s	Cork oaks exploited for tanning in Portugal
1300-1500s	Salt monopoly for crown of Castile
1309	King Fernando IV of Castile besieges Algeciras
1309	Guzmán captures Gibraltar on behalf of King Fernando IV of Castile
1309	Guzmán is killed, reportedly in a skirmish in the hills near Gaucín
1311-1350	Semi-wild cattle roam pristine Guadalquivir valley in

AL-ANDALUS *Appendix Three*

	reign of King Alfonso XI
1325	Tenochtitlán founded by the Aztecs
1333	The Merinid Emir Abu al-Hasan takes Gibraltar from the Castilians
1338	King Alfonso XI of Castile creates the Guadalupe monastery
1340	Merinids destroy Castilian fleet in the Strait
1340	Merinids and Nasrids besiege Tarifa
1340	Merinids defeated in Battle of Río Salado
1342-1348	King Alfonso XI writes the Book of Hunting
1342-1344	Siege and fall of Algeciras
1348	The Black Death
1350	On March 26, King Alfonso XI of Castile dies from the Black Death while besieging Gibraltar
1369	Prince Enrique de Trastamara kills King Pedro El Cruel of Castile and becomes King Enrique II (The Bastard)
1374	Gibraltar taken over by the Nasrids
early 1400s	Portuguese export cork to Flanders
1410	Castilians take Antequera
1415	Battle of Agincourt
1436	Enrique de Guzmán attacks Gibraltar and drowns in the attempt
1440	Juan de Guzmán secures Medina Sidonia by exchange
1441-1444	Revolt of the princes of Aragón
1445	Juan de Guzmán becomes 1st Duke of Medina Sidonia
1453	Fall of Constantinople
1462	Siege and capture of Gibraltar by the Duke of Medina Sidonia
1466-1467	The Duke of Medina Sidonia takes Gibraltar
1468	The first duke dies
1469	King Enrique IV of Castile legitimises by royal warrant Medina Sidonia's ownership of Gibraltar
1470s	Wolves enter city of Sevilla
1473	Sistine Chapel is built
1472	Merinid collapse in North Africa
1488	The second Duke of Medina Sidonia becomes first Marquis of Gibraltar

AL-ANDALUS *Appendix Three*

1492	In January, Granada falls to King Fernando II of Aragón and Queen Isabel of Castile
1492	The second Duke of Medina Sidonia dies
1492	Expulsion of the Sephardic Jews from Spain
1492	Columbus discovers America
1497	Gibraltar used by the third Duke of Medina Sidonia as military base for the invasion of North Africa
1497	The third Duke of Medina Sidonia captures Melilla in North Africa
1497	Expulsion of Sephardic Jews from Portugal
1499-1502	First Morisco uprising in Alpujarras
1500s	Flamingoes stop breeding in Ebro delta
1500s	Red and fallow deer and wild boar abundant in Guadalquivir valley
1501	On December 22, Queen Isabel issues a decree making Gibraltar Crown property
1502	On January 2, a royal governor takes command of Gibraltar
1504	Death of Queen Isabel
1506	Third Duke of Medina Sidonia marches on Gibraltar
1509	Reign of King Henry VIII of England
1517	Start of the Reformation
1532	Francisco Pizarro defeats Atahuallpa at Cajamarca
1558	Reign of Queen Elizabeth I of England
1567	King Felipe II issues edict forcing Moriscos to give up their way of life
1568-1570	Second Morisco uprising in Alpuarras and Axarquía
1571	Battle of Lepanto
1575	King Felipe II visits Daimiel
1577	Sir Francis Drake sacks the coast of Spain
1579	Princess of Eboli, mother of Doña Ana, is imprisoned in San Torcaz fortress
1579	United Provinces (Holland) proclaim independence from Spain
1580	Spanish conquest of Portugal
1588	Seventh Duke of Medina Sidonia leads the Invincible Armada – associated deforestation

AL-ANDALUS *Appendix Three*

1596	Effingham and Essex sack Cádiz
1600	Elizabeth I of England grants Charter to English East India Company
1603	James VI of Scotland becomes King James I of England
1608	Approval of expulsion of Moriscos from Spain in January during reign of King Felipe III
1609	Expulsion order announced on September 11
1610	Death of Doña Ana
1615	Death of the seventh Duke of Medina Sidonia
1620	Pilgrim Fathers reach Cape Cod in Mayflower
1640	Portuguese revolt against Spain
1642	English Civil War
mid-1600s	Deforestation of Doñana
1654	Wolves cause damage in eastern Doñana and Algaida pine wood is cut down
1666	Great fire of London
1681	Algaida reforested
1700s	Attempt to revive Villafáfila salt industry
1704	Duke of Marlborough defeats French at Battle Of Blenheim
1704	Isaac Newton publishes Optics
1704	Sir George Rooke and Prince George of Hesse-Darmstadt capture Gibraltar on August 4
1712	Queen Anne declares Gibraltar a free port
1713	Treaty of Utrecht signed
1717	Cádiz becomes sole port for trade with the Indies
1727	Thirteenth siege of Gibraltar
1737	First large-scale introduction of stone pine in Doñana
1745	Jacobite rebellion
1750	Cork stoppers first made in Cataluña
1750	Cork stopper industry takes off in second half of century
1755	Lisbon earthquake
1756	British lose Menorca
1763	British regain Menorca
1767	Captain James Cook discovers Australia
1773	Boston Tea Party
1773	Vineyards first planted in Doñana
1775-1783	American War of Independence

AL-ANDALUS Appendix Three

1778	William Garvey Power arrives in Jerez
1779-1783	Great Siege of Gibraltar
1782	Start of excavation of galleries inside Gibraltar
1782	Attack of the floating batteries on Gibraltar on September 13
1782	Lord Howe's relief of Gibraltar on October 11
1785	Doñana vineyards abandoned
1796	Napoleon Bonaparte invades Italy
1797	Jervis blockades Cádiz
1798	Battle of the Nile
1801	Battle of Algeciras July 6-13
1803	Wolves plentiful and hunted in Doñana
1804	Napoleon crowns himself Emperor
1805	Battle of Trafalgar on October 21
1807	Slave trade abolished in the British Empire
1808-1814	France occupies Spain
1809	Battle of Talavera in July
1813	Calpe fox hunt established in Gibraltar
1815	Battle of Waterloo
1817	King Fernando VII abolishes Medina Sidonia's fishing rights
1825-1838	Phase 1 of La Janda drainage
1830	Opening of first steam passenger railways
1837	Victoria crowned Queen of Great Britain
1838	Wolves reported a nuisance on outskirts of Sevilla
1830s	Cork industry extends to Extremadura
1840s	Cork industry extends to Andalusia
1844	Guardia Civil formed to counteract activity of bandoleros
1846	Potato famine in Ireland
mid-1800s	Last wolves in Guadalquivir valley
1848	Discovery of Neanderthal skull in Forbes' Quarry, Gibraltar, on March 3
1851	The Great Exhibition
1850 onwards	Peak exploitation of cork oak for tanning industry
1868	Fall of Queen Isabel II
1871	Trade Unions legalised in Great Britain
1872	Abel Chapman first visits Doñana on April 8
1873-1874	First Republic in Spain
1874	Verner arrives in Gibraltar for the first time

AL-ANDALUS *Appendix Three*

1876	Verner meets Irby
1877	Queen Victoria proclaimed Empress of India
1882-1884	Mano Negra episode
1889	Cecil Rhodes founds British South Africa Company
1891	Pablo Larios elected master of Calpe Hunt
late 1800s	Massive cork oak deforestation in Serranía de Ronda
late 1800s	Sierra Morena deforestation for charcoal and mining
late 1800s	Mass poisoning of wolves and vultures
1892	Portuguese ibex becomes extinct
1898	Spain and United States at war over Cuba
1899-1902	Boer War
1900	Pyrenean ibex becomes extinct
1900	Medina Sidonia sells Doñana to Garvey
early 1900s	Wolves gone from Subbetics
1901	Edward VII crowned king of Great Britain
1905	Death of Irby
1906	King Edward VII of Great Britain and King Alfonso XIII of Spain become royal patrons of Calpe Hunt
1907	Discovery of Gorham's Cave, Gibraltar
1909	Verner writes My Life among the Wild Birds in Spain
1912	Sinking of the Titanic
1912	Verner shows La Pileta cave to L'Abbe Henri Breuil and Professor Obermaier
1914-1918	First World War
1915	Closure of trade unions in Medina Sidonia and Casas Viejas
1922	Death of Verner on January 25
1922	Union of Soviet Socialist Republics formed
1924	King Alfonso XIII hunts in Doñana — no wolves are found
1925	Wolf extinct in Ronda and Grazalema mountains
1926	Dorothy Garrod excavates Neanderthal child in Devil's Tower, Gibraltar
1930s	End of Royal Calpe Hunt
1929-1954	Phase 2 of La Janda drainage
1930s	Wolf extinct in eastern Málaga and Granada mountains and in Cazorla, Baza, Gor and Filabres sierras
1931	Declaration of Second Spanish Republic in April
1933	Adolf Hitler appointed German Chancellor

AL-ANDALUS *Appendix Three*

1933	Casas Viejas incidents
1933	Last wolves in Sierra Nevada
1934	Last bandolero (Pasos Largos) killed on March 18
1935	Atkinson and friends visit Andalusia in search of the griffon vulture
1936-1939	Spanish Civil War
1939-1945	World War II tunnelling in Gibraltar
1950-1953	Korean War
1950s	Start of mass exodus of people from Castilian countryside
1950s	Some wolves descend to Guadalquivir valley from time to time
1951	Last wolves shot in Doñana
1952	Elizabeth II crowned queen
1954-1967	Phase 3 of La Janda drainage
1954	Last cranes breed in La Janda
1961	Yuri Gagarin first man in space
1963	President Kennedy assassinated
1965	Franco hunts in Daimiel
1969	Armstrong and Aldrin land on the moon
1970s	White-headed duck on the brink of extinction
1975	Death of General Franco
1980s	White-headed duck recovery
1982	Falkland Islands War
1982	Controversial skull discovered in Orce
1990s	Major recovery of the griffon vulture
2006	Last great bustard of La Janda killed on April 10
2006	First three captive-bred bearded vultures released in Cazorla
2007	Two more captive-bred bearded vultures released in Cazorla

AL-ANDALUS *Index*

Accentor, Alpine	186, 190	Argaric Culture	236
Aciscar, Laja de	38-39	Atahualpa	142
Albarracín Mountains	200	Atapuerca	64
Alborán Sea	51-52	Aurochs	39
Albufera	200	Axarquía	268-270
Alcalá de los Gazules	99	Baelo Claudia	110-112, 116-117
Alcalá Sidonia	99	Baetica	207
Alfonso I, King	195-196	Basti	236
Alfonso II, King	195-196	Batestania	236
Alfonso III (El Magno), King	128, 134, 138	Baza, Dama de	236
Alfonso VI (The Brave), King	245-248	Baza, Sierra de	229-238
Alfonso VIII, King	251	Benalup	152, 157-162
Alfonso X (El Sabio), King	94, 99, 157, 252	Berbers	195
Alfonso XI, King	14, 98, 123, 128, 136, 254	Betic Mountains	17, 260-275
		Biodiversity	282-284
Alfonso XIII, King	16, 178	Biodiversity, deterioration	284-289
Algaida, La	16	Bittern	162
Algeciras	102, 254-256	Bluethroat	186
		Boabdil	244
Alhambra	252	Boat Hoist Cave	239
al-Idrisi	118, 134	Breuil, Abbé Henri	171, 228
Almadraba	102, 118-124	Bronze Age people	112
		Buck, Walter	16-17, 98, 168, 182-186, 188-189, 208
Almohad	249-252		
Almonte	106		
Almoravids	245-249		
al-Mutamid, King	245		
Alpujarras	268-270	Bullfighting	39-40
al-Rahman I, Abd	211	Bustard, Great	129-120
al-Rahman II, Abd	214	Buzzard, Honey	58
al-Rahman III, Abd	214	Byzantines	118
Alta, Laja	112	Cádiz	219-221
Álvarez de Toledo Caro, Joaquín	107	Caetaria	117
Annual, Desastre de	40	Caliphate	214
Arab Invasion of Spain	193-194	Campiña	31
Ardales Cave	228	Cantabrian Mountains	188-190,

AL-ANDALUS Index

	195, 200	Cultural contact	302-304
Capercaillie	190	D'Arcon, Jean-Claude-Eléonore Le	
Carteia	117-118	Michaud	218-219
Carthaginensis	206	Daimiel, Tablas de	208-210
Carthaginians	114	Dehesa	136-138
Casas Viejas	152, 157-162	Despeñaperros	24, 251
		Devil's Tower Rock Shelter	171
Cazorla, Sierra de	14, 40, 64, 210	Dolphin, Bottle-nose	70
		Dolphin, Common	70
Ceuta	118	Doñana	14, 16-17, 33, 80-94, 98-99, 102, 106, 121, 210
Chalcolithic	234-235		
Chamois	190		
Chapman, Abel	16-17, 30, 98, 130, 168, 176, 182-186, 188-189, 208		
		Doñana, Palacio de	82-83, 106
		Doñana, sand dunes	92
Chaucer, Canterbury Tales	254	Drake, Sir Francis	219
Cid Campeador, El	248	Duck, White-headed	162-164
Cisneros, Cardinal	268	Duero River	206-210
Cold fauna	74, 278-280	Eagle, Bonelli's	39, 173-174
Conflict, territorial	307-309	Eagle, Short-toed	54-56
Conil	119-120	Eagle, Spanish Imperial	80, 84, 138
Convolvulus	39		
Córdoba	210-214	Eboli, Princess of	106
Córdoba, Caliphate	244	Ebro Delta	201-206
Córdoba, Great Mosque	214	Ebro River	200-206
cork industry	32-38, 40, 288	Edward VII, King	177-178
		Effingham, Lord	219
Cortés Pizarro, Hernán	142	Eisenhower, General	239
Costa del Sol	26	Elizabeth I, Queen	219
Covadonga	194, 196	Emerita Augusta	207
Crake, Baillon's	162	Enrique de Trastámara	102
Crane	136, 152-156	Enrique II (The Bastard), King	102
		Environmental resilience	302
Cueva de Nerja	111	Epidemic, Yellow Fever	222-223

AL-ANDALUS *Index*

Essex, Count of	219	Gibraltar, Strait as biological barrier	54
Euro-Siberian Region,	190, 196	Gibraltar, Strait of	50-60, 110-114, 123-124, 201
Extremadura	130-138		
Father León	122		
Felipe II, King	106, 208, 219, 268-270, 288		
		Gibraltar, tunnelling	238-240, 288
Felipe III, King	270-273	Gibraltar, uplift of the Rock	52-54
Fernando II, King	103, 244	Gorafe	229
Fernando III, King	252	Gorham's Cave	40, 67-75, 92, 114, 278
Fernando IV, King	118, 286		
Fernando VII, King	119		
Férula I, King	195		
First Europeans	64-66	Gravina, Federico	218, 223-224
Flamingo, Greater	202		
Flint, Edmund	67	Grazalema	200, 264
Floating Batteries	218-219	Gredos, Sierra de	182-188
Fonelas	66-67	Guadalquivir River	210-214
Forbes' Quarry	67	Guadalquivir River, birth of	14
Gallocanta, Laguna de	152-156	Guadalquivir valley	14-16
Garrison Library	67, 152	Guadiana River	134, 207-210
Garrod, Dorothy	171		
Garum	116-117	Guadix-Baza Basin, fauna of	66-67
Garvey Power, William	98, 107	Guardia Civil, founding of	260
Garvey, Guillermo	98, 107	Gull, Audouin's	201-202
Garvey, Patricio	98	Gull, Mediterranean	201
Gaucín, Sierra de	102	Gull, Slender-billed	201
Gibraltar Scientific Society	67	Harrier, Marsh	161
Gibraltar	103, 218-224	Harrier, Montagu's	138
		Heron, Purple	161
Gibraltar, Galleries	238	Hesse-Darmstadt, Prince George of	220
Gibraltar, Great Siege of	218-221, 238	Historical contingency	294-298
Gibraltar, opening of the Strait	50-52	Homo antecessor	67
Gibraltar, Rock of	40, 102, 238-241, 281	Homo erectus	64-66
		Hyaena, Spotted	72
		Ibex, Spanish	32, 176, 182-186

334

AL-ANDALUS Index

Ibis, Glossy	160	León, Kingdom of	128
ibn Tumart	249	Lerma, Duke of	272
Ince, Sergeant Major	238	Lusitania	200, 207
Inventiveness, human	304-305	Lynx, Spanish	17, 92
Invincible Armada	106, 219, 237	Macaque, Barbary	284
		Madinat al-Fath	250
Irby, Howard	38, 130, 151-152, 156, 168-169	Madinat al-Zahra	214
		Magpie	90
		Magpie, Azure-winged	80, 90-92
		Mancha, La	206-208
Isabel II, Queen	158, 260	Mano Negra	159
Isabel, Queen	103, 244	Manuel I, King	103
Iulia Traducta	117-118	Marisma, Seasonality	84-90
Jackdaw	90	Marquis of Gibraltar	103-106
Janda, Laguna de la	30, 38, 130, 146-164, 288	Marquis of Santa Cruz	106
		Martel, Charles	244
		Martinazo, Casa de	83, 90
		Medellín	142
Jebel Musa	50	Medina Sidonia	103, 158
Jebel Tariq	194	Medina Sidonia, Duke of	99, 103-107, 119-123
Jervis, Admiral	219		
Jesuits	122-123		
Jewry, Iberian	211	Medina Sidonia, dynasty	99
Jews, expulsion of	103	Medina, Laguna de	164
Jews, Sephardic	220-221, 275	Megaliths	229
		Melilla	103-106
Juan Carlos, King	178	Melkart	114
Juan de Austria, Don	268-270	Mellaria	117
Juan de Rivera, Archbishop	272-273	Merinids	98, 252-256
Juan, Prince	99-102, 254		
		Meseta	128
Julian, Count	193-194	Millares, Los	234-235
Kestrel, Lesser	130, 138-139	Monastery of Guadalupe	120, 136
		Monfragüe, National Park	136-138
Kite, Black	80, 138	Monk Seal	70, 124
Laja	30-31	Mons Abyla	50
Larios, Pablo	175-178	Mons Calpe	50
Latifundium	157-158	Montado	136
Lentisc	74	monte blanco	92

AL-ANDALUS *Index*

Montesinos Cave	208	Paradoxes, environmental	298-300
Morena, Sierra	16-17, 33	Paradoxes, human historical	305-307
Moriscos	268-270	Pasos Largos	260
Moriscos, expulsion of	270-273	Pedro (The Cruel), King	102
Mozarabs	211, 249	Pedro of Cantabria	195
Mudéjar	268	Pelayo	194-195, 196
Muhammad I, King	252		
Muhammad XII, Emir	244	Pérez de Guzmán (El Bueno), Alonso	99-102, 106, 118-119, 254
Murabit	245-249		
Musa ibn Nusayr	194		
Muslims, expulsion of	103		
Muwahhid	249-252		
Mycenaean Greeks	112	Phoenicians	112-114
Nazrid	252-254	Picos de Europa	188-189
Neanderthals	54, 67-75, 111, 171, 228, 280	Pileta, Cueva de la	171, 174, 228
		Pillars of Heracles	50, 112-114
Neanderthals, last populations	75	Pine, Black	264
Nelson, Lord Horatio	223-224	Pine, Stone	74, 80, 92
Neolithic people	111, 150-151, 229-232	Pinsapo	264
		Pizarro, Francisco	142
Niebla, Count of	102	Plata, Sierra de la	110
Niebla, County of	94, 120	Pyrenees	189-190
Oak, Cork	31-38, 74	Quixote, Don	207-208
Oak, Holm	136	raptor migration	57-58
olive monoculture	14, 24	Regulares	40
Olive	73	Religion, impact of	306-307
Orce	64	Retinto Cattle	39
Order of Alcántara	134-136	Rincón, Laguna de	162
Order of Calatrava	208	Rio Tinto, mines	33, 236
Order of Knights Templar	136	Rocío, El	80-82
Order of Santiago	134-136	Rock Lizard, Iberian	186
Osprey	172-173	Roderic, King	157, 193-194
Otero de Sariegos	138-139		
Owl, African Marsh	161	Romans,	115-118, 200, 236-237
Owl, Eagle	39		
Owl, Short-eared	138		

AL-ANDALUS Index

Roncesvalles	248	tanning industry	33
Ronda, Serranía de	33	Tarifa	99-102, 254
Rooke, Sir George	220		
Royal Calpe Hunt,	176-178	Tarifa, Vía de	123
Rudolph of Austria, Crown Prince of	169-170	Tarik ibn-Ziyad	157, 194
		Tarraconensis	206
Ruidera, Lagunas de	207-208	Tartessos	114
Saguntum	202	Tempranillo, El	260
Saint James	196	Tern, Lesser-crested	201
Salt industry	117, 128-129, 286	Tern, Whiskered	162
		Thrush, Blue Rock	173
		Toledo	211
San Bartolomé, Sierra de	110	Tolosa, las Navas de	251
San Lúcar de Barrameda	102, 120-121	Torquemada, Tomás de	103
		Trafalgar, Battle of	208, 223-224
Sancho IV, King	99-102, 123, 254	Treaty of Utrecht	274-275
		Trujillo	130-138, 142
Sancho, Prince	99		
Santa Fé	244		
Santa Olalla	92-94	Tuna industry	111-124, 286
Santiago de Compostela	196		
Sevilla	211	Valencia	245-248
Sierra Bermeja	264	Vanguard Cave	70, 92
Sierra de las Nieves	264-266	vega	39, 147
Sierra Nevada	264-266	Venta Micena	66
Silva y Mendoza, Ana de	106	vera	84,
Skylark	264-266	Verner, Willoughby	17, 30, 38, 130, 146-147, 156, 168-175, 228
Solana de Zamborino	67		
Species protection	289		
Spoonbill,	162		
Stay Behind tunnels	239-240		
Stork, Black	138		
Sultan Yusuf	99	Villafáfila	128-134
Suspiro del Moro	244	Vulture, Bearded	17, 44
Tagus River	200	Vulture, Bearded breeding programme	289-290
Taifas	244-245, 252		
		Vulture, Black	44, 138
Tajo de las Figuras	150-151	Vulture, Egyptian	30, 39, 44, 174
Talavera	136, 188		

Vulture, Griffon	14, 30-32, 38-40, 44-46, 84
Vulture, Ruppell's	44-46
Wall Creeper	190
Warbler, Bonelli's	32
Wellington, Duke of	176, 186-188
Western Spadefoot Toad	74
Whaling	124
Wheatear	264-266
wolf	14-24, 278
Woodpecker, Black	190
Woodpecker, Middle Spotted	190
Yeates, G. K.	147, 156, 202
Zahara	120
Zaragoza	245-249
Zarga, Laja de la	30
Zoñar, Laguna de	162